Walter Harris was born in London in 1 bridge, he left England to travel and Egypt, Yemen and South Africa befor of 20. He worked as a journalist, ever and continued to travel, like an English Indiana Jones, to areas of the Middle East never previously visited by Europeans, but his greatest love was for Morocco. His grave is in Tangier, where he died in 1933.

Praise for Walter Harris

'This book is brilliant – sharp, melodramatic and extremely funny.'
Rough Guide to Morocco

'Among the funniest and best-written books I have ever read.'
Byron Rogers, *Evening Standard*

'A portrait of dark and splendid vanished days, of combined magnif-icence and squalor, barbarism and culture.'   *The Literary Review*

'It remains an indispensible account of the Maghrib at the end of its ancient history.'   *The Emirates*

Tauris Parke Paperbacks is an imprint of I.B.Tauris. It is dedicated to publishing books in accessible paperback editions for the serious general reader within a wide range of categories, including biography, history, travel and the ancient world. The list includes select, critically acclaimed works of top quality writing by distinguished authors that continue to challenge, to inform and to inspire. These are books that possess those subtle but intrinsic elements that mark them out as something exceptional.

The Colophon of Tauris Parke Paperbacks is a representation of the ancient Egyptian ibis, sacred to the god Thoth, who was himself often depicted in the form of this most elegant of birds. Thoth was credited in antiquity as the scribe of the ancient Egyptian gods and as the inventor of writing and was associated with many aspects of wisdom and learning.

THE LAND OF AN AFRICAN SULTAN

Travels in Morocco

Walter Harris

TAURIS PARKE
PAPERBACKS

New edition published in 2011 by Tauris Parke Paperbacks
An imprint of I.B.Tauris and Co Ltd
6 Salem Road, London W2 4BU
175 Fifth Avenue, New York NY 10010
www.ibtauris.com

Distributed in the United States and Canada Exclusively by Palgrave Macmillan
175 Fifth Avenue, New York NY 10010

First published 1889

Cover image: 'Tangiers', Hercules Brabazon (1821–1906) / Private Collection /
© Chris Beetles / The Bridgeman Art Library

ISBN: 978 1 84885 573 1

A full CIP record for this book is available from the British Library
A full CIP record is available from the Library of Congress

Library of Congress Catalog Card Number: available

Printed and bound in Sweden by ScandBook AB

CONTENTS.

PART I.

A JOURNEY THROUGH NORTHERN MOROCCO.

PART II.

A JOURNEY WITH H.B.M. SPECIAL MISSION TO THE COURT OF THE SULTAN AT MOROCCO CITY.

PART III.

·A VISIT TO WAZAN—MY RIDE TO SHESHOUAN.

PART IV.

ABOUT THE MOORS.

CHAPTER I.

LIST OF ILLUSTRATIONS.

PAGE

PART I.

A JOURNEY THROUGH NORTHERN MOROCCO.

"The dry land appeared, not in level sands forsaken by the surges, which those surges might again claim for their own; but in range beyond range of swelling hill and iron rock, for ever to claim kindred with the firmament, and to be companied by the clouds of heaven."—RUSKIN.

THE LAND

OF

AN AFRICAN SULTAN.

CHAPTER I.

TANGIER.

"Ah Sidi Mahammed al Hadj. Ah Salama, Sidi Mahammed al Hadj, Salaam alikûm Sidi Mahammed al Hadj." [1]

We have rounded Cape Malabat and are in almost quiet waters again, and Tangier is in full view—a white clustering of flat-roofed houses on the steep hill-side, with its kasbah standing out against the azure sky.

Even the sea-sick American lady raises her head

[1] The usual salutation of the Moors to the patron saint of Tangier.

from her handsome courier's shoulder, where it has
rested ever since we left Gibraltar three hours before,
and pulls a small hand-glass out of her pocket,
arranges her hat, and remarks,—

"Well, I guess this is the cunningest place I've
ever seen.   Boston ain't no patch on it.   Angela, get
up and see Africa."

Angela raises herself languidly and watches the
shouting Moors who are alongside now in their
boats.

"Ma," she says, "I shall marry a Moor."

Her mother's answer is lost in the shouts of the
natives, who are clambering on board and seizing
every one's luggage, hurling it in the boats regardless
of ownership.

Two or three guides, decked out in the most gorgeous of native costumes, into which a certain amount
of "fantaisie" has been imparted by the introduction
of patent leather shoes and European collars, are
hurrying about in every direction, touting for the
hotels.

"Sebah-al-khair al assoui,"[2] cries a sturdy boatman
to me—an old friend—and a great brown arm is
reached up from a boat below, and my hand is given
such a shake as it did not forget for some time.

I go ashore in his boat.

I have no trouble at the Custom-house, no luggage
to open.   The three or four officials, who sit under the
arcade of horseshoe arches, know me well enough.
From under the rich folds of their silk striped haiks

---

[2] My nickname all through the Moorish Empire.   Aissoui
means follower of Sidi ben Aissa, the patron saint of snake-
charmers, &c.   My tame snakes won me the name.

they reach out a plump white hand and grasp mine, murmuring a few words of welcome.

My servant meets me here—my faithful Selim—and I really believe he is pleased to see me.

I leave him to look after my luggage and take it to my old quarters, while I pass on, up the steep hill, under the Bab al Marsa, past the great mosque, with its richly tiled minaret, to the Legation.

Jack Green meets me at the door, surrounded by a score of dogs, who welcome me as an old friend by nearly knocking me down.

They are at tea upstairs.

A few questions and a few answers, a few messages and the latest news told, and I feel myself no more a new arrival at Tangier, but that I have bridged over the four months I have been absent, and am continuing my old life in Morocco just where I left it off so short a time before.

I had come out a week earlier than the rest of our party, to make preparations, so that as soon as possible after their arrival we might start off for our trip into the interior to Mequinez and Fez, and about these preparations I set the next day with a will.

Men, mules, &c., had to be found; no very easy job in the winter sometimes; but my former experience, and my personal knowledge of most of the men who make a business of accompanying caravans, made it an easier task for me than it must be for most people; and, besides, I had the invaluable help of my friend Carleton, whose knowledge of the Moorish-Arabic language, of the people and country, is unequalled. We two together set to work, so that by the time the rest of our party arrived, nearly a week later, we were, though not in ship-shape order, yet prepared to some extent.

The day of their arrival dawned. I got a telegram from Ingram from Gibraltar to say that the *Arcadia* had arrived, and that they would cross that day. Somehow the *Gibel-Tarik*, one of the steamers that ply between Gibraltar and Tangier, started very late, with the result that they arrived after dark, a serious thing in Tangier; somehow it poured with rain, and somehow it was low tide.

I shall never forget that landing. I have landed and seen landings in some of the worst surf ports in the world, but never in my life have I seen anything so screamingly funny as the advent of our party,

The steamer had whistled, so Carleton and I went down to the " Marsa," or harbour, chartered a small boat, and in the pouring rain set out; set out, do I say ?—were bodily lifted off our feet from the steps of the little pier and carried some two hundred yards on the backs of the Moors to the nearest spot that the boats could approach to the shore.

Over the rocks tumbled and rolled the great sturdy Moors, while we clung on like grim death to their shoulders. Finally I was pitched headlong into a boat, and a minute later Carleton was bowled in on the top of me. My first idea, as soon as I was able to have any ideas at all, was to keep this boat for ourselves. However, the additional weight of Carleton and myself (I weigh nine stone three) put the boat so low that she could not be shoved off the ledge of rock on to which she seemed glued like a limpet. Meanwhile the guides from the hotels could be heard approaching. In the darkness we could see nothing, but I knew that very few boats would meet the steamer. Then came the tug of war. A moment later our boat was assailed by a well-known hotel guide, the gorgeousness of whose costume is one of the features of Tangier.

The two Moors who were carrying him tried their utmost, at his instigation, to put him on board. Carleton and I would not hear of it. We had engaged the boat, and no one should come in it, as we knew well enough that we should require all the boat's available room for our large party and their still larger amount of baggage.

A struggle ensued, Carleton attacking the two Moors, while I made for the more docile guide, whose struggles were pitiful to behold. There is nothing that a Moor hates more than cold water, and here was the poor fellow—in his best clothes too—swaying about like a see-saw on the shoulders of two men who were being attacked by Carleton. Suddenly I saw my chance ; seizing his patent leather boots by each heel, I gave a vigorous thrust upwards. There was a dull splash, then a few bubbles, our boatman gave one shove, the boat was free, and the guide could be seen by the light of our one lantern up to his shoulders in water and violently hurling curses— there was nothing else to hurl—at our heads.

And so we saved our boat !

Ten minutes or so stout pulling by our Moors got us alongside. We were the second boat to arrive, so got pretty close up to the side of the *Gibel-Tarik*. But here was Babel.

Shouting and screaming on the steamer and in the

boats, yelling of boatmen, men climbing on board and seizing every one's luggage—and they had almost to be thrashed before they could be made to drop it —and amidst it all the recognized voices of our friends.

A breakneck scramble, and Carleton and I were on board; had found Ingram, and were saving the luggage from being hurled pell-mell into the boats— or the sea. And all this in almost total darkness.

We were too late to collect all our party. Forestier had been carried bodily away by a couple of Moors, 'sans everything," as Shakespeare says, and could be dimly heard from the distance shouting that he was safe—safe in a boat full of sea-sick Jewesses and filthy Jews, being rowed he knew not where. There was a comic agony in his tones—comic at least to us. I shouted to him to wait on the shore.

After fighting and struggling for near an hour in the pouring rain, we managed to collect the baggage together; to get Rover, the retriever, and Don, the setter, into the boat, and start.

There was only one man whose calm behaviour never changed, whose features never moved a muscle, who showed no surprise at the way of landing, and that was Brookes, Ingram's valet, who merely with his eagle eyes watched that no one stole the luggage, and on any one taking it would gently but firmly take it from them again and in sepulchral tones, that made one's blood creep cold, remark, "Take care; that is not yours."

Montbard had one little adventure. So eager were the boatmen to obtain him as a fare—I think they thought they might charge twice over, a special

arrangement by weight—that a man in one of the
boats seized him when on the companion ladder
violently by the arms, and tried to lift him bodily into
his boat ; but nineteen stone—I beg his pardon, fourteen stone—is no light weight. Great was the surprise of that boatman when Montbard, with the
strength of a Hercules, lifted the man bodily out of
his boat and placed him in another boat with a
" Mettez-vous là, mon enfant."

The boats pushed away from the steamer's side, the
dogs barked, the boatmen yelled, the rain poured
down, and all was confusion. After ten or fifteen
minutes' rowing, the boat ran on the rocks, one of the
boatmen stepped overboard, seized each of us in turn,
and carried us ashore. Ashore ! Far from it ; they
carried us on to the rocky remains of the old mole,
full of deep pools and water, and covered with
slippery sea-weed. However, purgatory ends in
time, and an hour later we were eating dinner in the
hotel and had forgotten all the miseries—I thoroughly
enjoyed it—of landing, and our two dogs had retired
to rest in their kennels—nor was it late before we did
the same.

The following morning we spent in overhauling
the baggage and getting our caravan together.
Carleton and I took stock of the luggage, and considered that twelve or fourteen mules were the least
we could do with to carry our tents, &c. These we
were not long in engaging, in the hopes of being able
to set out on the following Saturday. My horse I
had already bought, Ingram preferred to hire one,
while Forestier, Montbard, and Marshall chose riding
mules with native saddles—a very comfortable means

of travelling. Brookes likewise rode a mule. Having engaged our animals, we set about getting the men. Antonio, a Spaniard, who took me to Fez two years before, was indispensable, as not only was he a hard-working man, but the keenest of sportsmen and a wonderful shot. We were taking no head-man, as I had undertaken to "run the show," but Antonio was all through my right-hand man, and helped me most considerably.

As a soldier, a more or less necessary precaution, I chose old Hadj Hamed, a dear old ruffian, whom I had known before, and not only knew him, but all his dodges.

This taking a soldier is a law ordained by the Moorish Government, and though on occasions when travelling alone in Morocco I do not take one, yet I should advise every one, unless able to make themselves comfortably understood in the language, to do so. The principal use of the soldier is as insurance, for, granted you have a Maghasni with you, anything lost in the ordinary run of affairs can be reclaimed, or its value reclaimed from the Moorish Government, whereas if you have no soldier they hold themselves responsible for nothing.

Having succeeded in obtaining the services of Antonio and Hadj Hamed, the ticklish work began, that of picking one's men, for so much of one's comfort depends upon the way one's men work.

I called all the Tangier men who make a living by accompanying caravans, and about thirty or forty having collected, with Carleton and Antonio I picked out eleven, all of whom I had known before, or were known to Carleton, and very successful we were with them, for only one of our original men had to be sacked during the eight weeks we were up-country.

Selim, who had been with me on and off ever since I arrived in Morocco for the first time, came as my own particular servant, and worked well as usual all the way.

We were detained in Tangier three days longer than we intended by a heavy downfall of rain, so we spent the time, all our preparations being finished, in showing our artists round the town.

It is a queer little town, with steep streets and no cabs or carriages, very dirty and very smelly, in fact, thoroughly moresque. From the Marsa, or harbour, runs a long, straight street, which ends at the Bab al Sok, or gate of the market-place, at the upper part of the town. In this street all the principal buildings of Tangier are situated. Here we find the large mosque —there are several in Tangier, but none of such importance as this—with its tiled minaret and prettily-carved doorway. No sight, however, of its interior can be obtained, for the fanatical Moors have erected a hideous green wooden screen to prevent the Christians looking in as they pass by. Contrary to Turkey and Egypt, one cannot enter the mosques in any part of Morocco, the penalty being probably a very severe thrashing from the Moors, a thrashing that might be so skilfully manipulated as to " stretch him for a corpse " in whatever place it might chance to be.

The mosque has two entrances, one out of the main street, another which faces a narrow tunnel-like passage, a short cut from the main street to the British Legation.

Often as I was coming from the Legation I passed this gate surrounded by odoriferous beggars, and my poodle, Balzac, hearing the gurgling water of the fountain within, would put all his religious prejudices on one side and enter the sacred precincts, catching me up by leaving the building by the main gate, which I had to pass a minute or two later. What cursings used to issue from the mosque as they drove him out. Sometimes he rushed forth with a howl, and a well-aimed slipper would follow him into the street. Finally he got tired of exploring, and gave up these little feats of daring and passed the mosque door without even looking in, though I am sure he used to gaze round the corner of his eyes on the look-out for the expected shoe.

A little further up than the mosques begin the shops, first those of the lawyers and writers, for writing is quite an unknown art amongst the lower classes, who one and all adjourn to the shop of a professional for their correspondence. Little box-like shops they are, just possessing room enough to allow the owner to squat down and count his beads, or, spectacles on nose, to read some heavy, both materially and physically, religious work.

A little higher up is a sort of open space known as the Little Soko, where the Jews congregate to congratulate each other on their sharp doings and to look out for Europeans to be dragged off to the bazaars, and taken in—in both senses.

Near this Little Soko is the British post-office, a small building of no pretensions. The street then proceeds up, every available spot being used as a shop. Gun-cases in red cloth, brown mountaineers' jelabas or cloaks rich in embroidery, fine white haiks, the toga-like garments of the richer Moors, daggers, powder-flasks, lamps, and Manchester goods, fill up the little bandbox shops, till one would almost wonder how the shopkeeper gets in and out.

The front of the shops are closed by a shutter, which when business is proceeding is fastened from above, while a rope is used to allow the shopman to scramble on to his miniature stage.

One or two fountains in very poor repair vary the scene a little. But it is the people more than the buildings that form the interest of Tangier. From all over Morocco they come. The Genouah, from Timbuctoo, with their head-dresses of shells and strings and their clanking cymbals. The Susi in dark blue linen, or black and brown jelabas, the mountaineers tall and fair, many with bright blue eyes, and by far the handsomest of the Moorish peoples. The men from the Gharb, or fertile plains, enveloped in the numerous folds of their coarse haiks, speaking with a strange accent, the Berbers, with their guttural tongue, absolutely different from Arabic. These are the original inhabitants of Morocco, and were Christians once. Amongst all this medley pass and repass the rich town Moors on horse or mule, gaudily caparisoned, or perhaps one may catch a glimpse of his Highness Sidi Hadj Alsalam, the Shereef of Wazan, of whom more anon, as he rides on a splendid grey horse through the Soko, apparently indifferent to the crowd of his devout followers, who kiss the hem of his garment as he passes, and so crowd round him as to render it necessary for his slaves to beat a way for him.

But in enumerating the peoples of Tangier there are some we must not forget, the Europeans. Here, there, and everywhere can be seen Spaniards, many of them half drunk, all of them most objectionable. There is nobody more charming than a Spaniard of the upper classes, but the dregs of the criminal population that they are now so vigorously pouring into Tangier are rendering the place unbearable.

They come, I believe, in the hopes of getting work. They get none. They starve. What is the result? Tangier, that once was as safe a place to reside in as any spot in the world, is full of burglars. Six houses were robbed in the months of March and April alone in this year (1889). But with the recent change of Spanish minister it may be hoped that this will be remedied, and that the wholesale introduction of starving Spaniards will cease. The difficulty of bringing crime to justice in Tangier is enormous ; all Europeans are under the laws of their own Consulates, and this international arrangement of tribunal —though all, I am sure, try to co-operate—is an exceedingly difficult matter, and generally results in nobody getting convicted of anything. As a rule, with the exception of these late burglaries, Tangier is remarkably free from crime, especially on the part of the Moors, who, though they despise the Christians and look upon them as unclean, yet know full well that they dare not insult them, more than to mutter some meaningless curse now and again, such as : " May God destroy your grandfather and your great-grandfather in the flames of the infernal regions." I sometimes answer when I hear their curses hurled at my head, " Go on, go on ; do you think God will listen to the curses of a dog of an unbeliever?" This expression, "Kaffirbillah," takes the breath out of their mouths; the very idea of a Christian using it to a Mahommedan being preposterous.

But to return to the main street of Tangier. A sharp turn to the right, under an archway near which men are shoeing horses and mules, another turn to the left past the shops of the mountain Riffs, another gateway, and one is in the Soko. In winter this Sòk is a vast expanse of mud, in the summer of burnt clay. Here all the native traffic of Tangier is carried on. On the right lie the camels, glad of their release, no doubt, from the heavy burdens they have borne from the far away. On the left are circles of men and boys listening to the story-tellers, watching jugglers, or perhaps a performing ape, and gazing in admiration at the oft-repeated and poor performance of a snake-charmer. A little lower down are the women from the villages round selling "rhibieh," green food for horses, thistles for the mules and donkeys, chickens, eggs, and bread. At the top of the Soko is a little shed, on the walls of which hang coloured waistcoats and kuftans, to tempt the young mountaineers, by their gaudy colours, to buy for their wives or daughters. Such is the scene in the Soko on a Sunday or Thursday morning, a motley crowd indeed intermixed with horses, mules, and donkeys, and with a stray camel or two, which have wandered away from their caravan and are foraging on their own account. While writing of the Soko, a story comes to my mind which I think is worth repeating here.

A well-disposed elderly gentleman was visiting Tangier some years ago, before the country was as

opened up as it is now. He, of course, visited the
Soko and was overcome to see the ignorance and
bigotry of its occupants.

Retiring to his hotel, he engaged a guide, to whom
he told his idea.

He was going to preach!

The guide, who knew the danger of such an adven-
turous proceeding, held his own counsel, but pointed
out merely the risk he himself ran in interpreting,
demanding a proportionately large sum, which the
benevolently inclined old gentleman at once promised
him. Arrived in the Sôk, the preacher mounted an
empty case and commenced his sermon.

Great was his delight to see a crowd quickly gather
round him as his guide interpreted his fervent words.
Larger grew the crowd—no one uttered a word—in
breathless silence they listened till the end, and then
departed.

So did the old gentleman.

The guide got his large sum of money, and not
many weeks later a leading English paper had a long
article on the missionary question in Morocco, re-
counting in full the patience with which this crowd
had listened to this sermon on the Christian religion.

I hope sincerely that the old gentleman will never
know that his interpreter was telling a story from the
Arabian Nights.

He might be annoyed.

Tangier possesses a fine old kasbah, or fortress, on
which are the Government buildings, the old treasury,
the courts of justice, the prisons, the palace, and one
or two other official residences. This kasbah lies to
the north of the town, and a steep climb it is up the

narrow streets till one reaches the once beautifully tiled gate, now whitewashed all over, that divides the official from the non-official town.

Almost the first sight that meets one's eyes is a court, cut as it were in the solid masonry, the roof supported by rows of columns with horseshoe arches, and presenting an appearance not unlike the boxes at a theatre. A flight of steps leads from the level of the ground to this treasury, for that was the original use of the building. All ruined it is now, with the tiled pavement torn up and broken, with the doors hanging on their hinges; nor is the place inhabited except by a beggar or two who during the heat of the day takes shelter there from the sun and doubtless sleeps there at night. To the left of this building and at right angles to it is a somewhat similar yard, where the flogging takes place, though it is not very often it is made use of for this purpose, being generally used as a resting-place by the soldiers attendant upon the Bascha. The pillars in this case are of marble, with marble Corinthian capitals. To the right of the treasury are the two prisons, the country and the town prison respectively, gruesome dens full of half-starved natives, most of whom are probably guilty of no crime whatever.

What a history could be written in the prisons of Morocco! What tragedies have taken place within their walls! One story, most curious of all perhaps, I cannot refrain from relating here.

Not many years ago there suddenly appeared in Morocco, a young Austrian, who spoke a certain amount of Arabic, and his secretary. His story was a strange one.

C

He made himself out to be a son of the late Sultan, or a most direct descendant of some former Sultan, I forget which; he said he had been kidnapped in his youth and brought up and educated abroad, thus his slight knowledge of his mother tongue. He travelled all through the country spreading this story, which made a great impression on the minds of the Moors. Whether he meant to attempt the throne, or merely to obtain money from the Moorish Government, has never appeared, but he was frustrated. The Sultan had him seized and thrown into Tangier prison. Here he was called upon by the Austrian Consul, who told him that he had only to allow he was an Austrian, and he would immediately be set at liberty. To every one's surprise, he maintained that he was a Moor.

Day after day he had the opportunity of freedom offered him by merely allowing himself to be an Austrian subject, a matter already known for certain at the Austrian Legation; but no, he still held out, till a month or so later, in the prison with Moorish murderers and robbers, he died of starvation and exhaustion.

A narrow lane leads to the gate of justice, and as one passes one can see the old grey-bearded Bascha, seated on his throne of judgment, trying cases. The plaintiff and the defendant are both kneeling before him surrounded by soldiers, both crying out their wrongs at the same time. Probably the one who can afford to present his excellency with the largest bribe, varying generally from a wax candle or a loaf of sugar to a five-pound note, will win his case.

However, the Bascha of Tangier is far above the

ordinary run of Moorish officials, and is popular both with Moors and Europeans. The work I have had to trouble him with—for I have been obliged to see him on business sometimes—as to the behaviour of my men, &c., has been satisfactorily settled, and I always found him most polite and easy to deal with. Not so, however, his Calipha, the second in command, who is hated all round, and who obstructs in every way in his power every small case a Christian may bring before him.

Beyond the gate of justice is the old palace. This palace has recently been restored, as it was rumoured in Tangier that the Sultan would visit that place. That he intended and still intends to come there can be no doubt, though constantly recurring war in other parts of his dominions keeps his attention and his presence elsewhere.

Word having been sent that the Sultan would visit Tangier in a month or two from that time, the Bascha set to work to have the palace redecorated, or rather to have all the exquisite Arabesque torn down, and everything, including the wonderful tilework, whitewashed. However, our minister, Sir William Kirby Green, with his usual energy, had a stop put to this work of destruction, and informed the Bascha that unless everything was restored and not destroyed, he would inform the Sultan when in Tangier of all the circumstances of the case. The result has been that the palace is one of the best specimens of Moorish architecture existing in the whole country.

The central court is fine, with great white marble columns and Corinthian capitals, a marble floor and fountain. On to this court open four rooms, each with tiled and marble floors, rich tile and arabesque walls, and magnificent ceilings in the style of Moorish design and carving known as stalactites. The ceilings have not been repainted in the bright colours now in vogue amongst the Moors, but the old painting has been retained, and merely certain parts regilded. Here again thanks are due to our minister.

The rest of the palace is even finer than the court, one minute courtyard with three small rooms being a perfect gem, so rich is the arabesque and painting, while some of the corridors that run round the small enclosed gardens are very beautiful. The exterior of the building, as is customary with all Moorish architecture, is devoid of any decoration. A mosque adjoins the palace, but this, of course, I have never seen.

Beyond the kasbah is a large flat open space of ground known as the Marshan, where there is quite a European colony. Here, too, take place the races, and sometimes polo. Beyond the Marshan flows, far below it, for it is an elevated plateau, the Wad-al-Ihoudi, or Jews' river, a pretty little stream, nearly dry in summer, but a roaring torrent in winter. Across this stream is the "mountain," another European colony where are several lovely houses, those of Sir John Drummond Hay, Mr. White, and Miss Reade being perhaps the finest. From the mountain there is a gorgeous view. Below one to the right lies Tangier, beyond which one's eye roves over plains and mountains till, some fifty miles or more away, one can see the snow-capped mountains of

Tetuan, and away to the south at a much greater distance the enormous crags of Sheshouan, a mountain over 7000 feet in height. In front of one lie the Straits, Gibraltar clearly visible at one extremity, and behind it the snow-peaks of Mulahaçen and the Sierra Nevada, and at the other extremity the bay of Trafalgar and Cadiz ; while the whole expanse of sea is dotted with vessels.

The fashionable resort of Tangier is the beach of

Tangier Beach.

great wide sands, where every one can be seen riding between four and five in the afternoons. A mile and a half from Tangier along the beach is a river, and beyond that the ruins of Tingis, the Roman Tangier, of which not much beyond the walls remains. As is usual all over Morocco, there are no bridges by which to cross this river at this point, and until quite lately, when the Spaniards instituted a ferry, it had to be crossed by fording, not at all a pleasant proceeding both on account of the depth and current and the treacherous quicksands that exist in parts

of it.   In the time of the Romans there was a bridge
over this river, the remains of which still exist.
Higher up there are two bridges, one of them on the
Tetuan road.   The surroundings of Tangier have not
been taken proper advantage of, and only the gardens
of Sinieh Hashti, one on the " mountain," and Lalla
Shaafia are good examples of what the soil and
climate of Tangier are capable of growing.

A few words—only a few—as to the history of
Tangier.

Tangier was taken by the Portuguese, 1471, and
remained in their possession till ceded to England as
part of the dowry of the wife of Charles II. in 1662,
soon after which we gave it back to the Moors.   It
has several times been bombarded, the last time in
1844, when the French stormed the town.   When
the next bombardment will take place, it is impossible
to say.

We beguiled our few days' waiting in Tangier by
seeing the sights by day and by a dinner-party or
two in the evenings.   Going out to dinner in Tangier
surprises those who visit the place for the first time.
It is often pouring with rain, and of course no cabs
or carriages exist, while the roads are generally so full
of mud as to render any attempt at walking futile.

The only means of proceeding are by mounting a
donkey, on a " burda " or flat native pack-saddle, and,
braving wind and rain, to proceed.   The residents
have got so accustomed to this means of progression
that they think nothing of it, and on rainy nights
every one turns out to a dance just as if it were a
warm summer evening.   Figures enveloped in mackintoshes and shaded by huge umbrellas can be dimly

distinguished threading their muddy ways through the Soko by the light of the fantastic-shaped lanterns that their servants carry. Strange to say, their frocks do not seem to suffer, and one sees as many smart frocks at a Tangier dance as one does in most quarters of the globe.

Society in Tangier is split up into three factions ; those who will know each other, those who won't know each other, and those who must know each other but don't want to. I do not know which is the nicest faction, but I know no other little town abroad where people are kinder and more hospitable than at Tangier. Picnics and cheery little dinners are of constant recurrence, while riding parties and impromptu teas—not at all like an English "at home"—are very common.

Another great source of amusement in Tangier are the pig-sticking meetings held at about monthly intervals through the winter and early spring.

Nothing can be imagined more charming than these little gatherings, where every one—Tangier's every one—turns out and camps for five or six days at Awara. The originator of this noble sport in this country was Sir John Drummond Hay, Sir William Kirby Green's predecessor, an indefatigable sportsman—and with the new minister the institution continues and flourishes. The camp is pitched on the hill beyond the lake of Shaf-al-akab, near a village called Awara, in a dense cork and wild olive wood. The camp varies in size. Our minister— keenest of sportsmen—always has his camp out, and is generally accompanied by his wife and daughter, while Sir John Drummond Hay, who continues to reside in Tangier during the winter, brings his camp and family. Round the minister's camp are pitched the camps of the various residents, while Ansaldo, of the Continental Hotel, supplies tents and food for those who are not already possessed of them.

The sport itself is glorious, though to one unaccustomed to it the riding seems very perilous, as in some places one is going at full gallop over ground full of holes, in another tearing through bushes some five and six feet high, and again in cork woods, where one has to keep a very keen look-out to prevent getting one's head knocked off. However, though falls are common, very few accidents occur.

I have not space here to go through a whole day's pig-sticking, so will only describe one beat—that known as the mud flats.

The beaters remain on the top of a series of hills, while the "spears" are sent on and posted on both sides of a dry lake, hidden in the bushes. A certain time is given for the spears to be posted, and the beaters begin their work, hitting the bushes with sticks and shouting loudly all the while.

A pig is sighted, blank charges are fired by the beaters, while the spears wait in anxiety to see where "piggy" will break. Suddenly out he comes, and then begins the chase. The two spears nearest to him on the side he breaks dash after him, while those on the other side trot gently forward and prepare to meet him. The going is good and very fast, but to get the boar he must be stuck before he crosses the open ground, or he will be lost in impenetrable bush. Some one touches him with a spear, a mere prick however, but enough to turn him; with a grunt like

a miniature roar, he swings round. How his white
tusks flash in the sunlight. He charges ; not the
horse as he hopes, but on to the full point of the
lance levelled to receive him. All is not finished
yet—he is a tough old boar—he extricates himself
from the spear and charges first one horseman and
then another, from each receiving a dig. One perhaps
misses his mark, but is made to remember it by the
gash in his horse's leg where the old tusker has given
a nasty wound. At last, worn out with wounds and
the chase, he gives in and lies down to die.

Sometimes five or six pigs are got out of one beat
alone, but this is very exceptional. The usual average,
I should say, is to kill two or three pigs a day during
the three or four days' sticking. The dogs used for
driving the pig out of the bush are a curious set of
mongrels, but wonderfully cute, as they very seldom
approach within five or six yards of their foe, knowing
that one thrust of his tusks will send them to another
land.

It is a charming sight to watch the beaters, some
fifty or sixty in number, at work. They are for the
most part men from Suaneh, a village near Tangier,
and wear, like all men from that district, the brown
jelab and small coloured skull-cap, or red gun-case
wound round their heads. The excitement that they
get into, their shouting and blowing on horns, the
firing of guns when a boar is just sighted, and the
wild surroundings render the sport far more enjoyable than if it were managed with the precision and
order of an English covert shoot.

Perhaps the best time out in the pig-sticking camp
is the evening, when, after dinner, we all sit round the

great camp-fires and tell ghost stories, or render the
night hideous by an impromptu band.   I play on the
bath with a Zulu knobkerry.   It has not, perhaps,
the tone and expression of a violin, but it makes more
noise !

Far into the night we keep up the festivities, till
the fire burns lower, and then, after watching the
athletic Moors leap over the dying embers, we creep
away to our tents to wake refreshed and happy at an
early hour, prepared for a good day's sport.   We
usually go out into camp on the Monday, and strike
on Saturday, one day being an off-day, to give the
beaters and horses a chance.

On the whole, very little sport is to be found in the
neighbourhood of Tangier, everything having been
killed off by Spanish professional hunters to supply
the hotels ; but in winter a good many snipe may
be found on the lakes at Shaf-al-akab, and a few red-
legged partridges round about, but the sport is not
really sufficient to bring a sportsman to Tangier,
unless he intends making a tour up-country.

Some years ago, I believe, the sport, even in the
immediate neighbourhood of Tangier, was very excellent ; but the constant shooting of the birds without
a close season or restrictions of any sort has destroyed everything.

A new sport has just been introduced into Tangier
—fox-hounds—and with wonderful success, some
splendid runs having been obtained ; the country is
good, the going particularly fast, and there are plenty
of foxes, the result being that all interested in the
introduction of the hounds have been pleasantly surprised, as, though we felt confident from the beginning

of good sport, yet the reality has surpassed our
happiest dreams. There ought to be no difficulty in
keeping the hounds through the summer, as the
climate at Gibraltar is a great deal hotter in the
months of July, August, and September, and there
the hounds manage very well. This opening up of
fox-hunting ought to attract many visitors to Tangier
who are fond of sport and are ordered abroad for
health.

But the rain has passed over, and January 7th
of this year dawned gloriously. Our mules were
brought early, but it took a long time sorting our
baggage and packing it so as the weights should suit
the various animals, collecting our men, &c. Carleton kindly helped me, and after much shouting and
hurrying, kicking of mules and neighing of horses, we
were delighted by about noon to see our long string
of animals set out and cross the Soko, then turn to
the left and disappear on the mountain road.

I felt satisfied—we all did, I think—there was
nothing more to do but to rest for a time. Everything had gone on, there was no more anxiety as to
getting away, and we had only to ride out late and
overtake our mules before they reached their first
camping-place, beyond Spartel. Though we were
proceeding to Fez, Carleton and I, who both knew
all the roads well, decided that our only means of
reaching it would be to travel by the coast as far as
Laraiche, and then strike inland, owing to the flooded
state of the rivers, which on the Fez road were quite
impassable. However, at their mouths there is not
so much water, or a ferry exists, as the case may be.

I rode down to bid them good-bye at the Legation,

and with all sorts of good wishes from every one, we mounted our steeds and, turning our faces away from Europe and civilization, set out for the interior.

"Ah Sidi Mahammed al Hadj. Ah salama Sidi Mahammed al Hadj. Salaam alikum, Sidi Mahammed al Hadj," cried our Moors, as the three white domes of the great patron saint of Tangier were hid from sight, and we turned the corner from Soko on to the Spartel road.

CHAPTER II.

TANGIER TO LARAICHE.

WE left Tangier by the way which leads to the mountain. The road takes one along the lower slopes of the Marshan, on its south side—a road full of mud and crossed by dozens of tiny streams ; but no adventure befell us, though once or twice the horses and mules were up to their knees in the soft clay.

We crossed the Wad-al-ihoudi by the new wooden bridge. Some of the mules for a time utterly refused to proceed. My horse passed over first and offered no resistance, so that I was able to look back and see Forestier and Montbard thrashing their beasts on, to persuade them to cross. Nothing, however, seemed to be able to make the mules comprehend that they were to go over. I believe they knew it perfectly well, but mules have a way—and a will—of their own, and they began thus early on the journey to show it. A few minutes later they crossed perfectly quietly, having changed their minds for apparently no reason at all, though I fancy I detected a smile on one of the white mule's thick lips, as much as to say, "Well, we kept you waiting for a quarter of an hour and are satisfied now ; but wait for the next river !"

They used to repeat this little game at various stages of the road, varying it now and again by bucking, and sending saddle—great heavy native ones—and riders on to the wayside, then refusing to be caught.

However, at length our caravan crossed the bridge, and we began the steep ascent of the "mountain." What a rocky way it is, over great boulders and loose stones, sloping slabs of slippery rock, between prickly pear hedges and great spiky aloes. At length the summit is reached, and, looking back, the wide panorama of Tangier and the country beyond, Apes Hill, Gibel Habib, and the Tetuan Mountains, is stretched out before one, the Straits looking like an azure river dotted with its numberless ships, while in the midday haze the shore of Spain seems almost an unreality—so soft an outline it has and so delicate it is in tint. Tarifa—Tariks Town—is clearly visible, the first landing-place in Europe of the great Moorish general—a clustering of white houses low down to the Spanish coast. Our road is now more level; we pass "The cottage," one of the last European residences on the Spartel road, and say good-bye to Tangier, which is soon lost to sight.

Almost as far as Cape Spartel the road runs along the summit of the ridge of mountains. It is a wild path; here and there high into the air rise great crags of rock, covered with fern, almost the only break in the monotonous mountain-tops. Merely a track the road is, cut through the thick brushwood of gum cistus—the lovely white flower of which is not yet in bloom. A little further on the view opens up on our left, and we look down to the Atlantic beach, the lakes of Shaf-al-akab, and the cork forests. Near the lighthouse one descends to a slightly lower level and proceeds along the face of the precipitous cliff. Here it is most beautiful of all, just a narrow path in the wall of the precipice. Here and there rise great rocks, strange masses like church steeples and grotesque animals ; wild thick brushwood, where lurks the wary boar, grows on all sides, even over the steep face of the slope. Sometimes this brushwood meets overhead, rendering the road almost tunnel-like in appearance.

I remember once riding along this none too pleasant road on a very fresh horse. I was accompanying two friends to Spartel, and was regaling them with stories of Morocco ; unluckily, just as I reached the point of each yarn, before I had time to bring it out, my horse would make a clean bolt, dashing along the precipitous path at a breakneck pace, and making me think that every moment I was to be hurled into the ocean hundreds of feet below. Besides, the whole effect of my stories was spoilt, which was annoying. The remedy was found, however, by Col. S., one of my friends, proposing that I should only whisper the point of the story so as not to allow my horse to know the moment to bolt. I found it most successful.

Suddenly the lighthouse comes into sight, a tall white pillar, on the extreme N.W. corner of Africa. How the sea dashes and foams around the rocks at the foot of the cliff, rushing in and out of the great boulders in a dance of mad frenzy.

We found our mules waiting for us here, and having despatched them to Gibeleh, a small village a little way further on, we enter the lighthouse, drink coffee with the keeper, and sit for an hour or so on the rocks near by.   It was a glorious afternoon, with just a fresh enough N.W. breeze to cover the sea with little white billows, and to render the sound of the waves as they burst on the rocks below a wild melody of music.

An hour though was all the wait I could allow, and then once more we mounted and proceeded on our way.   The road after leaving the lighthouse is much like the latter part we had passed over, but about half an hour's distance from Spartel, one descends the steep, rocky side of the mountain, and fording a small river, emerges on the sands.   What a gallop Ingram and I had.   My horse, a celebrated bad-behaviour brute, which no one could be persuaded to buy in Tangier, and which had been for sale and unridden for four months, had already been playing some little tricks on the road, so I took it out of him across that mile or two of sands.   Half an-hour later the road began a gentle ascent, then leaving the beach we turned a little inland, and an hour or so before sunset reached Gibeleh, where we found our mules already being unloaded.

Naturally, as it was our first camp, there was some confusion, but we all worked with a will, and before dark had the satisfaction of seeing our four tents pitched, a fire alight in the kitchen, on which stood a long row of saucepans and kettles, and our mules all tethered in a long line.

Half-an-hour after sunset Carleton turned up, having been detained in Tangier till four o'clock, when he had left the town and ridden out across country in the almost incredible period of two hours. It was late before we got our dinner, as stores had to be hunted out, and there was much to be seen to, nor were we sorry to turn in and seek refuge in sleep from the worries of a "first night."

Now having got fairly off on the road, a few words as to what is required for camping in Morocco may not be out of place ; however, the following paragraphs may be comfortably skipped by those who have no intention of visiting this land of an African Sultan.

To begin with one's kit. I find—after considerable experience—that one requires very much the same clothing camping out in the winter in Morocco as one does in England in early spring. I had with me on this trip two pairs of good strong cord riding-breeches ; a pair of "Field" boots, to lace up the front, of brown leather ; a pair of shooting-boots, and a pair of ordinary walking-boots ; one pair of knickerbockers and one of trousers, a blue football jersey ; two cloth coats and waistcoats ; a covert coat ; two mackintoshes; a pair of waders, and a considerable amount of underclothing, stockings, pijamas, &c. As to hats, small caps are excellent, but a shady hat or two must be bought ; I prefer the large soft felt hat to the helmet, as the latter are so difficult to pack.

My tent is a square one, with double flat roof, bamboo poles, and waterproof flooring. It is only some seven feet square, but I find it quite large enough. I always use, and have found most satisfactory, one of Silver's "Salisbury" beds, which pack up very small, are light, and when carefully treated

D

will last for years.   My bedding consists of two very
large Moorish blankets sewn into a bag, and a native
striped coverlet ; an immense Russian fur coat, which
I picked up during a trip to the White Sea, always
accompanies me on all my travels.   The bag of
blankets I find most excellent, as, being very large,
they form some eight folds, which one can vary
according to the weather, by sleeping with four at
the top and four at the bottom, or one at the bottom
and seven at the top.   My huge fur coat makes a
mattress.   Let me warn the intending " camper " of
one thing, that cold at night is not to be kept off
merely by thick coverings over one's bed, as it is
far more important that between one and the ground
there should be a great thickness of blankets or a
mattress—on account of the damp rising from the
earth.   Of all the important " articles " of camp life,
this is the first and by far the most important—a
camp-bed.   I do not care how many waterproof
coverings there may be between one and the ground,
it is unsafe to sleep on the ground.

Stores for the trip can either be obtained in Tangier or England.   I prefer the latter.   All the stores
we took on the tour I am now writing of, were supplied by the Army and Navy Stores, beautifully
packed into strong iron-bound boxes.   There is no
need, I think, to go through a list of stores.   The most
important are tea, coffee, candles, potted meats, tinned
soups, pepper, salt, mustard, tinned tongues and
hams, biscuits, liquor, &c.   These are the most important items, the rest depends upon the travellers,
whether they intend to camp luxuriously, and how
many mules they intend to take with them.   We

took four boxes of stores, some two feet six inches in
length, eighteen inches in width and height, but I
should advise any one else to take them the same
height and width, but only two feet in length, as
that size would fit better into the native "shuarries"
or paniers.

Saddlery, guns, and ammunition must be brought
from England ; a good saddle is a necessity, as sore
backs are very common amongst the horses; also it
is best to bring two bridles, breastplate, crupper,
numnah, &c. ; brushes and cloths can be procured
in Tangier. A headstall and chain are required for
tethering the horse, for though they are tethered as
well by the legs, yet I prefer the double precaution,
and do both. Tents too it is best to bring from
England, enough for oneself and a large tent for the
Arabs. I find that the only means of getting along
the roads without trouble from my men is to house
them well. As for the number of cartridges, I can
give no advice, it all depends on luck whether one
gets good shooting or no. Of course there are excellent spots to go to, but the birds vary very much
from year to year ; I believe myself the barbary partridge is migratory to some extent. The best shooting we obtained two years ago was in a secluded
spot near Fez ; this year we shot all day over pre-
cisely the same ground, and got nothing, absolutely
nothing, though our bag two years before had been
both varied and large. Nobody had shot the place
this year before us, and there seems no theory capable of accounting for the disappearance of game than
that they had tired of their old ground and sought a
new one elsewhere.

Cartridges can be obtained now at Tangier from Mr. Ansaldo of the Continental Hotel. A small-bore rifle is advisable for great bustard.

Now to return to our camp once more. We were very early astir on the 8th of January, and soon had our mules packed and ready to be off. Sending them forward, we proceeded to the caves of Hercules, to show our artists one of the sights of the neighbourhood of Tangier.

It is not surprising in a country that boasts of a pillar of Hercules to find caves dedicated to the same mythical hero, but it is surprising anywhere to find caves so fine as these.

Though situated on the water's edge, it is impossible, owing to the surf and precipice, to enter from the sea ; and the only means of access is through a long, winding passage some little way inland. When one has threaded a rather precarious path through this dark passage, one finds oneself in a really magnicent cave, about which are grouped, like sepulchral mummies, Moors, who earn their livelihood by hewing mill-stones out of the solid rock ; nor has the cave been to any degree defaced by this seeming desecration. On the contrary, the innumerable circles traced upon the walls and roof have, in the half-light, a weird appearance that reminds one of the days when astrologers covered the walls of their retreats with strange hieroglyphics.

It is a beautiful sight to stand on a piece of projecting rock near where the sea enters and watch wave after wave roll in, dashing through the narrow natural archway swiftly onward till stopped by a wall rock, over which, when it finds itself baffled, its throws its myriad drops of spray with a roar and a crash like thunder. And so day and night, though sometimes in calm weather the rush may be less, the sea will lash itself into fury again, till a thousand echoes are all crying aloud a chorus to the deep, dull roar below. No ; it is not difficult, in times like these, to imagine how the simple-minded Moor, ever ready to believe what he hears, should have the idea that within lived, and even lives now, some great spirit. As one sits on the dry ground above the cave and listens, he can imagine that below him, almost in the bowels of the earth, is being waged a war, the like of which mortal eyes have never seen or mortal ears heard ; and it is a battle, too, for the sea is fighting to wear away the rock, and the rock is fighting to keep back the sea, and the sea is getting the better of it ; for year by year it forces its entrance in further and further, and in the dim future perhaps will own all the disputed land, but that will be long after the Moors have ceased to hew mill-stones.

But I have heard another sound in the dim caves, a sound strangely out of place where one expects to hear nothing but the sea, the quiet hoot of the owl, or the squeaking bats ; I have heard the ring of merry laughter and the sound of happy voices. Readers, I confess at once I have heard the clashing of knives and forks, and the popping of champagne corks.

It is a great place for picnics in summer. Everything lends itself to enjoyment. The ride from Tangier, through valleys whose little streams are full of basking tortoises, the hills with the gum-cistus all in bloom, the steep descent through the village of Meduna, with its small mud-and-thatch houses and its hedges of prickly-pears and aloes, the blue vast ocean and the bluer vaster sky.   Nor is the ride home in the afternoon the least enjoyable part, especially if one return by Cape Spartel, past the lighthouse perched on the rocky promontory, along the edge of the cliff, over the mountains, till as evening approaches one sees Tangier at one's feet, crowned in the glorious rays of a setting sun, all gold and mauve, or one rides through the now quiet sôk, amidst sleeping camels, by the light of an African moon.

After this little outburst of sentimentalism we will return once more to our matter-of-fact journey through Morocco.

The road led us along the sea-beach, over hard yellow sands, for some distance, and many were the races Carleton and I rode, both feeling that intense sensation of freedom, which one can only feel in such countries as Morocco.   We found our mules waiting on the banks of the Wad Tsahadartz, an unpleasantly large river, which had to be crossed in two rickety little boats, behind which swam the mules and horses. This unloading the mules, piling the baggage into the boats and then loading them on the opposite bank is a tedious process, and we wasted much time over the crossing.   However, if Morocco possessed bridges all through the country, half the pleasure of tent-life then would be gone, for it is these great rivers that form one of the principal means of keeping Morocco in the state of " B.C." existence it enjoys now.

About four o'clock, the passage of the Tsahadartz having been accomplished without any mishap, we pitched our tents in a village of the Gharbia, on the side of a steep hill, near some charming gardens.

Our barometers fell fast—I mean the spirits of M. and F., our French artists. Evidently there was rain in the air. No longer did the cheering notes of " Gais et contents, nous allons à Longchamps " issue from their throats. Evidently, as I said before, there was rain in the air. About six o'clock that evening it began to fall, and fell as fast as the " barometers " had done. It rained in torrents all night, though in the tents we were quite dry. We tried to cheer those whose knowledge of camp-life was just commencing by prophesying fine weather for the morrow, but they still stuck to their new idea, that Morocco was the most horrible country they had ever set their eyes on· When coffee, liqueurs and cigarettes followed dinner, they cheered up a little, and we all began telling stories of sport. Ingram and I had told a good many when Montbard opened his mouth and told us the following:—

" The True Story of Montbard and the Burgundy Hare.

" There is only one country in the world," he began, " and that is Burgundy. Burgogne, c'est la France, Paris is its suburb and all the countries of Europe are as nothing compared with it. In Burgundy the fruit-trees bear fruit seven times in the year—there is no winter, no summer, it is always alike—and there is no close season for game. The country is full of game, swarming with it ! Why do you Englishmen go to Central Africa to shoot, why do you come to Morocco, when Burgundy is so near ? Why go to Norway to fish when our streams are full of big trout running from a pennyweight to two ounces !

" But enough !   Burgundy is the finest country in the world !

" One May, when everything looked its best, I took my trusty gun—for the blacksmith in the village had put the bent barrel nearly straight, and set out. I had broken it by using it as a brake to the pony-shay coming down the steep hill behind the village.   Well, it was May when, pipe in mouth, my gun over my shoulder, cartridge-bags and revolvers round my waist, I sauntered out.

" Why did I go shooting, you ask ?

" Because I am a lover of ' La chasse ' and because," here Montbard's voice was scarcely more than a whisper, "the people told me that a hare had appeared in the neighbourhood, and was devastating the country round.

" In the open country I put away my pipe, loaded my right barrel (the bent one) with shot and my left with a bullet, in case I missed with the first, and prepared for action.

" There was scarce a breath of wind in the woods, the leaves just rustled sweetly on the trees. Every now and again I waited to listen, but heard nothing.

" Steadily I crept forward, listening as I went. I hoped to find him asleep, gorged on the fowls he had eaten the night before. For nearly half an hour I walked, till, thoroughly worn out, I reached the further side of the wood, passed through a small gate, and threw myself wearily down in the orchard of a small farm-house.

" I must have slept some time, what woke me I do not know, but I think it was that feeling that Providence has vouchsafed to mankind to perceive when danger is near. I never stirred, but opened one eye slowly and looked out.

"A cold sweat burst all over my frame, but I never lost my head for a moment.

"Imagine," here Montbard was dramatic, "imagine my horror to see, devouring a cabbage close to my feet, the H A R E.

"I never moved. Livingstone, when under the lion's paw, knew his only safeguard was in remaining quiet. I did the same.

"The hare seemed quite unaware of my presence, and was calmly eating, but I could not help thinking how few moments it might be before he would change his diet of cabbage for one of human food. Still I never moved.

"All my life I will never forget that day, at night now I sometimes dream of it. Every line of that hare's form is as clear before me now as it was then.

"It was white—like a polar bear—with great scarlet eyes—a sure sign that it was of the man-eating species. Its teeth ground against one another with horrible reverberation, while the fiery glance of those scarlet eyes petrified me with terror.

"Yet I never moved.

"Presently the hare turned the other way. I raised my gun to my shoulder—and allowing for the bend in the right barrel—took a long and steady aim.

"My life depended on that shot, for the ferocious beast was only a yard away, and did I miss would be upon me at once!

"I fired—both barrels!

"When I dared to open my eyes the hare had disappeared!

" With a shout I rose to my feet, expecting every moment to feel his cruel claws tearing limb from limb, while his fangs extracted my inside—like Prometheus. Imagine my joy when I found I had killed him—not only killed him, but blown him to atoms !

" All that was left was a blue velvet collar with ' Jeanne ' embroidered on it—tied by a fine cord to a cabbage stalk—all do I say—no not all, for half an ear was found some fifty yards away—a veritable trophy !

" The people in the farm tried to make a fool of me, they said it was a tame Himalayan rabbit I had killed. But I was not to be fooled.

" I knew then, and I know now, that I had ridded my fatherland of one of its worst enemies.

" Who can tell how many herds and flocks might not have been destroyed before its death, how many children might not have been carried off, or graves dug up and corpses exhumed ! "

Montbard ceased.

I was the only one who dared speak.

" Did not Tartarin come from Burgundy?" I asked.

Montbard answered me with a look.

If the hare had seen that look, it would have died of fright.

We all went to bed.   None of our adventures compared with Montbard's.

All night it poured in torrents, and the following morning the rain was falling as fast as ever, so we decided not to strike camp, but to remain the rest of the day at the Gharbia village, so as to allow our tents, &c., to thoroughly dry.   Ingram, Carleton and I went out to try and shoot something, but had very poor sport, though it was not wasted time, as it gave us an excellent opportunity of studying our dogs. Mitza, a half-bred French pointer, belonging to Antonio, surprised us by her sagacity, and especially her skill at following up wounded birds. We walked all day over undulating hills surrounding a large marsh. The sides of these hills were covered with palmeto— a dwarf palm—which reaches the height of about two feet, and affords excellent covert for the birds. We only bagged four and a half brace, but our walk was a thoroughly enjoyable one. On our return to camp we found tea awaiting us, after which I spent an hour grooming my horse and initiating Selim into the mysteries of the curry-comb, &c.

A showery night succeeded a fine afternoon, but the next morning was bright and sunny, so we decided to make a move. There was no need to make an early start, as we had a tidal river to cross *en route*, and it was therefore eleven o'clock before our mules were all packed and the caravan moved forward.

An hour's ride brought us to the river, the Wad al Ghreefa, near which are the ruins of a Roman aqueduct. We had to wait some time before we could cross, as the water was yet too high. On the opposite bank we saw Mr. and Mrs. T. and Count H. on their way back from a trip to Laraiche. Carleton and I soon forded our horses across, though the water came over the flaps of our saddles ; Ingram and the others followed some few minutes later. On the south bank we joined the other party, and had a pleasant lunch all together. While this was proceeding our baggage was being brought across, for the most part on the mules' backs, but for fear of the ammunition and guns getting wet we had them carried over by men mounted on our saddle-horses. In this manner nothing got damp. An hour or so we spent on the beach, and then our party broke up, Mr. and Mrs. T. and H. proceeding on their way and we on ours.

An hour or so later we reached Arzeilah, a small walled town on the seashore, very picturesque, very old and very dirty. There is little doubt that this town is on the site of the Roman Zilio, the name alone going far to establish this theory. It has suffered the varied vicissitudes that nearly all the Moorish coast-towns have passed through, having been the scene of many a bombardment and many a battle. Portuguese at one time, Spanish at another, Moorish now, and rumour even speaks of it having been English at one period.

We pitched our tents not far from the town, on a site I had often occupied before, overlooking the sea. Our party split up, some going after sport in the neighbourhood, while I undertook to show our artists the ins and outs of the little place.

Probably the population of Arzeilah is not more than 800 or 1000, but from the important look of its solid turreted and betowered walls one would think it at first sight to be a place of far greater importance and size. We entered the town by the principal gate, a curious old Portuguese structure, which answers not only the purpose of a means of exit and entrance for the population, but is also conveniently situated, being on a steep slope, to carry away the drainage of the town. However, we succeeded in wading on ; and called upon our consular agent, a Jew of the name of Bensheetah, whose acquaintance I had made when passing Arzeilah on my return from visiting the Sultan at Morocco City with the British Minister. Contrary to most Jewish houses, we found his residence very clean, and it was a pleasure to sit and drink coffee with the handsome old gentleman while we discussed Moorish and European affairs in Spanish, a language I am very slightly acquainted with. However, I succeeded in making him understand, though I had to vary my statements, without strict accuracy to truth, to suit my knowledge of the tongue.

Within the town walls there is little to see but dirt, a not uncommon sight in Morocco ; the smells, too, seemed to affect all our senses at once, so extremely powerful they are. Arzeilah possesses many Jews, who are, as a rule, as dirty here as elsewhere.

Between the town and our camp, about 150 yards from the main gate is the tomb of a great Moorish saint, and the " saint-house " belonging thereto. It is certainly one of the most beautiful " Marabouts " in the whole country, and the clustering palms and creepers greatly enhance its appearance. Over or through this luxuriant vegetation peep the little horse-shoe arched door, a milk white dome, and the green-tiled roof.

We took tea in the open air. The view looking towards the town was very lovely. In the foreground was the saint-house, beyond it the battlements and towers of Arzeilah, a dull grey mauve against the sunset sky, a perfect harmony of colouring, while the sea gently lapped along the yellow sands.

A gorgeous moonlight night succeeded a fine, though chilly day. Shortly before dark our sportsmen returned, having picked up some three or four brace of partridges. Next morning we were off be-times, and leaving our mules to be packed and brought on under the charge of our soldier, we set out *à la chasse*. A showery day, and the fact that we were not yet far enough away from Tangier, rendered us satisfied to return to camp with only four and a half brace of birds, two pigeons, and a rabbit. Our camp was pitched on the summit of a steep hill overlooking a small lake; close to our tents were large groves of oranges, in which we sauntered during the evening, stealing the fruit and shooting wood-pigeons. The orange-trees were very large and covered with fruit, though it was too early in the year for them to be really sweet. However, we managed to eat a good many, and suffered accordingly. Next morning I was disgusted on rising to find the rain coming down in torrents, and with every likelihood of its continuing to do so all day.

Our barometers—the Frenchmen—down again, down very low. " Could we not turn back, this was too awful. Why, it was better in London in fog and snow, than in Morocco with only a tent to cover one's head, and the rain coming down as if a second flood were about to take place," &c., &c. But we paid no attention, knowing that this rain was an unusual occurrence, and that it must soon end.

Carleton had been seedy all along ; he left Tangier unwell, and what with getting very wet shooting and utterly refusing to cover himself sufficiently at night, his cough had increased to such an extent as to make us all exceedingly uneasy. Much against our will he set off for Tangier in the pouring rain the follow-ing morning—a ride which took him some thirteen hours. He feared an attack of inflammation of the lungs in the camp, and risked all on this perilous ride. It was not till our arrival in Tangier that we heard how narrow an escape he had had in swimming his horse over the Wad Ghreefa, which was in flood ; or how he reached Tangier some time after dark, half-fainting from fatigue, or how he was confined to his bed for days with congestion. The same time as he swam his horse over the river two Moors trying to swim across were carried out to sea and drowned, and Carleton almost suffered a like fate. Had not his horse been a powerful one and its rider a most perfect horseman, both would have been lost.

Sunday being fine, we struck camp, and making a tolerably long march of some seven or eight hours on a tiresome path—as we constantly had to deviate from the road on account of torrents and mudholes—pitched our camp half-an-hour before sunset at Sahal-al-Khemis. The road had tired us all out. The ups and downs of the mountain track, through great high brushwood and withered olive-trees, had been very dull and monotonous, nor were we at all happy in our minds about poor Carleton.

At Sahal we found Captain T. P. and his son encamped—the former laid up with gout. These two instances of illness may tend to frighten sportsmen from the country, but the weather had been so exceptionally bad as easily to account for them.

Sahal-al-Khemis is a typical Moorish village of the better class, with square mud-huts, for the most part thatched, great hedges of prickly pears and cacti, and storks everywhere. Scarcely a house there was that had not a stork's nest, commenced already, on its roof, while the birds strolled about quite tamely, clacking their beaks as if to say, " No one touches us, we are sacred—so take care." The Moors never destroy the storks, as the following fable is accepted all through the country concerning them.

" They are men," say the Moors, " who have come from islands far away to the west, upon the great ocean, to see Morocco. Like all the world, they know there is no other land to compare to it, so they even abandon their outward form of men to come and see it. We will give them hospitality, we will not harm them."

This idea that Morocco is the only country of the world worth anything, is well illustrated by a story told by a French author, a man who knows Morocco well.

The Sultan, wishing to be like the Sultan of Turkey, gave an order to a French firm to design and manufacture for him " Orders." This was accordingly done, and the Orders arrived. On one side was a drawing of the sun, a circle in the centre, with rays spreading in every direction. On the centre was engraved in Arabic, " Al Maghreb," the native name for Morocco, while each of the deviating rays contained the following—London, Paris, Moscow, Stamboul, India, and others. The Moors do not know the European countries except by the names of their capitals.

This naturally pleased the Sultan, but the design on the other side struck him still more, and must have added much to his knowledge of astronomy and geography, for written in decorative Arabic were the words:

" The sun never sets on the Shereefian Empire."

The Sultan never made use of these Orders, as he

feared they would call too much attention to his country and create jealousy.

We pitched our camp on one of my favourite spots in all Morocco, the edge of a precipice overlooking a rich fertile valley and the ocean beyond, while to the north rise wooded mountains of considerable altitude, and rumoured to be full of wild boar.

The following day G. T. P. joined us in a small shoot over very rough plough. It was hot work, and we found two hours of it enough, killing nine and a half brace of partridges, one hare, and a pigeon· Near the sea-coast we bade adieu to our friend, who returned to his camp, while we rode on by the sea beach to Laraiche, a large town only some two hours' ride beyond Sahal. The view as we crossed the sand-hills and caught sight of the town was a particularly pretty one. The winding river, the Koos, rushing in over its foaming bar, while its waters are like glass within, is a river of no mean pretensions, and even at Alazar, some twenty miles up, is no insignificant stream. On the further bank is Laraiche, a rather European-looking town, as the Jews, of whom a large proportion of the community consist, have taken largely to European ways and habits, bar cleanliness. Above the town the river turns sharply to the north, and here lie a few small European sailing-ships. Thence the river changes its course considerably, running in serpentine windings in and out of the low marsh ground. A mile from its mouth, on the north bank, is a high hill, the site of Lixus, while on the south bank are low mountains covered with orange and olive groves, one of the many sites of the Gardens of the Hesperides.

E

Our mules were awaiting us at the ferry across the river, as were also Montbard and Forestier, who had found it too warm for shooting, but had done good work in their sketch-books.

We soon had our mules safely conveyed across in barges, and it was not long before our camp was pitched at the top of the town, on a small disagreeably scented piece of ground just outside the south gate.

What there is to see in Laraiche we spent the following day in seeing, but there is little of any great interest. It is more owing to the situation that Laraiche has the reputation of being a picturesque town, than to any of its buildings or decorations. The Soko within the town walls is certainly pretty, though scarcely oriental, the long colonnades of pillars and arches on either side of the square savouring strongly of the Portuguese. At the end of the Sôk, however, there is a purely Moorish archway of the usual horseshoe type, in good preservation and of fine workmanship. Passing under this arch, one enters the kasbah, or fortress, in which all the official residences are situated, including the prisons, as gruesome as usual. The gate of Justice is certainly fine, and not unlike that of Tangier. Here we called upon the Governor, a pleasant-spoken old gentleman, though his reputation is not exactly a good one. He is the Bascha of the town, and his rule extends over the whole district of Laraiche, including all the Koos plains and the town of Alcazar, where he is represented by a Calipha.

The exterior of the fortress is fine, surrounded as it is by a deep moat. The walls are high, and are of solid masonry, the top decorated with small towers, through the buttresses of which peep a few old Portuguese guns. Laraiche has been the scene of many a deadly fight. From century to century it changed hands amongst the Moors, Portuguese, and Spaniards ; from the latter it was captured just two hundred years ago (1629) by Moulai Ismail, one of the greatest and most cruel of Morocco's Sultans. As late as 1860 it was bombarded by the Spaniards in justification of some wrong, and previously, in 1830, it was nearly knocked to pieces by the Austrian fleet.

But Laraiche has a history far more ancient ; when the Spaniards were still barbarians, the Portuguese still more so, before ever Austria possessed a fleet (!), Laraiche and the country round was a flourishing Carthaginian colony. At Lixus, only about an hour's ride from the town, on the north bank of the river, one can see great walls they raised, stones sixteen feet in length, four wide and four thick, piled one on the top of the other. But exploration here, on the very small scale that exploration can be carried on amongst these ruins, is much impeded by the density of the vegetation. On this visit to Laraiche I did not have an opportunity of visiting Lixus, but I had spent some hours there on a previous occasion. We grovelled about in the earth a little, and found some small pieces of mosaic and a little stucco fresco-work, on which the colours were still in brilliant preservation. Doubtless were one able to overcome the prejudice of the native officials and obtain permission to dig, many interesting remains would come to light.

The ruins consist for the most part of walls, though here and there the remains of a forum or temple can

be traced.   As I said, however, the place is too overgrown with brushwood to allow one to gain any clear
idea as to the extent of the remains.

The steep streets of Laraiche with their uninteresting semi-European buildings, and filthy smells, do
not tempt one to remain, so that we only stayed one
day, long enough to have some of our mules reshod
and a panier or two mended.   One incident happened
the day after our arrival there.   One of our men—
Ingram's gun-bearer—succeeded in abstracting the
silver end off Ingram's walking-stick, and selling it to
a Moorish woman for half a peseta ($4\frac{1}{2}d$.).

Proofs were clear against him.   He had been seen
stealing and also selling it.   At first we thought of
taking him before the Bascha, but we could not
harden our hearts sufficiently to let him lie for an
indefinite period in the filthy prison.   I therefore took
from him what money he had, which had been
advanced to him on leaving Tangier, and his new
brown jelab in part payment thereof, and gave him
five minutes to get out of sight, telling him if he had
not disappeared by then, I would take a shot at him
with my pistol.   In five seconds he was gone.   I
replaced him by a brawny nigger who had been loaf-
ing about the camp, and whose services I afterwards
dispensed with at Fez, as he did not hit it off with
my other men.   Ingram and the others, to whom
Arabic names were rather a mouthful, had by this
time nicknamed all our men.   Very naturally our
nigger passed as "Sambo;" while Gil Ali, a fine
strapping Moor, a servant of Carleton's, was called
"Jubilee;" Selim, my own man, Fondak, on account of some trouble he had given Ingram

and myself, some two years before, at the Fondak, or Caravanserai, half way between Tangier and Tetuan. Abdurrahman, a handsome young Moor, of most gentlemanly habits, and features of pure Roman type, went by the name of Cæsar. He was a charming youth, and the most satisfactory man I have ever had to do with, working always with a will, and ready to do anything to please one. I took him later on to Wozan, on my second tour in the interior this year, and found him as good as ever. One elderly man we had with us possessed only one eye, and accordingly went by the name of Cyclops, while another was called Sindbad. They soon got to know their nicknames, and called each other by them, though some got strangely muddled in their pronunciation, Cæsar becoming " Seissors " and Sindbad " Shinbaek."

On January 15th we left Laraiche for Mequinez.

CHAPTER III.

LARAICHE TO MEQUINEZ.

WE left Laraiche on January 15th. It was the first really hot day we had yet experienced and the

Peasant Girl.

"barometers" were up accordingly. The sun streamed down upon us and seemed to thaw the cold in our bones, the result of a week's wet. I know no feeling more exhilarating than to ride under a warm sun after suffering from cold—one can almost feel the warmth forcing its way into one's inside and warming the very "cockles of one's heart," though I believe it puzzles anatomists to fix the exact location of that portion of the organ. About an hour after leaving Laraiche we entered a grand forest of cork and wild olive-trees, which here reach a great altitude. The scene was lovely, the branches overhead sufficing to keep off the almost too powerful rays of the midday sun, which pierced, however, the thick foliage here and there, shedding slanting lines of brilliant light on to the green sward. Every now and then the forest opens up into delightful glades, where were feeding cattle, while on every side gambolled and danced the lambs and kids—and the soft notes of the shepherd boy's pipe and the rich song of the birds added to the perfect enjoyment of the pastoral scene. But this forest has also a darker side, as it is said to be infested with robbers, who plunder the small caravans as they carry their merchandise to and from the coast. We spent an hour or so shooting in these woods, and got a few brace of partridges.

We pitched our camp before sunset some way on the further side of the forest at a minute village called Ein-Buileh-Sidi-Muhktar. The long name I suppose was to add to the importance of a few mud and thatch huts and a "ghima" or two—the brown canvas tents of the Arabs proper. This was the first encampment of "ghimas" we had come across, and clearly told us that we had said good-bye to the hills and were entering the plains, where the wandering Bedouins have their abode.

These tent villages are usually pitched in a circle,

each tent touching its neighbour, so that there is no
way into the circle except by the one entrance, closed
at night by a high stack of brambles.   Into these
villages at night the flocks and herds are driven, as
raids by other Bedouins are not uncommon.

A wonderful life these Bedouins live, wandering
from place to place, a month here, a year there, a week
somewhere else.   Passing their days as their ancestors
passed it when Rebecca was found at the well, simply
pastoral, simply poetical, simply filthy.   O dirt, what
would artists do without thee ?   What an addition thou
art to the picturesque !   Wash the Bedouin lady, undo
the tangles of her hair, give her clean clothes and a
dress improver, and all her beauty is gone.   It is one
of the most poetical sights in the world an Arab
" duar " at nightfall.   The sun has set, yet the Eastern
sky is a blaze of crimson and silver with the after-
glow.   Slowly winding their way from the well are
the women and girls, bearing on their heads their
heavy pitchers.   Over the hill-top come the lowing kine
and the bleating herds, driven by little boys who dance
along to the music of their reed pipes, not shrill and
harsh, but with soft, low-sounding strains.   From the
" ghimas " can be heard the sound of the corn-mill as
the women sit and turn with never-ceasing arm the
heavy stone, while here and there from the encampment a thin coil of blue smoke ascends pillar-like into
the breathless air.   Glorious must be the life of a
Bedouin.

The Skeikh of Ein-Buileh-Sidi-Mukhtar called on
us, bringing a present of some milk and two chickens.
We found him most pleasant, but like most Moorish
visitors he stayed too long, and all our plots and plans

to dislodge him failed, so that at last I had to tell him that we wished to go to bed.

The next day witnessed one of those changes of temperatures one sometimes—often even—experiences in Morocco, and was bitterly cold. The road was a dreary, treeless one, over great prairies, with nothing to relieve the monotony, but marshes, a few duars, and rain. It rained in torrents, but we decided to push on. We had already been detained long enough on the road, and now braved Providence and refused to give in to her, shaking our fists in her face.

Early in the afternoon we pitched our camp in a highly picturesque village on the left of the road, the name of which I was unable to discover, as none of the natives I inquired of knew it. However, it is a place of some importance, and possesses the shrine of a very holy man—a white-domed saint-house, with a mosque adjoining. One by one our men, as we passed in the pouring rain, reverently knelt and kissed the doorstep or lintel of the tomb, calling blessings from above on the head of the dear departed.

The saint business is a grand thing in Morocco. When every other business has failed a man usually takes to being a saint, and as all Moors are brought up with the most extraordinary ideas as to honesty and morals, they generally succeed in gaining an average fortune in the "saint line."

Saints are seen everywhere. Often distinguished by peculiarities of dress, generally by the fact that they carry battle-axes, and always by the reverence they obtain from their fellow-men, they are easily distinguishable. Every visitor to Tangier will have noticed an old gentleman with long grey hair and beard, a pale blue cloak and a breast covered with such charms as tin match-boxes and tooth-combs. He is a great saint; and the goodwill of his business would be well worth purchasing. He was, so it is said, a tolerably respectable man, but one day for amusement he killed his wife, for which he was hamstrung. Finding himself incapable of work, he promptly and wisely took to the saint business, and is now a rising star in that profession.

Towards evening it cleared up, and the setting sun dried our tents. A big bonfire blazed till late at night in camp, and many were the ghost stories we were told by our men, or told ourselves. Arabic is a wonderful language for story-telling—powerful in the extreme. One story I told my men—half founded on a tradition of the Moors and half invented in my imagination—caused an unexpected move on the part of Selim.

I told them that once camping with Aleck Bereus near Alcazar Sorehr in the Anjera, close to a spot called the Haunted Ford I had seen a ghost.

This is what I told them.

" THE HAUNTED FORD.

"Not long ago Bereus and myself were encamped in Anjera. We had pitched our tents on the steep bank of a fast-flowing river under the shade of some lofty olive-trees, for, although it was early in the year, the sun was powerful. On the evening of which I am speaking the sun had set stormily, and the moon's rays could only now and again pierce the filmy clouds that appeared to be running races in the sky. My friend and myself were seated in front of our camp fire, and were just thinking of turning in, when a ghostlike voice, proceeding from the wood behind us, said in Arabic, ' Who dares to pitch his tent at the haunted ford ? ' Thinking that this might be some trick to call our attention away—for the place was infested with robbers—we stuck to our posts, merely drawing our revolvers. The voice repeated its words for a second time, and then there issued from the wood into the full glare of our camp fire the strangest figure I have ever yet set my eyes on. An old man, nearly bent double with long grey tangled locks hanging wildly over his haggard, sallow face, scantily clad in a torn 'jelaba,' and bearing a battle-axe. But the strangest feature of all were his eyes—black fiery eyes that never stood still, but gazed every moment in some new direction. I instantly recognized that we had nothing to fear from our aged friend—and that he was only one of the mad shereefs [1] —who wander over the country begging their way —and reverenced on account of their madness.

"' Who dares pitch their camp at the haunted ford ? ' he said again.

"' I do,' I answered.

" He turned quickly towards me—gazed at me for a moment and said, ' You speak Arabic ? '

"' Yes,' I responded, then added, ' Sit down by our fire and warm yourself, and we will give you something to eat.'

"' I will sit down,' he said, ' but I cannot eat at the haunted ford.'

[1] A man who is " hamak " or " silly " obtains much reverence in Morocco, as in the East.

" He sat down by the fire and stretched his bony hands over the sparkling embers. Suddenly a thought struck me.

"'Tell me,' I said, 'the story of the haunted ford.'

" He got up and changed his position—seating himself opposite to us on the further side of the fire, so that every detail of his face and person was illuminated; and a strange creature he was. As he looked half starved I again pressed him to eat.

"' He dies,' he mumbled—half to himself, 'he dies who eats at the haunted ford,' but in spite of this he ate some bread, mumbling the while, ' I shall die for it. He dies who eats at the haunted ford. I shall die for it.'

" Then he began his tale, in strange poetical language such as all the Arabs use when narrating their weird stories :—

"' Two hundred years ago, on the very spot where your camp is now pitched, was fought a great battle, and many were the slain and many the wounded ; for a portion of the Sultan's army, with the Sultan's brother, Sidi Mahammed al Fileli at the head—was attacked by the mountaineers. Now the Sultan's brother fought like one of the royal line, and here, there, and everywhere in the fray could be seen his great white horse charging to and fro while every blow the Prince dealt was a blow of death. But the mountaineers were too many, and all the Sultan's army were slain and the Sultan's brother himself was taken prisoner.

" When evening came on and the mountaineers were singing and shouting their songs of victory, they led out their prisoner into their midst and just where your tent is now pitched they beheaded him   No sooner was his head severed from his body than his horse broke loose from its tethering rope and dashed into the circle of mountaineers.   Then from the pool of blood arose the body of the Prince, and lifting on high in his right hand his head, mounted his horse and galloped away up the bed of the river, while the mountaineers'—he stopped suddenly. He was bending forward over the camp-fire till the flames almost licked his dishevelled grey locks.

"' Continue,' I said.

"' Listen !' he shrieked, ' listen ! '

"' It is only the rain,' I said, for I heard a splash, splash, splash down the river—but it was not the rain.

" Suddenly there was a flash of lightning, then a crash of thunder echoed and re-echoed a thousand times on the mountain-tops—then there was silence again.

" Splash, splash, splash in the river ; louder and louder the wind howled in the trees. With one accord we turned to the river tearing its wild course along below us. Again a flash of lightning, for a moment the flash quivered in the air, then died away, —but we had seen enough, for by the momentary flash there was revealed to us, a white horse tearing past at full gallop over the rushing stream ; on the horse was seated a Moor—headless, his haik and jelaba stained crimson with blood, while high above his severed neck in his right hand he bore—his head.

" For a moment my senses left me, then a sickly

smell of burning brought me to myself. I looked at
the old shereef; he had fallen into the fire dead,
struck down by the last flash of lightning.

" Before daylight we had left the horrible spot, and
were well on our road homewards."

I finished my tale half, as I said, from imagination,
half from an old fable. The men had listened in
breathless silence.

" Is it true ? " one of them asked.

Before I had time to say anything, Selim had given
the answer:

" Yes," he said, " it is true."

" How do you know ? " asked one.

" Because I was there and saw it all," responded
Selim.

I was staggered. I had exaggerated averagely in
my tale, and was rather proud of the effect it had
produced upon the men, but Selim's ready lie took
my breath away.

The night was gloriously fine, the moon being particularly bright, and our evening of ghosts, of hidden
treasures, of djins and fairies, passed most pleasantly.
When I " turned in " the moon was sinking to rest,
but her soft cool beams still fell over the plain around
us, till every marsh and every puddle looked like
plates of beaten silver.

We pushed on the following day. The weather
was bright but cold. I held a consultation with our
men in the morning, which resulted in our deciding
to abandon the direct route to Mequinez on account
of the late rains and present mud, and by taking a
course over the low hills to strike the high road
between Alcazar and Mequinez, near R'hmus. Our

change turned out well, and we found but little mud
as far as R'hmus, though a great deal afterwards,
between there and the Sebou plains.

We were not able to ·reach Hurbasseh, as I had
hoped, that night, but after a long ride we pitched
our tents near the tomb of Sidi-Aissa-beni-Hassan,
at a village of the same name. It is situated just on
the borders of the plains formed by the river Sebu,
an · immense prairie, dotted with Bedouin encamp-
ments, and exceedingly fertile, the soil being immensely rich. The village itself is a picturesque
little place on the side of a steep hill overlooking the
plains, which stretch almost as far as the eye can see
in every direction. It was a decidedly more lively
camp than our last in every respect, as we were now
on the caravan road, and our camp was surrounded
by camels, mules, donkeys, Arabs, and fleas. The
four former kept to themselves, but the latter came
early and stayed all night.

The camels kept up their "bubbling" all through
the night. It is a horrid sound and sight. The
noise can only be compared with crossing the channel
on a rough day with many sea-sick passengers around
one ; while the sight is worse, as the camel, apparently
for no reason, protrudes a large portion of its stomach
—like an inflated bladder—from its mouth, and
swallows it again with apparent difficulty.

We witnessed an example of Moorish law being
administered here. The Sheikh of the village had
sent a man, as is customary, from his village to guard
our camp during the night. This was a precaution
always taken by the head of the villages ; the fact
that a soldier accompanied our caravan, made him

liable for any harm that might befall us. The man refused compliance with his chief's commands, as he said it was too cold. Being hard pressed, he drew his dagger. In a moment he was seized and thrown to the ground, while the Mokaddam of the village and our soldier—Hadj Hamed—lay into him with knotted straps till their victim yelled with pain.

I did not think it necessary to interfere, as the matter had nothing to do with me, and I try and push my nose as little into Moorish affairs as I can, except where I am directly interested. Though the flogging he got was of a severe kind, and the term of imprisonment he entered upon the following day a period that might extend over any length of time from a week to a year, yet his punishment cannot be compared to what he would have got in England for the same offence, i.e. drawing his knife on his superior officer, with evident intent to murder. Once or twice I was tempted to interfere in such affairs, and have several times been successful, by petitioning a Kaid or Sheikh to get a man out of prison. Once already on this journey, between Arzeilah and Laraiche, we had suddenly found the door of our tent surrounded by some dozen Moors leading a sheep, which, before one could say a word, had been sacrificed. After a sacrifice of this kind, it would be a " hashuma "—a word we have no translation for, except, perhaps, to invent an opposite to " comme il faut "—to refuse to listen to their petition, and to press it, together with a small bribe— which, generally, does not need much pressing—upon the Kaid or Sheikh.

The man in question had been imprisoned for some trivial offence, which, probably, he never committed, and we were successful in gaining his release.

About two hours after leaving Sidi Aissa, the following day, we passed through the little town of Hurbasseh, which stands on a slight elevation—the only one—in the Sebou plains. There is nothing to see there, nor on a former occasion did I find the Kaid particularly pleasant.

An hour and a half later we reached the river Sebou, a stream of some size ; one of the largest, in fact, in Morocco.

It is a sluggish, muddy river, not unlike the Nile at parts, flowing between steep clayey banks. The passage of this river is one of the things in Morocco most liable to try one's temper, as all the beasts have to be unpacked, and pack-saddles and animals ferried across in clumsy great rafts. On this occasion we spent three hours and a half over the crossing, during most of which time I stood on the further bank, waved my gun, and shouting the most horrible language in Arabic at the boatmen on the other side, all to no avail, for not a word could they hear, as the river is over a quarter of a mile across, and the wind was blowing from them to me. I tried to make them understand that our animals were to cross first, and that the various caravans waiting to be ferried across must come afterwards. I had engaged all the boats for our passage, and therefore naturally was annoyed to see camels and various beasts of burden being shipped while ours were kept waiting. Finally, I made them understand by sending a man back across the river with a message that I would shoot the first animal that did not belong to us that I saw enter a

F

boat. My man crossed, and as I saw him deliver the
message I raised my 20-bore shot-gun to my shoulder
with threatening attitude. They did not know how
useless a shot-gun would be at that distance, but the
desired effect was accomplished, and the camels were
speedily withdrawn from the boats. However, the
passage was a novelty to the artists, who sat on the
bank and sketched while I swore. Three hours and
a half of swearing did not put me in the best of tempers, especially as Arabic swearing is difficult, the
pronunciation of some of their antediluvian words
being impossible. I call them antediluvian words,
because they are as far removed from our ideas of
language as the animals of " pre-floodite " times are
from the beasts of to-day.

It was night when we pitched our camp in a small
Arab duar, and confusion reigned supreme accordingly
till a late hour. At length things got sorted, or sorted
themselves, and we settled in comfortably for the
night. The dogs of the village barked at the moon,
or because there was no moon, or at nothing—I did
not ask them which—the livelong night. One barked,
then another, then a chorus, finally there was silence
in camp for the space of—a minute, then a miserable
puppy—may it never rise to years of discretion—
yelped, and all set off again. We found, next morning, the reason of their proximity to our camp ; we
had planted our tents quite close to the decomposing
carcase of a some ten-day-dead mule, whose highly
flavoured and scented inside formed the dinner, supper, and breakfast combined of the canine tribe. The
wind changed in the morning, so we made the discovery quite early. There was no need to go outside

and look. Oh, no ; that mule had a knack of making his presence felt within the tents, without troubling us to come out. The Moors never clear away the dead beasts from around their villages. Even at Tangier, only just outside the gates, I have seen dead horses, oxen, mules, and camels left to rot in the most casual way imaginable. One gets used to it in time, however.

We camped at Sidi Cassim the following night, a village of importance on account of the size, and from the fact that it is the residence of the Kaid of the neighbouring district—a very large one. The road between our dog-and-dead-mule village and Sidi Cassim is a dull level one, which gave my fiery black horse an ample opportunity of showing his temper, and me also, for I spent my day in galloping and thrashing him, while he spent his in galloping and bucking. However, it was one of the last tussles we had, and I fancy he learnt then that I was to be the master.

At Sidi Cassim the Calipha, the second in command, called, and I renewed the acquaintance of two years before. So few Christians do these Moors see in the interior, that though I only spent one night there exactly two years before, he recognized me at once and welcomed me as an old friend.

The Kaid insisted on supplying us with all our wants ; food for ourselves, and for our horses and mules barley in abundance. He very kindly presented me with a fine Moorish greyhound, which, though not to compare with our prize-bred dogs in England, yet do very well in Morocco.

The Kaid himself called, mounted on a large grey

F 2

horse, trapped in crimson, while the old gentleman himself wore a pale blue burnous and fine white haik. He was accompanied by four mounted soldiers, each bearing a gun.

We had an amusing example of the swagger these officers of the crown like to exhibit on all possible occasions. We had been showing our guns to the Calipha, who of course only possessed a flint-lock. A caravan was just settling in for the night near us. The Calipha asked for a cartridge, and, raising the gun to his shoulder, fired in amongst the incoming caravan, hitting his mark, however, and shooting a hound that was barking at the strangers. Without a word or even a look he returned the gun saying it shot very well. Certainly *he* did.

I tied my newly-acquired greyhound at night to my tent-pole, but spent a miserable night in consequence ; for when she was not howling and whining, she was busily engaged in biting through the ropes of my tent in vain attempts to escape. Finally I let her go, and off she scampered back to her late master's house, only to be returned next morning.

Sidi Cassim is situated at the extreme southern extremity of the Sebou plains, and we were not sorry, on leaving next morning, to ascend the mountains once more, the dreariness of the muddy level road being depressing. The ascent was very steep, but the view from the summit superb, looking down over the two villages of Sidi Cassim, and its winding river, a tributary of the Sebou. The village is almost worthy of the name of town, and possesses a remarkably fine mosque and minaret, and some charming private gardens on the river banks full of shrubs and palm-trees. Beyond the village lay the great plain, stretching north, east, and west.

Far away, Hurbassen was plainly visible, a streak of white on the dull green, while beyond the mountains rose in faint blue outline against the bluer sky. At the summit we had our choice of two roads ; without a moment's hesitation we chose that of the Zaroun, so called from the mountains it passes among, as by that road we should visit the Roman remains of Volubilis, and see, though of course not enter, the sacred town of Moulai Idrees.

On our arrival some hours later at a suitable camping-ground near a small river, we pitched our tents, and, as some daylight yet remained, took our guns and sauntered out. However, though there were plenty of birds, we obtained but little sport, as we were accompanied by a score of Moorish dogs —far too keen sportsmen—who kept running on ahead and putting up the birds in the most aggravating way.

Near our camp were some Roman ruins, not as fine, of course, as Volubilis, which we visited the following morning, in fact merely the foundations of some large building.

Next day, keeping to the small river, on the banks of which our tents had been pitched, we proceeded on our way. About three hours after leaving camp we arrived at Volubilis, by far the finest Roman remains in Morocco. We had shot all the way from our camp and picked up some eight or ten brace of birds, and in the ruins themselves shot some blue-rock pigeons.

There is not very much remains standing of the

ruins; two archways, each of great size, and in mode-
rately good preservation, alone tell of the grandeur of
the old city, while acres and acres of land are strewn
with monuments and broken sculpture.   A few
isolated pillars also remain, and an immense drain or
aqueduct, not unlike the Cloaca Maxima at Rome,
opens on to the little river below. We spent an hour or
two crawling over the huge stones and trying in our
mind's eye to picture the old place as it once must
have been, a minute Rome in the midst of a barbarian
country.   Above the ruins on the steep brow of the
hill, at the summit of a precipice, is situated the town
of Moulai Idrees, called after the same great saint as
founded Fez.   It is one of the most sacred towns in
Morocco, and therefore very strictly forbidden to
Christians.   The town is one of some size, with steep,
hilly streets.   There is not much to see within it
except the shrine of Moulai Idrees, father of the one
buried at Fez, which is most gorgeously decorated,
and ranks as a " first-water " shrine all through the
country.   The little city has a most romantic situation, as it is built at a great height and on a very
steep slope, rising to a point at the top, while all
around are olive and cork forests and precipices.   It
is a great place for pilgrimages, and I was surprised
that none of our men took advantage of being in the
neighbourhood to visit it.   All they did was to mutter
a few prayers as they first saw the town, and a few
more when it was hid to sight behind a brow of a
hill.

The Moors call the ruins of Volubilis—as they do
most things of great antiquity—Pharaoh's castle,
though, on asking who Pharaoh was, I could obtain

no answer beyond that he lived a long time ago, and
was probably a great man, and a Christian !

About mid-day we mounted our animals and set
off for Mequinez. Finding it would very probably
be dark before we arrived, Ingram and I decided to
ride on with our soldier and procure a house from the
Governor, to whom we bore a letter of introduction
from Si Torres, the Moorish Minister of Foreign
Affairs, resident at Tangier. However, our soldier
utterly refused to ride on with us, the excuse being
that his horse could not stand fatigue. I therefore
took the matter into my own hands, and Ingram and
I rode on without him, a very unusual and scarcely
to be recommended plan. As we crossed the ridge
of hills a wonderful view opened before us. A steep
rocky decline led to the plains below, which stretched
far away in every direction. Beyond to the south
rose a range of low mountains, their tops speckled
with snow, while more to the east glistened in the
sunlight the snow peaks of the northernmost portion
of the great Atlas range. Though the name of Atlas
has been bestowed upon some of the south Algerian
mountains, it has been done so without any cause,
as the Atlas proper are an isolated range, and not in
any way connected with the mountains of North
Morocco or the Algerian ranges.

On the plains below us, surrounded by groves of
olives, lay the great town of Mequinez, spread out as
in a panorama, with its mosques stretching towards
heaven their minarets of green and gold. We saw
that a long ride lay before us yet, so we pushed our
horses on at a good pace. The country surrounding
Mequinez is well known for its fanaticism, and our

pushing on in this way was not an over-safe plan,
though all the natives who met us on the road
responded to my salutation cordially, and laughed
when I answered their inquiries as to the whereabouts
of our soldier, and on my telling them how he
refused to push on, so we had come without him.
Many asked me if I had a revolver, which of course I
had, and slung too in a very prominent position.

While crossing a small river I chanced to turn my
head, and caught a glimpse of Hadj Hamed pushing
his old chestnut, with an expression on his wicked
old countenance of perfect devilment. We pushed
on accordingly, but finally allowed him, cursing and
grumbling, to overtake us. A queer old figure he
was too, that soldier of ours, with his great turban
of white linen and terra-cotta coloured suit, almost
hidden in the folds of his graceful new white sulham
and his disgraceful old blue one, which had almost
lost any traces of colour it might once have possessed.
His crimson peaked saddle too was not in the
best condition, though much of its antiquity and
"minuses" were covered by a prayer carpet, which,
I must say, I never saw used for its proper purpose,
though the old boy was rather fond of praying when
he had a sufficiently large audience.

His temper soon pacified down, and he began
telling marvellous stories of the game in the neigh·
bourhood, of the Sultan's army, and of his own importance. One remark on cooking—for he was a
gourmand—is worth repeating. "There is only," he
said, " one kind of game worth eating in Morocco—
wild cat. Its taste is as the taste of all other varieties
of game mixed. When once you have tasted wild
cat, never will you eat anything again with pleasure."

Probably not, I should think it is enough to poison most people, but I dared not say so. I merely proposed in a weak voice that I preferred owl stewed with mustard and sand. He said that ought to be good too, but he had never tried it.

An hour or so later we approached Mequinez by a richly wooded park-like valley, full of gardens and ruins. Crossing a bridge of some beauty and great size, which was, however, fast falling into disrepair, we ascended through more gardens, a steep hill, passed the lovely saint-house of Sidi Ali ben Hamdouch and fountain pertaining thereto, and found ourselves face to face with one of the glories of Mequinez, the north gate.

I will not describe here what lies within or about the town, I will leave that for the next chapter.

We rode to the gate of the Bascha, or governor's house, where our soldier presented our letter. Meanwhile, Ingram and I waited without, a small crowd collecting round us. They seemed utterly unconscious that I understood a word of their language, and their remarks were often more personal than polite, some even venturing to call down curses on our unoffending heads. Our black retriever excited much curiosity, which gradually grew into a party dispute, one section asserting he was a dog, the other that he was a black sheep. Christians are a rare sight in Mequinez ; thus the attention we excited. A good kick from my horse dispersed the crowd, and a moment later our soldier arrived with some of the Bascha's people to escort us to our house. This lending of a house during the stay of Europeans in the larger towns is not so much a compliment as a safeguard for the Bascha, who is responsible for any

harm that may befall one during one's residence in
his town.   Our house was already inhabited, but the
Bascha's soldiers made quick work in bundling the
inhabitants out, who dragged their furniture with
them as fast as they could.   Men, women, and
children, beds, and cooking-materials, saucepans and
kettles, stoves and tables and rugs streamed out of
that house for upwards of half an hour.   They
removed to next door, which belonged apparently to
the same owner.   They seemed quite annoyed at
having so hurried a notice to quit, but were quite
pleasant to us.

We found the house large, roomy, damp, and
smelly, but very picturesque, some of the wood
carving of the " patio " being of very fine workmanship, while the balustrade of the balcony of the upper
storey was of old " musheribeyeh " work.   A fountain
too of rich tile-work enhanced the scene and the
smell, as it seemed to have served for drains as well.
We had the house well washed down, and bought
charcoal-pans, which we placed in the various rooms,
furnishing them with our camp furniture, and really
we were very comfortable all our stay.

We had been a fortnight reaching Mequinez, a
distance of not much over a hundred and thirty miles
by the main road, but we had come a long way
round and been much impeded by rain and mud on
the road ; nor had we hurried, as we were in search
of sport and pleasure, and not hard up for time.   The
weather the first week had been very bad, but the
second week was glorious, almost too warm to be
pleasant in the mid-days, but frosty at night.

CHAPTER IV.

THE CITY OF MEQUINEZ AND THE JOURNEY THENCE TO FEZ.

" AH Sidi Ali ben Hamdouch, ah Sidi ben Aissa,
Assalamkûm." [1] We are in Mequinez, installed in our
house. The fountain bubbles in the court, night
comes on, the clouds come over, the rain comes
down, the water comes in, and the smells come up.
Such is our house at Mequinez. Oh! inhabitants of
civilized countries who fill your houses with rich
treasures of the East, how far you fall short of true
reality! Not till you have totally done away with
drains, except as a means for the entrance of rats and
smells, not till you have taken out your glass and
put in musheribeyeh work, through which rain trickles
delightfully, not till you have paved your floors with
slippery tiles and built your staircase one foot wide
with no windows and your ceilings of blotting paper,
not till you allow rack and ruin to reign supreme on
every side, will you realize the glorious pleasure of
residing in an Eastern house. But we forget our
discomforts, we are in Mequinez, in one of the most
sacred and one of the most fanatical cities in the
whole country, surrounded by the wild tribes of the

---

[1] Patron saints of Mequinez.

Zarounis and Zimmouris, the city of the ferocious sects of the Hamdouchis and the Aissouis. However, no ill befalls the stranger, here as elsewhere the Moor has resigned himself to the presence of Chris-

A Corner in Mequinez.

tians, though of course none are allowed to reside for any period.

A wonderful old city Mequinez is, bearing in every street, in every corner, the impress of its former grandeur and its present ruin—a city of the dead. Trade has fallen away, and unless the Court

be in residence, one can walk through the long
narrow bazaars with their wooden roofs, and pass
scarcely a soul. Typical of the whole Empire—a
grand, a very grand ruin, held up merely by props,
the jealousy of foreign countries and the now vanish-
ing reputation of former power. Yet Mequinez
possesses some of the finest remains that exist in the
whole country—notably the northern gate of the
city, the gates of the Kasbah, and the immense
blocks of masonry that alone remain to tell of the
magnificence and size of the palaces of Moulai
Ismael and Moulai S'liman. From the day we
arrived in Mequinez to the day we left we never
seemed to lose the extraordinary feeling of depres-
sion that must come once over any one who visits
the town—provided the Court is not in residence,
when things may be gayer. Otherwise, as I said,
Mequinez is a city of the dead, half the shops are
empty or crumbling away, the mosques fail to draw
full houses, and there is a look of despair written in
every face. We spent several days there. I took
our artists all round the town, pointing out its beauties and its curiosities. Like all who visit Mequinez,
they were most pleased with the gates, which are, I
think, as fine in their way as anything to be seen in
the Alhambra—the Alhambra at Granada I mean.
Again, I infinitely prefer gates when one knows that
there is no restoration, and when one feels certain
that one is gazing on the true and original, and not
on the stucco and plaster. The northern gate of the
city is particularly happily situated, as the approach
from without the walls is by a wide ascent directly
facing the archway. It is a perfect specimen of

sixteenth or early seventeenth century arabesque and
tile-work, the delicacy of which bars description.
The arch is a pure Moorish one of the horseshoe
type flanked by two massive buttresses. Round the
arch itself are coloured tiles intersected by delicate
tracery in arabesque, while above runs an inscription
in ornamental Arabic, black letters on dull green
tiles.   Standing near the tomb of Sidi Ali ben
Hamdouch, itself and its adjacent fountain both of
great beauty, and facing the gateway, no more
striking scene can be imagined. The sandy road,
the azure sky, low walls over which peep the tops of
dull green olive-trees on either side, the great gate
in front, its tiles glistening in the sunlight, an
emerging caravan of camels and Arabs, all present a
wonderful scene, the very contrary to the dark
covered streets and deserted appearance of the city
within.   Beautiful as this gate is, it is surpassed by
that of the Kasbah, a massive block in much the
same style, which though perhaps inferior in grace,
yet far surpasses it in its effect of grand solidity and
power.   It is almost overpowering, this great gate,
with its open square before and its winding arcade
and seats of justice within.   Delicate in colour it
is, too, the dull grey stone standing out in relief
from tile-work of an indescribable shade of green.
Above this filigree runs an inscription as on the
North Gate, in black letters on green tiles, while
below the arabesque pattern varies, forming itself
into panels each filled with exquisite designs in
coloured tiles.   On either side of the great arch are
columns of white marble, each of single piece, sur-
mounted by Corinthian capitals.   However, the Moors

never built any two things alike, and this peculiarity is nowhere better shown than in this gate, for on the right is a covered chamber or arcade, with pillars supporting the roof, evidently intended for, and used now as, a seat of justice, while the left is bare.

There are many stories as to the building of this gate. Some say that the architect had his eyes put out because he said he could build something better, some say he had his head cut off, but the tale I prefer is the following :—

The Sultan on the completion of the gate rode out to see it, accompanied by the architect.

" It is a magnificent building," said the Sultan from under his crimson umbrella. " I am very pleased with it."

The architect bowed his thanks, and said he was glad the Sultan was pleased, and if his Majesty could propose any improvement he (the architect) would immediately carry it out.

The Sultan looked for some time at the gate, then added,—

" Well, I may be wrong, but I think it wants something to set it off at the top. I know! I will write and ask her Majesty Queen Elizabeth of England for the old statue of the Duke of Wellington from Hyde Park Corner."

Whereupon the architect in desperation committed suicide.

This story is not very authentic, but is probably as true as any of the others.

Within the Kasbah Gate is another large open space much resembling that without. On to this square look the roofs of the Tomb of Sidi Moulai

Ismail, a deceased Sultan who reigned some two centuries ago, and who, having killed more men, Christians and Moors, than any of his predecessors, having wasted more money on impossible palaces and such-like than could ever be counted, and, when tired of a wife, having her for amusement tortured and killed before his very eyes, is now reverenced as one of the greatest saints of the Moorish religious calendar.

"Ah, Moulai Ismail," cry the Moors, "may God shower blessings on thy immortal soul. Peace be with thee, Moulai Ismail."

Good old Moulai Ismail !

There is one little idea of his I cannot help mentioning here. He complained very much of the road—a mere track—between Mequinez and Morocco city, and as a remedy commenced to build a wall from one to the other, along which he intended to drive in a carriage, a distance of some two hundred miles. The wall, needless to say, was never completed, though some hundred and fifty yards of it still stand. It is nearly sixty feet in height, and varies in breadth from twenty-two to twenty-five yards. The natives grow Indian corn on the top, which seems to flourish well.

A village near this wall still bears the name of the Christians—doubtless slaves—who inhabited it in former times, for "the sons of the Christians" it is to this day called. No doubt, it was the piece of land put aside by Moulai Ismail for his Christian captives, who, becoming Moors and marrying Moorish wives, gradually merged into the native race, no difference being now appreciable.

Near this village is a great reservoir, in working order, too, full of beautifully clear water, on which on my first visit was a boat, though now this had disappeared. Near this tank, which is of great size, are some curious and inexplicable ruins, one of which contains between three and four hundred columns; of course the roof has fallen in, there is scarcely a roof in Mequinez that hasn't. The calm disregard with which Moors look after the safety of their houses is nowhere else in the world surpassed. Predestination in everything. A house falls down and kills a dozen or so people.

"It is written," says the owner as he begins to build it up again, or more often to let it lie where it fell.

"It is written," say the people who are killed by its fall to each other.

When a Moor sits down on a pin he doesn't swear. He says, "It is written," and as he extracts the pin he does not wince; he merely says, "God is great," and puts the pin back for some one else to sit on, or to sit on again himself. Not so the Moorish Jew; he sits down on a pin and swears, then smilingly draws the pin out, and sells it to an unsuspecting Moor as silver.

To everything the Moor says, "It is written." When he catches the small-pox; when he beats his wife; when his house is robbed, or he robs some one else's; when his horse falls down and breaks his leg, or he puts poison in his friend's tea, he says, "It is written," and takes it as a matter of course.

Close to the tomb of Moulai Ismail, under the open square, are a series of great subterranean vaults, as

G

inexplicable as most of the ruins of Mequinez. We descended, as I had done once before. One "glissades" down; the first time I glissaded down I alighted on a skeleton of a camel, and bruised my knee, this time on the decomposing carcase of a cow. It was softer, but I preferred the camel. These dungeons extend to a great distance, the roof being supported by massive columns; the long black arcades in which flit the squeaking bats, and the refreshing odour of carcases in every stage of decay have inspired the Moors with awe, and the popular belief is that these vaults are the residence of many a "djin" and devil. On this account our Moors were very reluctant to allow us to descend, though Selim came with us, his intercourse with Christians having destroyed some of his superstition. Beyond the square which contains these unpleasant remains is a gateway, of no great beauty or size, passing through which one finds oneself in a long, straight road, shut in by high walls, the object of which cannot be gathered. It is certainly over a quarter of a mile in length, and, like many roads in Morocco, leads nowhere. It is generally used now as a camping-ground for some of the Moorish troops, whose tents and tethered horses vary the otherwise monotonous scene. The ground at one place is strewn with marble columns, no doubt brought there by Mouli Ismail from Volubilis.

Mequinez is surrounded by ruins, though most are great masses of tabbia without any pretensions to beauty. It would take weeks to properly examine these remains, nor do I think the work would repay the trouble.

Within the town little is to be seen, though the half-deserted main street, which by-the-bye contains a magnificent mosque with beautiful bronze gates, is picturesque, but so much rain having lately fallen, we found every street filthy, which did not add to the charms of the place.

The carpet and haik bazaar was a constant source of amusement to us of an afternoon, and we picked up some pretty carpets and embroideries at remarkably low prices.

The scenes in the streets much resemble those in all the Moorish cities; there are a great many beggars, though they scarcely worry one at all; mountaineers in their picturesque garb pass and re-pass, audibly cursing the dog of a Christian. Here is a blind negro whose eyes have only been torn out with hot irons a few days before and over whose cheeks still trickle tears of crimson blood—there is a wedding procession all gaiety and music and torches. Such is life in Mequinez.

Our house was constantly invaded by troops of dirty Jews who tried to sell us poor curiosities at perfectly impossible prices, and whose cringing, whining ways and tone thoroughly disgusted us. Finally we ordered our soldier not to allow a single son of Israel within our door.

The Mellah, or Ghetto, at Mequinez is as dirty as anywhere, though some of the Jews' were fine houses. The Mequinez Jewesses' dress is perfectly hideous, the tawdry gold braiding and high cap, with its black silk imitation hair, being grotesque in its ugliness. The Jews are treated in Mequinez much as they are in Fez, and on the whole have little to complain of except dirt, and they seem to revel in that.

A curious circumstance happened in Mequinez during our stay, namely a heavy fall of snow. Snow, though not unknown here, for it is generally visible all through the winter in the neighbouring hills, very seldom falls in the town, and this particular snow-storm no doubt formed the topic of conversation in the cafés for many a long day to come. Not only did snow fall, but it lay, and the view from the terrace of our house was very curious, the surrounding plains and olive groves being completely covered with it, as were the flat roofs of all the surrounding houses, while the emerald green mosque towers wore night-caps. Our Moors were surprised beyond measure, as being for the most part Tangier men, where the snow never lies, this was their first experience of it ; nor did their surprise abate when a carefully aimed snowball hit our old soldier just below the ear and trickled down his neck. At first he thought he was shot, and was seized with fright, which increased when he dis-covered it was water which was slowly threading its course over his skin. Not being familiar with cold water, or any kind of water for the matter of that, the sensation was startling, and for a time I thought he would have a fit.

From the terrace of our house we obtained a charm-ing view, looking over the whole city, and the plains beyond. The outer walls of the town can clearly be traced all around. There are three distinct high walls at various distances from the town wall proper, each consisting of tabbia, while the enclosures thus formed are full of olive-trees, or cultivated with grain.

As Mequinez is the seat of the two most fanatical sects of the Mohammedan religion in Morocco, I will here describe, as far as I can, their religious rites.

These two sects are respectively the Aissoui and the Hamdouchi. The former are the followers of Sidi Ben Aissa, whose remains rest at Mequinez, as do those of Sidi Ali Ben Hamdouch, the patron saint of the other order.

I have had the good fortune to witness the strange rites of both sects on several occasions, and can therefore vouch for my description of their performances. The Aissoui are not unseldom seen in Tangier, and I have also seen the Hamdouchi there *en masse*, though very seldom. However, a stray follower may turn up in the market upon occasions.

Who Sidi Ben Aissa was, it is difficult to say, but he lived co-evally (and probably co-evilly) with Sidi Moulai Abdul Kader, not the celebrated Mohammedan saint whose remains lie in Baghdad, but a Moorish namesake.

Whoever Sidi Ben Aissa may have been, we know what power he is said to have possessed, viz. that of rendering harmless the bite of serpents and reptiles to those who are his followers. Any one, any Mohammedan, can become an Aissoui. The inauguration is simple. He journeys to Mequinez, calls upon the present representative of Sidi Ben Aissa's family, to whom he offers prayers and money especially money. This over, the priest blows upon him, and the devotee arises and sets out in the firmest belief that however many venomous snakes may bite him, however many scorpions sting him, no harm will befall. How discomforting the disillusion must be at times! The

believer who sits down on a scorpion soon discovers
that he has given the priest of the Aissouis more
power than he is justified in receiving—and more
money.

The great feast of the Aissouis generally takes
place about our Christmas time, though the date
varies considerably.   From all sides collect the
fanatics, crowding the market-places of the towns
throughout the country.   With heads uncovered they
form into rings, some thirty or forty perhaps in each
ring.   Drums and fifes and tomtoms are brought out,
and the hideous music begins.   Slowly they rise and
fall in spasmodic jumps to the sound of the music,
which gradually increases in time, finally becoming a
wild burst of discord without any attempt at tune.
By this time the spell has begun to work, and the
Aissouis' little jumps have become hideous leaps.
Their long hair, a sign of the sect, flies wildly around
their heads, while horrible cries rend the air in every
direction.   They have doubtless put themselves into
a state of wild frenzy or madness, and seem totally
unconscious of what is going on.   One falls in a fit—
green in the face and foaming at the mouth—the
rest leap and dance over him in a terrible ecstasy.

A live sheep is thrown amongst them by some
onlooker.   In a second it is torn limb from limb,
and each is wildly tearing the raw flesh with his
teeth, smearing his face and limbs with crimson
blood.   It is a scene that writing cannot describe, that
needs seeing to realize.

Another strange rite connected with this religious
outburst of fanaticism is the sacrificing of a sheep.
Sacrificing animals is not uncommon all through

Morocco, no doubt an old Pagan custom which existed in the country long before the Arab conquest. The sheep's throat is cut at Tangier at an enclosed N'Sala, or "praying-house." The moment the knife has severed the jugular vein, an Aissoui seizes the struggling beast with either hand, holding it aloft above his head, and with a continual stream of blood flowing upon him, runs as fast as he is able to the great mosque in the main street, a distance of about a quarter of a mile or more. If he succeeds in bearing the sheep alive to the mosque, it is a sure sign of a successful year ; if, however, the sheep dies *en route*, it brings ill-luck. Woe betide the Christian or the Jew who approaches near the Aissouis when they are performing their horrible rites. So terrified are the inhabitants of the town of these fanatics that shops are shut and doors barred during the days they are about ; nor do the Jews venture into the streets. I know as an undoubted fact, that three or four Jews were torn to pieces and eaten by the Aissouis in Mequinez this last winter. However improbable such an event may seem, yet it is perfectly true, as not only was I told of it by the relations of the victims in Mequinez itself, but heard it from official sources, both European and native.

The rites of the Hamdouchis much resemble those of their fellow sect, though instead of preserving them from snake bites, they are enabled to wound themselves without suffering any after result.

I will not enter fully into the details of a Hamdouchi festival, as the sight is too loathsome even to describe, and it will be sufficient, I think, to say, that when in a state of frenzy they cut their heads open with fast falling self-inflicted blows of battle-axes, and gash their bodies with knives. I have seen Hamdouchis, stark naked, covered with blood, blue in the face and foaming at the mouth, their heads a network of long cuts, and daggers passed through their cheeks, rolling in the sand and biting stones.

A former servant of mine I once saw in this state amongst many others. The occasion was the visit of the head of the sect to Tangier. The " Saint " was mounted on a splendid grey horse gorgeously trapped, stationed on the market-place of Tangier. Each side of him stood standard-bearers, carrying crimson and yellow flags, while behind him were the musicians. He was dressed all in white, his haik being of fine silk. In type he is a particularly poor specimen of a Moor, his expression being both low and sensual. In front of him were the devotees going through their horrid performance. Though mounted on my horse, I kept a fair distance off, especially as one or two of the Hamdouchis, armed with battle-axes and knives, kept volubly cursing me and looking most unpleasant.

The following day I found an excuse to call upon the man who had once been my servant, and who had surpassed the others in frenzy, and found him very chippy, in fact more dead than alive. I examined his wounds, which were all flesh wounds, though some were deep and all severe. He tried to keep up his spirits and pretend he suffered no ill, but to no avail, as the nineteen gashes on his head alone must have caused him unutterable agony, not to mention that he had been some hours with a dagger-blade through both his cheeks and was covered with wounds all over.

Another favourite pastime of the Hamdouchis is to throw cannon-balls and heavy stones into the air and to allow them to fall upon their clean-shaven heads with a thud that would knock the brains out of most men. There is no trickery about any part of the performance, the whole affair is too horribly real.

No doubt both the sects of the Aissouis and the Hamdouchi are closely allied to what are known as the howling dervishes in Turkey and Egypt. I have seen them in Constantinople and elsewhere several times, and though the sight is very disgusting, particularly as highly respectable Turks take part in it, yet for morbid horrors it is not to be compared with the two sects of Mequinez.

On Friday, January 25th, we left Mequinez, passing out by the gate of the Fez road. Near this gate we met the Bascha of the town, mounted on a beautifully caparisoned mule, and attended by some dozen armed horsemen. The group formed by the Bascha and his suite was a striking one, the old white-bearded man in his cloak of pale mauve forming the centre, while the horsemen's gorgeous raiment and long guns completed the picture. His Excellency was very polite, telling us to camp near his country seat, and that everything would be supplied for ourselves and our beasts. I thanked him for his kindness (purely imaginary) during our stay and rode on. Leaving the city we passed over a bridge, in tolerably good condition, that spans a small stream. Here washing was being carried on on an extensive scale, hundreds of women, for the most part negresses, stamping or jumping on the white or parti-coloured linen, and singing as they worked. The men's washing was more simple, as they merely stripped stark naked, and then washed the clothes they had previously been wearing, sitting still in a state of unblushing nudity, while the clothes dried in the warm sunlight.

It reminded me of a story of a Scotch Professor, which though absolutely unconnected with Morocco, I think worth telling here.

A Reservoir, Mequinez.

A large party were shooting on some moors in Perthshire, amongst them an elderly Scotch Professor. It suddenly came on to pour with rain, nor was there any protection in the neighbourhood. As the rain was falling too fast to permit shooting, the sportsmen merely sat down and got drenched. As soon as the shower had commenced, however, the Professor had wandered off, and during the whole hour or so for which the rain fell was not seen. It cleared up in time, and, to every one's surprise, the Professor reappeared perfectly dry, not even a drop of rain on his clothes.

The rest were annoyed, and asked him where he had found shelter, but on this subject he was very reticent. At last they persuaded him to tell them how he had kept dry the while.

"Directly the rain came on," said the Professor, "I stripped, and sat on my clothes till it ceased."

The story is not, I know, a new one, but I fancy it is not generally known.

To return to our road from Mequinez. Having crossed the bridge, the road ascends, turning slightly to the right. From this spot a wonderful view of Mequinez is obtained, the whole town lying slightly below one on a gentle slope. A turn in the road soon hid the city, and for the following three quarters of an hour we passed through groves of olive-trees, evidently cultivated here with great care.

Three separate walls of the town we passed by, each situated at equal distances from the other two, and all three in a state of disrepair. Beyond the last of these walls we entered upon open country, for the most part uncultivated. After four hours' ride we arrived at a small village in the district of Jedida, where I had camped two years before. Two hours' daylight yet remained, so, leaving our camp to be set up by the men, we strolled out, and three guns picked up ten brace of birds in under the two hours, also a quail and a landrail. We determined to take the journey to Fez very slowly, as the plains between the two towns contain some of the best shooting to be found in all Morocco ; so accordingly the following morning, leaving our camp to be struck and taken on by our men, we started off on foot, and for two hours walked through low palmetto bushes,

most excellent covert for the partridges, of which
we obtained sixteen brace and a half, one quail,
seven snipe, and a pigeon. The barbary partridge
takes a great deal of shot, and we lost many run-
ners. They do not fall like an English wounded
bird, lie for a moment, then run, but the moment
they touch the ground—almost before they reach it
—away they go, often doubling back between the
guns. After two hours of sport we left the covert
behind, and entered cultivated ground, where our
animals were awaiting us. A little later we arrived
at an immensely deep ravine, with precipitous walls
of clay and a river dashing through its midst. On
my former visit I had crossed this ravine by a bridge,
but the last winter's rains had completely carried it
away, and one had now to proceed some way higher
up and cross on an extemporized bridge of logs,
against which the river rushed with tremendous
force, seeming as if each moment it would carry the
rickety structure away, and wash bridge and all
over the high waterfall below. However, we crossed
in safety, and, keeping to the edge of the ravine, proceeded to a large village of Jedida, where was the
residence of the Kaid of the district. The view looking down into the valley was very grand. The
narrow ravine descended some hundreds of feet pre-
cipitously, the walls being of bare clay, while the
river below rushed, and tumbled, and foamed over
great boulders of rock, from amongst which rose tall
pampas and bamboos. Thousands of blue rock-
pigeons filled the air. I tried once or twice to descend, but found it impossible to get below a ridge
about a hundred feet down, where were planted

several groves of orange and olive trees, almost overhanging the river below, like some of the farms on
the fjords of Norway.

I called upon the Kaid on my arrival, accompanied
by Hadj Hamed, but so insolent was he in manner
that I was obliged to use severe measures to bring
him to his proper level. I never saw a man so taken
aback as he was when I spoke to him seriously, though
not kindly, and finally exerting all my sarcasm and
theatrical force, I worked myself into a delightfully
ungrammatical peroration which exhausted all " bad "
Arabic, at the same time flinging at him a small paper
document. He picked it up, opened it, started nearly
off his feet, kissed it reverently, and pressed it against
his forehead, then turning to me, held out his hand,
exclaiming, " You are very welcome." I answered
nothing, refused his proffered hand and with a half-
muttered " Kelb "[2] strode away. A minute later his
Excellency was at my tent door ; I refused to admit
him, but allowed him to be seated outside, while he
took down a list of the provisions, &c., for men and
beasts that I should require from him, free of cost.
They all duly arrived in time with numerous messages
from the Kaid, begging me not to report him at head-
quarters at Fez. With the exception of a quarrel
with the Bascha at Fez a few days later this was the
only inconvenience we suffered all the road from
native rulers. If one behaves decently towards them,
one has nothing to fear on their part, and I pride myself that all the months I have at various times travelled in Morocco, with the exception of my ride to
Sheshouan, I have never had any serious trouble ; on

[2] Dog.

the contrary, on the well-trodden paths of Northern Morocco, and even in the out-of-the-way fanatical mountains beyond Wazan, untrodden by any one, I believe, till I entered them this year, I am always well received, and in the evenings my little tea-parties in my tent are fully attended.   In this way I have friends all over Morocco, and it is a great charm added to the delights of travelling on entering a village, instead of being received with frowns, to hear " Mahabee, al Aissoui, Mahababee." [3]

I do not go so far as to say that one should give in to Moorish prejudices in attempting exploration in Morocco, for these prejudices are the prejudices for the most part of officialism and not of the people themselves, but I will say this, that exploration amongst the Moors requires far more tact than courage.   I do not speak as an explorer, for what little work I have done in that line has been of no consequence ; but this year I was enabled, sans disguise, to travel in perfect safety and comfort in the hitherto unvisited regions of the Beni M'Sara, Ghruneh and other mountain tribes, which country always has had the reputation of being one of the most fanatical districts in Morocco. But I will describe my short journey through these districts in my chapters on " A visit to Wazan."

The following morning I was awakened at an early hour by a great noise, and on rising to see the why and wherefore, discovered that all the village was up in arms, and that men were collecting from the other villages round on the war-path.

---

[3] " You are welcome, Aissoui, you are welcome."   The name Aissoui has always followed me all through Morocco on account of my fondness for snakes and reptiles.

On making more careful inquiries I found that a battle was about to be fought at no great distance away between this particular tribe and some Berbers. I dressed hurriedly, and buckling on my revolver and taking my small-bore rifle, burst in upon the crowd, informing them that I was going to accompany them to see the affair.

At first they were quite pleased, and examined my rifle and pistol with much curiosity, but finally I was not allowed to go, our soldier having informed the Sheikh of the village that if any harm were to happen to me, he would hold him responsible. I am glad now I did not go, as I was informed afterwards on good authority that probably each side would have forgotten his quarrel in their endeavour to take such a good advantage of shooting a Christian, afterwards each party accusing the other of having done it. An hour or so later the warriors started, setting off at a brisk trot. A grand hundred men they were, with all their finery on, and their long, useless-looking guns with barrels cased in silver and flint locks.

What was the ultimate result of the row I cannot say, but I rather suspect when it came to the point there was no fighting at all, and that the whole affair was settled, as on inquiries in Fez I could learn no news of any battle having taken place.

The result, however, of every man and every boy who was capable of holding a gun leaving the village was a very marked one, as no sooner were the warriors hidden to sight, than the ladies of the tribe began to make their appearance, and there being no one to restrain them, their curiosity led them into our camp, though the appearance of a, to them, infernal machine in the shape of Ingram's photograph camera, soon dispersed them.   However, by Selim's ingenuity and some small bribes we managed to persuade some to stand for us, and were successful in obtaining some very pretty groups.   They did not in the least seem to care that their husbands and brothers might all be shot and never return ; on the contrary, the village wore quite a gala air, and laughter and singing were heard on every side.

The treatment of women in the East, like the slavery question, is a very difficult one to touch on, especially for those who know a little of it, and do not write the astounding articles which appear in some of the papers dated from the offices of the " Societies " they belong to.

Missions for the enlightenment of women in Morocco are very different from the Zenana mission in India, one of the noblest of all our institutions in that Empire.   In India we raise, or try and succeed too, to raise the women from their low station and make them the companions and the friends of their husbands instead of their slaves.   India belongs to England, and in governing India we have taken under our protection its inhabitants ; we are able to watch day by day the progress that our example is making amongst the natives.   We are responsible, in fact, not only legally but morally, for the welfare of our people there.   Where all are striving with the same object in view, we may confidently look for success.   Not so in Morocco.   A solitary missionary or two spreading the doctrine of the equality of men and women does no good, no, he does much harm.   It but impresses upon the minds of the women a fact that they have till now been totally unaware of, namely that they are, to our ideas, degraded, coarse, and of no intellect ; that their husbands are their equals, if not their inferiors.   A very little sets the Moorish mind on fire, and a woman who has once heard these words shapes out her life accordingly ; she tries it on, she fails, and if troublesome is removed by sale, or by poison.   She learns nothing of the ideality of Christian womanhood—she must go to the East End on a Saturday night to see that,—she is merely imbued with a contempt for her husband and with discontent for herself.

I have written strongly, as I feel strongly—far more strongly than I write—on these questions.   I have seen the work in many lands, I have found one fact, that where missionaries go, goes also drink.   Now allow that the Mahommedan religion is in every way inferior to ours, an allowance I do not make in every case of the tenets of the two, allowing for climatic differences, yet the Moors live in tolerable peace. Crime with them is not nearly so rife as crime with us.   Now let us, for a moment only, Christianize the whole Moorish nation.   What is the result ?   The natives let their hair grow instead of shaving their heads : the result is disease.   They drink wine : the result is crime—with which they are entirely unable to cope on account of possessing no police—and drunkenness and death.   They eat pork, and suffer with scrofula and horrible diseases at once.   In fact, in introducing Christianity as it now exists, or is supposed to exist, we would only be hurrying a fallen nation more quickly to its grave.   We might, it may be argued, introduce some of their customs, such as

H

teetotalism, the shaving of the head, and the abstin-
ence from pork amongst them, but it is not for us to
alter what Christ has so plainly laid down.

It is a serious question—a most serious one—but it
is a question I have studied to some extent.   I have
met with missionaries in many parts of the world and
I am not satisfied.   Though no great friend of the
Church of Rome, I have found among the Catholics,
amongst the Jesuits particularly, the most devout, the
most striving of all missionary sects.   They give up
their lives to their work, they live single, they have
no worldly cares, no thought for worldly things, nor
have they that desire which so many of our missionaries have expressed to me, of some day returning
home and dying in comfort in England.   I think
that the best remedy that could be found would be
to make all our volunteer missionaries to foreign
parts go through a three years' training in the East
of London or in some low home district first.

At present Fez and the other great cities of
Morocco are in a far higher state of civilization, and
less given up to crime, than any of the poorer quarters
of our metropolis.   It is safe to walk in the streets—
for a Christian as well as a Moor—by day or by
night—yet there are no police, nor does one see the
flagrant immorality that exists in even our most
fashionable quarters of a night.   Far be it from me
to preach, but comparing the two capitals, London
and Fez, together, and seeing the advantages and the
disadvantages of both, I say, without hesitation, and
after careful thought, that it will be an evil day for
the Arabs and Moors if ever they become Christians.
It will be but the kicking away of the few steps of

the ladder that exist between them and destruction.

That comment will be made on these words I know—just as comment was made on what I wrote on the slave question in Morocco two years ago—and which brought down on my young and inoffensive head a letter in the *Times*, a letter from an individual who commenced by saying my words were "statements of a misleading nature," and who concluded by contradicting me on one or two points altogether. Since then two years have passed, and of those two years I have spent the greater part in Morocco. I have studied more closely the slavery question there, and when the time comes shall not only reiterate my former statements but write still more strongly on the subject.

To return to more pleasant subjects. We paid a visit to the deep ravine at Jedida before leaving our camp that morning, and I could not help being struck at the adaptability of the place for a fourth-act suicide on the stage. Everything that could be required is there, a precipice, grand scenery, a rushing river. All it wants is to be set up, say at Drury Lane, and a heroine who nightly would sacrifice herself in a melodramatic way to save a lover or two —a fine ending for a play. We left camp about ten, as usual allowing our mules to overtake us on the road. We shot for an hour and a half, and obtained seven brace of partridges. The country was much the same as that we had travelled on the previous day, undulating plains partly cultivated, and partly covered with a thick growth of palmetto and asphodel. Away to the north lay the steep rocky mountains of

the Zaraoun.   One peak is crowned by a building,
and on inquiring from the men the object of this, I
was told that it is a most sacred spot, there being a
large deep hole in the ground from which ascends
air with great force, so great indeed that if one
throws a stick into the hole it is promptly ejected
again to a great height into the air.   Of course the
place cannot be visited by Christians, or I should be
by this time able to give a more minute account of it
than can be gathered from the men ; however, I
believe the tale to be perfectly true, nor do I see any
reason to disbelieve it, as at Moulai Yakoob, near by,
are marvellous hot springs with great heating pro-
perties.

An instance of the *bonâ fide* power of Moulai
Yakoob water came under our notice at this very time.
One of our men, Abdullah by name, had been suffering from a terrible eruption on his leg, which was
one mass of deep-rooted boils, causing him extreme
agony.   During our stay at Fez I insisted on his
visiting Moulai Yakoob, which he did.   I watched
with interest for his return.   He had walked some five
hours to the spot, and five back, so did not arrive till
late at night.   The following morning I examined his
leg, and found it far worse, the morning after it was
still worse, fresh places having broken out, but the
third morning it commenced to heal, and on our
leaving Fez, ten days later, he was completely cured.
Kaid Maclean told me many instances of wonderful
cures that had come under his most direct notice,
some being servants in his house.   From our men
I was able to learn something about this spot.
The water rises in a pool near the white-domed tomb

of Moulai Yakoob, a great saint, and flows into an open, oblong tank, some fifty feet long. In this the men bathe, while the women use a second tank, supplied by the overflow from the men's. The whole place is situated in a small circular valley, that seems to answer the description of the crater of an extinct volcano. The time may come when Moulai Yakoob will replace Homburg and Baden Baden, and a band will play on the esplanade at three, and every one will go to Brahe's for ices. On our road we passed a charming spot, where a fine bridge, richly decorated, and in good condition (marvellous to state) spans a stream of clear running water. Here, under the shade of a palm-tree, we waited for lunch. Just below the shady spot the river widened out into a little marsh, in which we obtained some excellent snipe-shooting on a small scale. Shortly after leaving the bridge the clouds cleared that had been over the great Atlas range away to the south-east, and their glittering summits of snow towering into the azure sky were fully revealed to our wondering and admiring gaze. The Atlas range at this point does not reach nearly such an altitude as it does near Morocco city, but the snow and the soft white clouds suspended above formed a lovely picture.

We pitched our camp near some lakes, or rather marshes, in the hope of bagging some snipe and duck, as on a former visit I had obtained excellent sport at this spot; but, strange to say, though we rested the following day there, we shot absolutely nothing at all. But our visit was not without a little adventure, for the second night a house in the village took fire. We instantly hurried to the spot, and

found the natives doing absolutely nothing to ex-
tinguish the flames. The men were shouting, the
women screaming, and that was all. Every one said,
"It is written," and it would have been "written"
with a vengeance if we and our men had not arrived on
the scene, and after half-roasting our hands and faces
in pulling the burning house down, saved the whole
village from destruction.

The days were very hot about this time, but the
nights bitterly cold, and many were the mornings we
were obliged to break the ice on our buckets before
we were able to wash. However, in the tents we did
not suffer at all.

At this spot I spent a long and wearying afternoon
in stalking four great bustard. From our camp
Antonio had seen them settle in the open ground on
the opposite side of the lake. I at once seized my
rifle and set out. I walked over plough under the
burning sun for half an hour or so, then waded through
water up to my knees for half an hour more, and
then the stalk commenced in earnest. The country
was very open, and my only chance of approaching
the wily birds was by crawling along the edge of the
lake on my—well, chest. This I did for upwards of
half an hour, now in mud, now creeping through
thorns that ran into me everywhere. However, the
excitement of the sport made me forget all else, and
I persevered. On and on I crept, from little scrubby
bush to little scrubby bush. I never obtained a
glimpse of them, I dared not look up, as the covert
would not hide my head; half-fainting with fatigue
and anxiety I crept on. At last I reached a patch of
scrub I had noticed from the other shore ; raising my

rifle to my shoulder, I prepared to fire, at the same
time lifting my head gently and peeping over the
bushes; there, not twenty yards from me, was a cow ;
the bustard had cleared off twenty minutes or so
before, and I never even got a sight of them. Reader,
I said a naughty word, a very naughty word, but it
was in Arabic, so it doesn't count, at least not for
much.

I was glad of my tea on my return to camp,
and had soon regained my crushed spirits in one
sense, but not the broken bottle of maraschino that a
mule had kindly rolled on that morning. However,
our high spirits were soon down to zero, for we
witnessed that evening one of the few sights that
render travelling in Morocco sad.

A little caravan in single file wandered past our
camp. Just a dozen or two men in high relief
against a sunset sky, a few soldiers on horseback, and
a few camels, and chained to the camels by cruel
fetters the head-men of the Beni M'Tir tribe, who
had revolted against the Sultan the year before and
been captured. Eight of these poor fellows there
were dragging their heavy chains behind them, on
their way to Morocco city, hundreds of miles away
across the monotonous plains, to die in the rank
dungeons of a subterranean prison. So noble they
looked. There was no cringing about them, they
toiled on, with head in air, along the dusty way. I
doubt not they fully deserved their punishment, all
rebels do, but one could not but feel sorry for them,
and regret that such splendid-looking men had no
more future before them than dungeons and death.
They had played the stake. Fortune had turned the

wheel and they had lost. They must have known
the risk. . . . " It is written," said one to me, as we
gazed on him, " it is written."

"Peace be with you," I answered.

Alas ! poor the peace, I fear, that they would
find.

The following day we rode into Fez. The approach to Fez from the Mequinez road is not fine,
as the city, sloping down from this point, one only
obtains a view of its upper or western part, which
forms a long, low line on the near horizon, above
which rise a few minarets.

Immediately outside the gate are the ruins of the
old palace, commenced by Moulai Ismail, situated on
the banks of the Wad Fas. Before reaching this,
one obtains a view, and passes close under, the walls
of the Sultan's new palace, but little of it can be
seen from without. A few scattered tombs and a
stunted olive-tree or two vary the monotony on the
other side of the road.

Passing through a small and insignificant gateway,
one enters the city. A hundred yards or so down a
crowded, narrow street, and one turns sharply to the
right, under two large but coarsely-decorated gates,
into the city proper beyond. We proceeded at once
to the house of my friends, Kaid and Mrs. Maclean,
and it was with real and sincerest pleasure that I
renewed the acquaintance of two years ago. Of
their great kindnes to us in Fez I will speak anon.

CHAPTER V.

FEZ.

FEZ, Fas it is called by the Moors, is the capital, or northern capital, of Morocco, and is by far the most important town in the empire, not only on account of its size and the number of its residents, but also as being one of the official residences of the Sultan and court, and on account of its trade. Certainly no town in the country boasts such a situation as Fez. The City of Morocco is as picturesquely, or even more picturesquely, situated; but whereas the latter owes more to its surroundings, the former is in itself superior in position, for the town lies on the slopes of the Wad Fas, a small, fast-running stream, an affluent of the Sebou, and is thus, both as regards health and our ideas of situation, far more advantageously placed. The two capitals have much alike, however; in fact there is much that pertains equally to all Moorish cities, the total want of restoration, or even repair, the dirt, the smells, and the rough muddy or stony roads, full of holes leading into what little drainage there is; but perhaps these holes are there on purpose to point out to the traveller the fact that drains do exist. This I know, that though two years separated my visits to Fez, yet I remembered the holes and took special guard to keep my horse out of

them when riding through the streets for the second
time ; and there they were, a little larger perhaps from
the number of horses, mules, and donkeys that must
in that period have stepped into them, and perhaps
broken a leg or two.

Street in Fez.

The history of Fez is composed of wars and
murders, triumphs of arts and sciences, and a good
deal of imagination.

Even the founding of Fez is a matter of doubt ; but
authorities seem to agree in giving 800 A.D. as about

the probable date. Leo Africanus, if I am not mistaken, gives A.H. 185, which brings it very close to 800 A.D. But though the date of the foundation is more or less a guess at hazard there is no doubt as to the founder.

Moulai Idrees was the grandson of the Prophet Mahommed, who wandered far from his native land ; we are not told whether it was on account of his having got into trouble there, but I rather think it must have been, as surely the " saint business " must have been good enough in those days, and a grandson of Mahommed would never have wanted for £ s. d. ; however, he came to Morocco, and recognizing that the slopes of Gibel Salah would form an estimable site for a city, planted himself and his followers there, though it was not till his son, Idrees' time, that the foundation of the city of Fez can be said really to have taken place.

Whether this Idrees was as interesting an individual as his cousin Haroun-al-Raschid it is difficult to say, but he succeeded in gaining a very large amount of reverence, probably far more than he deserved, from the Moors, and it was not long after his death that Fez began to grow into the " beautiful and Holy City " that it now is.

From that time till some two centuries ago it increased rapidly, became a seat of learning to which even Spaniards were sent to finish their education, where astronomy was to some extent understood, where medicine was progressing in rapid strides, and where poets were putting upon their vellum scrolls, and in vellum books the old songs of Spain. How things are changed now ! The roofs have fallen from the colonnades of the colleges and mosques ; astronomy has

given place to the lowest ideas of astrology ; medicine
is but the concoction of a filthy potion, or a few words
scrawled on a small piece of paper, and worn round
the neck, vellum is unknown, and they use kitchen
paper instead ; poetry has disappeared, and has given
place to lewd verses ; while the Spaniards have to go
elsewhere to be educated, or as seems rather to be
the case to-day, to let education " slide " altogether.

Yet Fez is a charming old city.   After all it is only
as if we let Cambridge fall a little more to ruin, give
time to the statues on Caius gate to gain respectability
by age, and to allow the grass to grow in full luxuriance over the John's and Trinity tennis-courts. We
should love Cambridge just the same then, I think ;
perhaps more, and I am sure I should prefer the
wicked, idle Fez of to-day to the bustling Fez of two
or three centuries ago.   There is not a great deal remaining in the Fez of to-day to tell of these brighter
and happier times, but two mosques of great beauty
still stand almost intact, those of the Kairouin, and the
sacred shrine of Moulai Idrees.

The former is probably by far the largest mosque
in North Africa, and what glimpses we were able to
obtain of its interior did not belie Leo and Rohlfs,
both of whom rave about its magnificence. Row
after row of columns and arches, dusky colonnades
only half-lighted by the coloured lamps that hang
suspended from the roof, a great sunlit court full of
worshippers, two exquisite erections of tall, graceful
columns with carved roofs shading a marble fountain-
basin with its ever-gurgling water, such is the mosque
of the Kairouin.

By passing a small side gate we were several times

able for some minutes at a time to stand and gaze
upon the impressive scene, to watch the long line of
worshippers prostrate themselves and rise again at
the voice of one who read the Koran in a particularly
nasal accent. This mosque boasts a fine minaret,
from which the muezzin calls to prayer at the appointed hours.

Fez loses much beauty by the fact that its minarets
are not the splendid palm-like structures as at Constantinople and Cairo, but square or octagonal towers
rich enough in brilliancy of colour, but still not to
compare with those of the true orient in grace.

The mosque of Moulai Idrees is the most sacred
shrine in Morocco, so sacred indeed that the streets
surrounding the tomb of the great saint are forbidden
to the dog of a Christian, and one way is even pro-
tected by chains put across to prevent Jews or Christians passing by. However in spite of these stringent
rules Christians have succeeded in reaching and
entering, in disguise, of course, the holy building.
The mosque of Moulai Idrees is not nearly so large
as that of the Kairouin, but it is kept in far better
repair. The small room that contains the holy remains of the saint is a wonderful sight with its
paintings, delicate tracery and rich embroideries, for
the most part " haities " or wall hangings of coloured
velvet embroidered in gold, and gorgeously decorated
roof supporting hundreds of small lamps and one very
large one.

Of the other mosques of Fez one cannot say much,
except that there are a great number of them.

The city is divided into two parts, Fas Jedid and
Fas Bali, New and Old Fez. The former is the fashion-

able quarter, in which are situated the Sultan's palace and most of the houses of the richer classes.   These houses are for the most part surrounded by gardens, and are gloriously situated, the great attraction being that each is supplied with running water, drawn skilfully from the Wad Fas, and supplied to nearly all the houses of the town by means of small canals.   The gardens are full of orange-trees ; and flowers too grow luxuriantly in many, but very few Moorish gardens are at all our ideas of gardens, as they are allowed to grow pretty much as they like.   No doubt it was these gardens and the running water that led the poets of old to sing so extravagantly the praises of Fez.

Fas Bali, or Old Fez, is the commercial part of the place, the " city," so to speak, and contains the Fondaks and the shops.   The streets here are narrower than in New Fez, but far more picturesque, for instead of the tall garden walls on either hand there are the little box-like shops, full of rich colouring and dirt, smells of incense and dead cats, and containing also the shop-owner, who sits cross-legged, counting his beads perhaps, and scarcely paying any attention to his business or the rare sight of Christians.   I seldom yet saw anybody buying in Morocco ; every one seems to have things for sale, but no one buys and no one seems to care much whether he sells or no.   Casual beyond anything are these town moors.

One long street, roofed in from the sun, forms the highway of Fez.   It runs from New Fez right through the town, ending opposite one of the many gates of the Kairouin mosque.   In this street are exposed for sale almost every article one can imagine, but curiously enough the shops that contain one variety of goods are all together, for instance there are a dozen shops full of old iron and metal, old brass and copper kettles, bolts, chains and screws ; the next cluster, if one may speak of a cluster of shops, contains old daggers, swords, and knives, while a little further on is a district of shoe shops. Others again are full of Manchester goods, linens and calicoes, cretonnes and beads, and many an item besides, while a whole street is given up to pottery. These shops are for the most part only some few feet square, so that there is not room for a large stock, and the selling is carried on in an old-fashioned process. No one is " selling-off, must be cleared in three days. To-day last day of sale ; everything at immensely reduced prices." In fact, the art of advertising is scarcely, if at all, known.

The floor of the shop is elevated some few feet above the level of the street, and boarded over ; on the boards is a carpet, and on the carpet the shop-keeper. The front of the shop is a shutter that opens upwards. A piece of rope is used by the shopman to scramble in by. Altogether the *tout-ensemble* more resembles those little Japanese shrines containing an idol that we are all acquainted with now, rather than a place of trade. We have seen the outside of the shop. Let us go shopping now. We are in search of curios, buying old rubbish, little scraps of embroideries for instance.

We approach a likely-looking place and salute the owner.

" Salaam alikum," I say.

" Salaama," he replies, carefully avoiding repeating " alikum," a word never used to the dog of a Christian.

" Have you any embroideries ? " I ask.

" I may have," he replies.

" Let me see them."

" They are at my house, not in the shop."

I propose that he should send for them. He responds by asking me if I will promise to buy. This, of course, I refuse. After perhaps a quarter of an hour's discussion, he shuts up his shop and disappears in the crowd, reappearing in another half-hour or so with a large bundle.

Once more the shop is opened. I examine his wares and pick out three or four small pieces for purchase.

" How much will you take for these three ? " I ask.

" Name your own price," he replies, smiling.

" No, tell me how much you will take."

He examines the embroideries carefully, and after pointing out all their good points mentions a fabulous sum.

I turn away disgusted without a word and proceed down the street. Ten yards from the shop I hear him calling me back. I return.

Then it is my turn, and I point out that the embroideries are in anything but good condition, and put my fingers through various holes ; discover suddenly some defect, apologize for the trouble I have given him, and tell him I am sorry but I don't want them at all, they are too torn, or too faded, as the case may be.

Once more I go away.

This is repeated for half an hour or more, and finally I buy the wares at my own price, usually about a fifth of what the owner first asked.

A great deal of trade is carried on in the Kesserieh, or auction-market, where the auctioneers every day at midday run through the narrow ways of the bazaar holding out their goods and crying the latest bid. It is marvellous to see the way the bids go up when a Christian appears! I have known a man selling an embroidered cushion to call it out at a dollar till he caught sight of me, when it suddenly rose to five, however I purchased it for a dollar and twopence eventually. In this Kesserieh we spent an hour or two every day. Selim always accompanied me, and between us we managed pretty well. On one occasion I was very pleased with an exceedingly fine piece of embroidery I had bought for four dollars (sixteen shillings). Selim's face when I told him was a picture. Unutterable scorn was written on every feature. "Four dollars," he said sarcastically, "why you could buy a house for that in Fez;" then added, "tell me where you bought it." I was quite annoyed at my bargain being treated in this way, and told him it was very cheap.

"But where did you buy it?" he asked again.

"In the next street," I answered, "two shops down from the top on the left-hand side."

Selim disappeared.

A few minutes later he came to me smiling, and handed me a dollar.

"What's this for?" I asked.

"Oh," he said casually, "I went back to the shop and told the man I was your servant and that he had swindled you, and also informed him if he did not give me a dollar's commission I would bring you back to return the stuff and take back the money."

I

" And he gave you a dollar ? " I asked in surprise.

" Certainly," he responded, " and here it is."

Even I who speak the language to some extent get swindled, knowing as I do the Moors and their ways. How much more must a stranger be done who has to speak with an interpreter, who, of course, must have his commission, and a very considerable one it generally is.   On the whole there is very little to be bought in Fez, nor do the Moors yet understand that an Englishman will buy anything that is old and ugly, or at least fantastic.   They try, unavailingly of course, to tempt one with Manchester calicoes of brilliant hues, or very poor modern silver work from Mequinez. The old striped brocaded silk, long since ceased to be manufactured, is very beautiful both in texture and colour, but is very difficult to obtain in anything like good condition.   " Haities," or wall-hangings, of coloured velvet panels arranged in the form of Moorish arches and embroidered in gold, can sometimes be picked up, and now and again a good old Spanish sword, but the whole country is very devoid of *objets d'art*, and what there is is usually much poorer in design and execution than the work of India, Persia, Damascus, or Egypt.

But we have done our shopping, and will return once more ; not by the high-road this time, but by little winding lanes with tunnel-like passages under the overhanging eaves of the houses ; through a small open square or two, past a few richly-painted and carved doors of mosque or tomb, and so on once more to New Fez and its gardens.

The inhabitants of Fez are a peculiarly fair race. I do not, of course, mean to say that in Fez the gene-

rality of men are fair, because so few of the people of
Fez are really natives of that town, the tribes round,
and the constantly arriving caravans, forming the
chief part of the visible population, and again, the
intermarriage of these original inhabitants with black
or dusky wives has greatly changed their colour.
Yet amongst the old Fez families that have kept
distinctively to themselves, and have intermarried
amongst themselves, the rule is to find the men with
blue eyes and fair beards. Doubtless their origin is
from the far north, for they could never have settled
in the country at the time of the Arab invasion.
This same light type is found also a great deal
amongst the Beni M'Sara, and other mountain
tribes.

An important feature in the trade of Fez are the
Fondaks, which answer, perhaps, more to our corn or
coal exchanges than to any other of our institutions.

These Fondaks are often very beautiful buildings
of several storeys in height, open in the centre with a
" patio," and surrounded by galleries in carved wood.
One especially at Fez is remarkable for its great
architectural beauty, not only with regard to its
interior, but also its magnificent gateway. They are
now almost entirely in the hands of the Jews, who
trade in various European goods. There are other
Fondaks of far less pretensions, which answer more
to the caravanserai, and where the weary animals,
who have borne their burdens from some far-away
corner of the country, rest during their sojourn in the
city.

While on the subject of the buildings of Fez, I
cannot pass on without slight mention of the public

fountains.   Though I have seen no fountains in Fez
to compare in beauty or workmanship with those in
the southern capital of Morocco, yet there are some
of picturesque design.   The excellent manner in
which water is supplied to the city of Fez renders
these fountains in the northern capital of not so
much importance as those in the southern, where
water is only procurable at certain spots.   However,
in spite of the "waterworks" of Fez, the fountains
are well patronized.

There still remain in Fez some relics of the great
libraries that in former times were the chief ornament
of the place, but the books have been worm-eaten
almost to dust, and decay and damp have set their
indelible seal upon the manuscripts.   Nevertheless
there must be still works of great value hidden away
in the recesses of the library that adjoins the Kairouin
mosque, which probably will never come to light till
some European power takes possession of the country.
I am thankful that I shall not be a school-boy in
that day, for rumour says that the lost books of
Euclid—are there such things as the lost books of
Euclid?—lie hidden there, together with some of
Livy's hitherto undiscovered works.   Probably not.
Probably when the libraries are opened, as they
undoubtedly will be some day in the future, nothing
but musty Arab manuscripts will be found, the others
having been destroyed by the bigotry and ignorance
of the native rulers.

It is quite impossible, of course, for any Christian
to force an entry into these libraries, as, pertaining to
the mosques, they are held religiously sacred, and therefore must never be defiled by the feet of Christian or
Jew.

During my two visits to Fez I made several charming excursions outside the city walls, on one occasion riding completely round the city—a ride of some four or five hours' duration. The views from all sides are lovely, one especially so, when one has reached the higher ground of the cemetery to the south of the town. On all sides are the domed tombs of the saints, while here and there a change in the scene is given by the presence of dark green olive-trees. Far below one lies Fez, the whole city clearly visible. To the left is New Fez, with the Sultan's palace and park, and the many gardens with their white houses half-hidden in the trees; to the right lies Old Fez, one mass of flat roofs, in which scarcely a street can be traced, so narrow are they. Here, there, and everywhere, rise the minarets of the many mosques. Between the cemetery and the town is a deep gully, through which flows one of the branches of the Wad Fas. High above the stream, on the summit of the steep bank, are the walls of the town, great stone and "tabbia" erections of immense height, but fast falling to rack and ruin. Picturesque though in the extreme they are, half-covered with creepers, while on the old turreted towers have sprung up big trees and vines. In one place the whole wall and a tower have slid into the stream far below, and there they lie to-day, the water forming a pool above them and rushing over the crumbling stone in tiny cascades.

Unlike Mequinez, Fez does not boast very fine gates, the principal entrance of the town being most insignificant, though the two gates of the Kasbah are finer. The great builder of gates, Moulai Ismail, did not turn his attention much to Fez, but rested content with his works in Mequinez.

The sôks, or markets, of Fez are well worth visiting. These sôks are held on two days of the week on a large piece of ground just outside the city walls.

Here one sees exposed for sale all manner of native manufactures. Auctioneers run screaming up and down amongst the crowd, hawking embroideries, swords, pistols, and all manner of second-hand goods. Women sit veiled and cross-legged, selling under-clothing and rough mountaineer's haiks and blankets. In another quarter is the market for horses, mules, and donkeys ; and here the professional riders gallop up and down on the sturdy little barbs, crying out the latest bid. Another quarter is given over to the sellers of corn and barley, while in every direction are the caterers for the public amusement—snake-charmers from the Sûs valley, story-tellers from everywhere, powder play by the mountaineers, a Hamdouchi hacking holes in his head with a battle-axe, acrobats and musicians. But let us wander through and look at them more closely.

A large ring of people surrounds a snake-charmer from far-away Sûs. He stands talking to the people, while his three musicians render anything but sweet music on tomtoms, gimbris, and shrill pipes.

"Ah Sidi ben Aïssa,"[1] he cries. "Sidi ben Aïssa will not allow me to be hurt. He will guard me when I draw forth from this basket the terrible Lefah[2] of the Sûs. Come and see him," he cries, forgetting the religious part of his performance in his endeavour to increase his crowd. "Come and see

---

[1] Patron saint of snake-charmers, &c., buried at Mequinez.
[2] Puff-adder.

the Lefah, with fangs two inches long. In the name
of Sidi ben Aissa, charity ?"

Many are the small copper "flus" thrown to him
by his admirers, when he draws out of a reed basket
a Lefah. A shudder runs through the crowd. I
notice how very careful our friend is not to allow the
Lefah to get a chance of biting him. He holds it
safely by its neck as he hands it round for inspection.
Certainly its fangs are there, and very large they are
too. He plays no tricks, however, with his venomous
pupil, who is soon returned to the basket ; but with
other and harmless snakes he performs a few poor
feats. Holding a snake at arm's length, he shakes
his head—clean shaven except for one long lock—
violently to and fro, at the same time groaning and
crying to himself. This is supposed to charm the
snake, as well as to put himself into a religious frenzy,
during which he can suffer no harm.

Suddenly he puts his tongue out, the next moment
the serpent has fixed its long sharp fangs into it, and
the charmer is running round the circle with the snake
suspended from his mouth. More money is thrown
into the ring, and our friend moves off to another
part of the sôks to perform elsewhere.

The next crowd we pass is round a story-teller.
Wild indeed are his gesticulations as he alternately
flourishes his arms over his head, and springs forward
with spasmodic gestures. His story is just finished.
A tambourine is passed round, into which his admiring
auditors drop their offerings. Five minutes later he
tells another story.

This is his *modus operandi*. Round goes the tambourine first, but not much is dropped in. Then a

couple of musicians strike up a little music. That ceases. The tambourine is handed round once more, and the story commences.

"Long ago," he says, "in the time of Moulai Idrees and Moulai Abdul Kader"—here he kisses his hand, as a sign of reverence, as do all the crowd—"there was a poor man, a Shereef,[3] who lived a very righteous life, nor ever did he commit any sin. But he was very poor, and had not wherewithal to supply himself with food. One night, as he lay asleep on his bed, a vision appeared to him, and he saw standing before him"—[here the tambourine was passed round with some success]—"the Prophet Mahommed, the beloved of God, the Head of God"—[more hand-kissing]—in a flame of fire. And the Prophet said to him, 'Abdullah,[4] I have seen thy poverty, and am come to help thee. I have seen how, even in the days of starvation, thou hast never stolen, nor borrowed not to return,[5] and now I will give thee great wealth. Go early to-morrow to thy friend Achmedo, and borrow his white horse. I will put it in his mind to lend it thee ; and take this horse and ride to the pass of the lost lamb, and then leap on thy horse from the precipice, and surely thou wilt find great wealth.'

"Before Abdullah had time to thank the Prophet— God shower blessings upon his holy beard—he had vanished. Early he arose and donned his jelab, and set forth and begged the loan of the white horse from Achmedo, his friend. After three hours' ride,

[3] Descendant of the Prophet Mohammed.
[4] Slave of God.
[5] Abdullah must have been very different to most Moors.

he reached the pass of the lost lamb, and gazed over the precipice. A hundred feet at least in height it was. Gathering his reins in his hand, he galloped at the brink "—[round goes the tambourine with still more success]—"but on the edge he reined in his horse for fear.

"Five times he essayed to go, but each time his courage failed him. While he was sitting on his horse, he suddenly heard a great noise behind him, and, turning, saw "—[tambourine again]—"the Holy Prophet himself, seated on a snow-white horse, with fire bursting forth from its nostrils and mouth, coming towards him at full speed.

"'Weak man,' he cried as he passed, 'and hadst thou fear? Follow me!'

"A moment later the Prophet and his horse had disappeared over the edge of the precipice. A moment later, too, Abdullah had followed his example. It seemed an hour he was in the air, but suddenly he alighted; his horse never fell, but merely tore up the turf with its paw.

"He looked round; the Prophet had disappeared; but in the hole that the fall of the horse had caused, lay "—[tambourine with evident success]—"an iron ring.

"After some hard work, Abdullah succeeded in raising from the ground an iron chest full of gold pieces, and so lived in luxury till the Holy Prophet lifted him into his bosom and placed him near to God.

"And so are the righteous rewarded." [More tambourine.]

Close by are a party of mountaineers at their

powder play, or as they call it, "lab-al-baroud."
Splendid figures they are too, as they half-leap, half-
dance round in a circle, waving their long-barrelled
guns on high, and uttering loud cries.   Suddenly they
throw their guns in the air, catch them again, and
set them spinning at arm's length above their heads.
Faster and faster spin the guns, till the silver-mounted
barrels are only as a flow of light in the brilliant sunlight.   Suddenly the spinning ceases, the guns are
given one fantastic spin and fired.   Not as picturesque,
perhaps, as the "lab-al-baroud" on horseback ; but
these tall fair men, with brown embroidered jelebas,
gorgeously coloured powder-flasks, belts and shot-
bags, and a red gun-case wound round their heads,
are very fine.

From the wild heights of the Beni M'Sara, Beni
M'Sgilda, and Ghruneh they come, country almost
untrodden by Christian feet.[6]

But time is gliding on, the sun has risen high in
the vault of heaven, and the heat is intense in the
sôk.   Business is slack now, except for the half-nude
water-carriers with their goat-skin bottles and brass
cups, whose cry of "alma-alma"[7] is more heard than
ever, and the "genouah"— niggers from the far
Soudan and Timbuctoo—with their strange head-
dresses of feathers, shells and matted cords, to whom
the heat is as nothing compared with their own
country.   What grimaces the thick-lipped hideous
old fellows make as they clap their noisy cymbals
and hop first on one leg and then on another.   The

[6] I believe I am the only European who has visited those
mountain fastnesses.   I was there in March and April, 1889.
[7] Water.

songs of these genouah are curious. Arabic, of course is not their native language, and is only acquired on the long way from Timbuctoo to Morocco. The first words they learn are naturally of food, and thus their favourite song is merely :—

> " Colou jedada,
> Colou patata—
> Makleia."

In other words, " Bring the chicken, bring the potatoes—my food."

This is their highest ideal of poetry.

One is always surprised in Morocco not to find more beggars. Certainly the place, especially Tangier, is not devoid of them, but in the interior they are very little trouble. They sit round the mosque doors, crying in monotonous tone, " In the name of Moulai Idrees, charity ; in the name of Moulai Idrees, charity," but they never impede one's traffic as they do in Southern Europe.

The saint-business of Fez is a very extraordinary one. One never does anything in Fez without naming Moulai Idrees. He is the patron saint of the children, of sweetmeats, of everything. When a man sits down he cries, " Bismillah, Moulai Idrees ;" when he gets up he does the same. Every town has its saint. Morocco city has Sidi bel Abbas ; Mequinez Sidi Ali ben Hamdouch, Sidi ben Aissa, Sidi Abdurrahman M'jdoub, and Moulai Ismail ; Laraiche has a lady, Lalla M'nana ; while Alcazar has a very holy saint indeed, Sidi Ali bu Rhaleh, whose shrine is one of the most beautiful in the country.

I was never able to see the Sultan's Palace at Fez.

The first time I was there the excuse given was that his Majesty was away, therefore it was impossible ; the second time, that his Majesty being then in residence at Fez, the palace was of course invisible. Such are the Moors, they always have an excuse. Instead of saying straight out, " What! defile our Sultan's Palace by allowing a dog of a Christian to put his feet into it, not we, Kaffir-billah!" they apologize with the utmost courtesy.

The sultans who have left most impress on Fez by their works are Almanzar, Moulai Ismail, and Sidi Mahommed, the father of the reigning sovereign, who built the new palace, and Moulai Yezid, who raised or began to raise a palace which was to be the biggest in the world. However, only one room was anything like completed, and it never possessed a roof. The remains of this chamber form one of the largest squares in Fez, some two or three hundred yards in length, a hundred in width, with walls nearer eighty than seventy feet in height. I fancy it would have puzzled the Moorish architects of his day to roof in this "banqueting-hall." Some of the ruins just outside the walls of Fez are very pretty, probably the remains of some unfinished palace, in and out of which flows the River Fas.

Between the districts of New and Old Fez are a great many water-wheels used for raising water. One especially large one which I had seen on my first visit to the capital in 1887 had disappeared two years later—crumbled away,—and it was about time too, as probably it was the one mentioned by Leo Africanus.

A little beyond the place of the water-wheels the

Sultan is engaged upon enclosing for himself as a garden a large piece of open ground, traversed by numbers of little streams. As his Majesty is no mean landscape gardener doubless he will make a very charming place of it.

It was most interesting to see the high wall that is to enclose this new park being built. Tabbia, a kind of poor concrete, is, as usual, the material employed. On the summit of the half-built wall, already some fifteen or twenty feet in height, stood a long row of Moors and black slaves, with heavy mallets in their hands. As they worked they sang a curious monotonous chant, and at the repetition of some particular word, every minute or so, down came the hundred or more mallets in perfect unison.

It is close to this spot that the royal barracks are situated, and, as during my visit to Fez in January and February, 1889, his Majesty's troops were in the town, I saw these barracks full. There is no house at all, merely three sides of a large square enclosed by walls. At the bottom of the wall is a sort of rough façade, divided into small square chambers, into which there is just room to squeeze a man, and into some a horse.

While on the subject of the Moorish army a few details may be interesting. The army is divided into two parts—the Askari or regulars, and the Maghasni, the militia, or more properly, yeomanry.

The Askari were, and are certainly now, a wild lot, but what order and regulation does exist amongst them is due entirely to the energy and untiring attention of a Scotchman, Kaid Maclean, who for some twelve years has exiled himself from civilization and followed his imperial master and his troops through every vicissitude.

In what state Kaid Maclean found the troops on his arrival in Morocco one can only surmise, but probably all the world over there was not a more ruffianly set of robbers and thieves than the soldiers of his Imperial Highness the Sultan of Morocco.

However, under Maclean's guidance things quickly changed—very quickly compared to the alteration and progress of other Moorish departments—and from a wild horde the troops became a comparatively well-drilled set of men. Their numbers were increased, and probably at the present moment the Sultan has some thirty-five thousand regulars at his disposal, and another sixty or seventy thousand irregulars (very), which he could call out if occasion necessitated it.

The Askari are armed for the most part with Winchester repeating-rifles. Their uniform—a most inappropriate word, as anything less uniform I have scarcely ever set eyes upon—consists, or is supposed to consist, of red tunics with yellow braid, blue baggy trousers *à la* Turk reaching to the knees, bare legs and yellow shoes, and a crimson "tarboosh," or fez. However, this costume is much varied. Some have pawned or sold their unmentionables, many their tunics, shoes are few and far between, not so the holes in the few the men do possess. Their pay, which by-the-bye they very seldom get, is extraordinarily small, I am afraid to say how small, and on this pay they have to supply their rations, &c. However, I fancy they make up their want of pay by pillage and robbery. Yet in spite of all this these

men fight well, and go through their drills with regu-
larity. It seems that while morally the Moors have
sunk to the lowest depths compared to their ancestors
of the thirteenth and fourteenth centuries, yet they
have succeeded in retaining some of that innate
courage and love of warfare that existed in those days.

Many are the stories I have heard of the pluck
of these men, and they have ample opportunity for
showing it, for every summer they are engaged in
active service against some revolutionary tribe, and
these tribesmen fight with desperation.

The last great wars in Morocco were those of a
few years back, when the Sultan, at the head of his
troops, crossed the great Atlas Mountains and devas-
tated the Sûs Valley and its rebel inhabitants ; again,
in 1888, there was considerable fighting in the tribe
of the Beni M'Guild.

The manner of warfare practised is to march
through the offending country, to burn their villages,
to kill and to pillage, to kidnap or enslave every one
or everything they come across. But it must not be
thought that the tribes offer no resistance to the
uninvited presence of the Sultan's troops ; on the
contrary, they fight till they are able to fight no
longer ; and to give an idea of their courage, I will
tell one anecdote of an event that happened only
last year (1888) in the Beni M'Guild. Twenty-seven
of the head-men of the tribe were taken prisoners
towards the end of the war, and were brought into
the Sultan's camp. Chained to one another in a
long row, they were brought forward before the
whole camp. One of the Sultan's soldiers approached the poor fellows and asked :—

" Will you acknowledge the Sultan or die ? "

" Die," replied the man, and his head was hacked off with a dagger.

All twenty-seven gave the same answer and were similarly treated, even to the twenty-seventh, who had seen the twenty-six men, some of whom were his brothers, to whom he was chained, brutally killed. If this is not pluck, what is?

But enough of the horrors of war.

There is another division of the Sultan's army that needs describing, the Maghasni or "yeomanry." For the most part they consist of well-to-do men, and are all mounted. They are armed with flint-locks of native manufacture, fight very little, and are very picturesque. Their pay is slightly higher than that of the Askari, when they get it at all, but being mounted they travel about, and so have far more opportunity for practising their diplomatic skill. Instead of open robbery and pillage, at the very mention of which they would be horrified, they satisfy their consciences and their stomachs by obtaining food and money under false pretences. There is a sliding scale in crime, just as there is in everything else, but I must say I prefer the out-and-out thief.

It is one of these Maghasnieh that accompanies the European traveller during his journeyings in Morocco, though I confess I have on several occasions put international law on one side and travelled, greatly to my advantage, without one. There is nothing I think in Morocco more picturesque than these old soldiers with their long white flowing garments, gorgeously caparisoned horses, and guns

with barrels like a hop-pole. They are one of the
commonest sights in the country ; all along " the
road " one is passing them, generally with a slave
riding a mule which bears the Kaid's—they all call
themselves Kaid—luggage, amongst which one can
sometimes catch a glimpse of a wife, hidden away in
rugs and bundles. There is yet a small body of
men to be dealt with, not deserving of being called
a division of the army, yet in their own opinion of
the vastest importance, a not uncommon idea in
Morocco amongst everybody. These are the Bok-
hari, or black body-guard of the Sultan, all negroes,
mounted on black horses and dressed in long white
haiks and sulhams. A very fine body of men they
are, too, upon ornamental occasions ; but I doubt, in
spite of Lord Wolseley's paper in the " Nineteenth
Century," their capacities in warfare, as they ruin
their nerve and constitution by the enormous amount
of kiff—hemp—and hashish that they respectively
smoke and take.

A great institution at Fez are the Hummum or
baths, but as I shall in my chapter on Morocco City
give an account of a visit I paid in disguise to the
Dukala Hummum there, I will not touch upon the
subject here.

The prison of Fez is well worth a visit. There is
a great deal written and said about the horrors of
the Moorish prisons—a great deal too much in fact
—for I must confess I cannot in everything agree
with those philanthropists who desire to make the
prisons far more convenient and comfortable than
the very houses of the Moors. Of course I am well
aware that the prisons that one sees above ground

K

are but a very small portion of the place, and that
below ground are the reeking dungeons where men
are left to rot to death or to sink and perish by
starvation.   Now no influence brought to bear upon
the Moorish government will alter these subterranean
cells ; all that they will do will be to improve the
prison yard above ground, which is not necessary.
Certainly the treatment of the prisoners is not gentle
or kind ; one sees them chained to one another by
heavy iron chains at times, though most of them
are not thus made fast.   A certain number of these
prisoners are no doubt innocent of offence, and many
cases of mistaken identity must occur, but most
have committed heinous crimes.   The enclosure in
which they are confined is not over clean, but I have
seen many and many a dirtier house amongst the
richer Moors, while in the prisons the prisoners are
allowed to smoke, and are all in each other's company,
and not in solitary confinement.   On one occasion,
in Fez, I asked permission of the Bascha to visit the
prison.   He told me to go the following Friday.
However, mistaking the day, I went on Thursday
and found them at work cleaning it up for my to-
morrow's inspection.

    After all, the Moors are not far removed from
savages.   They possess very little feeling of any
sort ; love little but their women—whom they treat
as an English costermonger treats his donkey—and
sport, and were we to try refining punishments upon
them, we should altogether fail in carrying out the
ends we are striving after.   It is the fashion, of course,
to be given up to philanthropy at present with
regard to Morocco and other like countries.   It is

the fashion to try and raise the women from the
only sphere they know, to try and Christianize the
Moors and introduce drink, in fact by every means
in our power to overthrow the social system of
another country in which we have no other interest
than as an object for our philanthropy. If instead we
would attempt, as some are attempting, to root out
the seeds of evil that we Europeans have introduced
into the country, to do away with the indiscriminate
protection to low Jews by one or two powers who
use this protection merely for the sake of robbing
the Moors who have it not; if we were to make the
introduction of Spanish robbers and cut-throats into
Tangier a question for an European conference, and
by checking it render the houses of the Europeans
less likely to be robbed, and the Europeans themselves less likely to be garotted; if a strong check
were to be given to the liquor traffic, and if the
Christians in the country would learn that the Moors
are men and not beasts, then and then only we
might have some reason—some excuse—for expend-
ing philanthropy and money in Morocco.

There is but one more institution in Fez that
needs, I think, mentioning, and that is the Mellah—
or Ghetto—and its inhabitants. If one were to
spend a year in London in collecting all the most
abominable filth and piling it in a narrow street, just
cutting a pathway through the centre, and then
sprinkling over it to the thickness of about one foot
the drainage of ill-drained houses, the corpses of
cats, the heads, legs, and wings of chickens, and on
the summit of all this setting half a dozen scabby
children to play, one would have some idea of the

Jewish quarter in Fez. Nor morally are the Jews of Morocco better than they are domestically.

Like all others who visit Morocco, at first I was shocked at the treatment the Jews appeared to suffer, and pitied them most sincerely ; but it soon passed off, and I have come to recognize, through intimate knowledge, that there is no tribe of men more degraded, with less amour-propre, or more ready to rob and plunder, than the Moorish Jew. Of course there are exceptions, and from some of the Moorish Jews I have received great kindness, and learnt a great deal as to the internal history of Moorish affairs.

But though I speak strongly as regards the Jews, yet it is not difficult in looking back over their past history to find their excuses ; they have always been, especially in Spain, whence most of the Morocco Jews originally came, a persecuted race, and there is nothing that bemeans a people more than a long period of persecution. However, in writing against the Jews here, I do not go so far as some, and desire to totally abolish the only safeguard the Jews have from the hands of the Moorish government. Every one who has watched the Morocco question during the last few years, cannot have missed perceiving the battle that is waging pro and against " consular protection."

The state of the case is simply this. Protection must exist until the Sultan and the Moorish government can be trusted to rule in such a way as renders it unnecessary. It has lately been asked in an article in one of our London papers, *re* the scandal which came to light only two years ago as to the

selling of this protection, " How comes protection to
be a saleable article ? " The answer is as simple as
the question. Because the obtaining of protection
is the only means by which Jews and Moors alike
can escape the rapacious plunderings of the Moorish
government.

Of course I do not argue that this protection has
not been much misused, that the sale of this protection by men who are representing their country
in Morocco is a most degrading fact, yet taking its
advantages with its abuses, I have no hesitation in
stating that the abolition of " protection " in Morocco
would at once destroy not only the safeguard of
property, but the safety of lives.

I do not wish, however, in this work to enter at all
into Moorish politics. My one object during my
visits to Morocco has been and always will be to
keep myself free from the petty squabblings and
party strife that exists amongst the Europeans there,
so that with these few words on Protection, I will
return once more to the Mellah at Fez, not that
one often returns there after having once visited it.
The Mellah is a walled portion of the town, with
several gates, which are closed at night. Certain
restrictions are laid upon the Jews—the unprotected
Jews, of course—by the Moorish government. They
are not allowed to ride on horseback, or to wear
shoes in the Moorish quarters, though this does not
affect them much, as most are too mean to buy
them.

Beyond mentioning their love of swindling, their
vice and drunken habits, the utter filth in which they
live, their bemeaning and cringing ways, I think

there is little more to say about them. Amongst
the general Jewish community domestic morality is
not at a high standard. Yet, as skilled workmen,
the Jews far surpass the Moors. They are the
workers in silver and gold embroideries, tailors, and
minters, though none of their work can compare in
delicacy or design with the work of India, Persia,
Damascus, or Egypt.

CHAPTER VI.

No adventures happened to us during our stay at Fez, though I had a quarrel with the Bascha, or governor, that at one time threatened to be serious.

On our arrival in the city, I had proceeded to the Governor's official residence to deliver the letter of introduction we had brought with us from Si Torres, the Moorish Minister of Foreign Affairs resident at Tangiers, and in compliance with the terms of this letter to ask for a house during our stay in the city. This house was immediately promised, but evening set in without any definite abode being allotted to us. I again called upon the Bascha and asked that a house should be given us before nightfall; this he promised, but again no house was forthcoming, and the Bascha sent word without our knowledge, that our tents were to be pitched in an open space of ground, situated between New and Old Fez. This was done by our men, who spent the night there, Kaid Maclean's brother, Captain Alan Maclean, very kindly giving us shelter in his charming little house in New Fez.

First thing in the morning I again called upon the Bascha, who was sitting in court surrounded by his officials and soldiers. He took no notice of my presence at all, and continued hearing case after case,

and keeping me waiting.   This was too much, and I
pushed my way into the court and demanded a house,
a demand that was refused.   On hearing this refusal
I ordered my soldiers to take down all my camp and
remove tents, animals and all, without the city walls,
and there pitch just under the windows of the Sultan's
palace.   Then turning to the fat, disconcerted old
Mussulman, I added—

"I shall fire guns all night, and doubtless his
Majesty will inquire in the morning what it was for.
I will then inform him of your behaviour."

The old boy knew that this would never do, and at
once sent one of his soldiers to find me a house.   I
followed the man, and was shown into the filthiest of
filthy stables—doubtless meant as an insult.   The hot
weather and this combined made me lose my temper,
and returning to the court-house, I assailed the
Bascha with such choice language, as probably he
had never heard before.   This attack brought us a
slightly better residence, good enough at least for our
men and baggage, though I myself would have
rather slept in the street than in that cesspool of a
residence.   For this abode the Bascha demanded a
rent of a dollar a day, a rent unheard of in Fez.   On
leaving Fez I visited him once more, and jingling the
dollars in my hand, demanded first a receipt.   This
puzzled the old gentleman, as he knew perfectly well
that if he gave a receipt it would be handed over to
our Consul at Tangier, and by him to the native
Minister of Foreign Affairs.   He therefore refused,
and I likewise refused to pay the money unless I obtained a receipt in full.   So the matter ended, I promising to pay the money into the Consulate at

Tangier on my arrival there, and promising also that
he would receive a letter from our Minister that would
open his eyes. Thanks to the kindness of Sir William
Kirby-Green, a letter was sent, and such a letter as
did doubtless open his eyes. The epistle was not
sent to the Bascha himself, but to Si Gharnet, the
Minister of Foreign Affairs at Fez, nor before leaving
that city did we allow the opportunity to slip of
having the Sultan informed of how we had been
treated. The following day his Majesty interviewed
his Bascha, but what passed between them I know
not.

One other incident at Fez is worth mentioning, as
showing a trait in the character of the Moors which I
cannot but admire.

We were shopping one day, and passing one of the
little booths, Ingram saw some embroideries to which
he took a great fancy. On approaching to ask the
price, the man informed us that he regretted he could
not sell to Christians, as he was a Shereef, a descendant of Mahommed's. Ingram was much taken with
the man's convictions, even proof against money, and
the kindly way he apologized for not being able to
sell, and especially by the man remarking as an after-
thought, " I cannot sell to the Christians, but I can
drink coffee with them," and straightway he ordered
a cup of coffee which Ingram drank. The following
morning Ingram took the man some carpentering tools
as a present, with which he was much pleased. Every
morning he wished us a hearty "good-day," as we
passed, and on our leaving the city brought us a present of a basket of dates.

On the 9th of February, we bade adieu to our kind

host and hostess, and left the city. I cannot find words to thank Kaid and Mrs. Maclean and Captain Alan Maclean for their kindness to us during our whole stay. We lived with them all the time, and turned their house into a sort of mixture between a bear-pit and an old curiosity shop. Had it not been for their presence in Fez, and with the scant civility we received from the Bascha, I verily believe we should have been compelled to leave the city the day after our arrival.

We brought away many things from Fez, haities, or wall-hangings in velvet embroidered in gold, old Hispano-Moorish swords, Moorish manuscripts, some beautifully illuminated ; carpets, and embroideries galore, yet there is not very much to buy in Fez, or rather not very much variety. As a rule we were able to obtain things very cheap by bargaining.

Our mules and horses had all been re-shod, our saddles and harness mended and repaired, and all that remained was to organize our men once more, who had fallen into lazy habits during our residence in the town.

However, after a hard morning's work we saw our mules depart towards one o'clock on the 9th of February, and we ourselves followed an hour or so later.

A ride of an hour and a half brought us to our camping-ground, where we found our tents already pitched. On nearing the spot, we put our animals to a gallop, with the result that Forestier's mule—the white one who wouldn't cross the bridge the day we left Tangier—commenced bucking, finally pitching the great heavy saddle, and Forestier himself, of course, on to the soft, clayey road. Luckily no damage was done beyond a broken strap or so on the saddle.

Morocco is the country in which to study mules. As a rule they do not carry out their reputation for stubbornness; on the contrary, one generally finds them simple-minded and lady-like in their behaviour. Now and then, though, one comes across a brilliant exception, a sufficiently marked exception to prove a million rules.

I once knew slightly—I never gave it the opportunity of a very near acquaintance—a mule who—I cannot say which, it was too human in its habits—would lie down in every river it forded. However, in the end, like the naughty little boys in the tracts, it suffered for its waywardness, for it smilingly laid down in a deep river with a heavy pack on its back, and was carried out to sea and died. Since this disastrous affair there has been a marked improvement in the behaviour of the Tangier mules.

To return from mules to Morocco. Forestier's animal having been captured and its saddle readjusted, no further adventure befell us, and we reached camp in safety.

I was called away in the evening to see a poor man who was very ill. The Moors have such belief in the doctoring capabilities of all Europeans, that one is besought at nearly every resting-place to visit some sick person. In ninety-nine cases out of a hundred, one could do no good, but still I never was heartless enough to say so, but gave the patient a harmless dose of something or other, and with a "Trust in God, He is all-powerful," or some such common Moorish remark, would leave the sick person to his fate. In this village the man was lying sick of dropsy. I told his relations I could do nothing, but they implored me for medicine. I therefore gave him a rhubarb pill, and some permanganate of potass to wash his eyes with, which were inflamed and sore, and with a heavy heart returned to camp.

The following day we left early, and keeping to the slopes of the Zaroun Mountains, travelled for some five or six hours in a north-westerly direction, finally pitching our camp on a slight eminence in a little village of Mekis.

How glorious the cool evenings after the heat of the day were, when, dinner finished, we drank our coffee and liqueurs under the light of a brilliant moon! A bonfire generally blazed before our tents, sending its myriads of sparks, each like a miniature fire-balloon, into the dark blue sky. What a life one spends in camp ; nowhere in the world, except at sea, is there anything to compare to it. The freshness, the freedom, and even the comfort of a well-arranged camp cannot be surpassed. One wakes in the morning refreshed after sleep. There is no need to get up and light the gas because of the fog ; a splash in cold water, a cup of coffee and a cigarette —and bliss.

We often spent our evenings in our men's tent, and amusing evenings they were, what with tea-drinking and listening to the notes of the gimbri, a small two-stringed instrument. A game they often played, simple enough in itself, pleased us much. One man would hide his eyes while the others agreed on some particular object in the tent. Then one would take the gimbri and strike up a few monotonous notes, repeated again and again in fast

recurrence. To this accompaniment the seeker of
the object would say over and over again, " Ah tsimmah, ma shey tsimmah," " Here it is, it is not here ! "
one syllable falling on each note. While repeating
this, the searcher would move about the tent, pointing to various objects. On nearing the object chosen,
the music increases in pace, and by the careful
omission of one note and a slight alteration of time,
the words no longer run smoothly, while "tsimmah,
tsimmah, tsimmah," [8] fit in perfectly, and this continues, sometimes the latter music, when the searcher
is near the object, sometimes the former, when he
seeks in the wrong direction—until the object is discovered.

Next morning we crossed the bridge of Mekis,
close to which was seated a most picturesque group
—a Kaid and a few soldiers, accompanied by their
servants on their way to the court.

They were resting for breakfast near some palm-
trees. The old Kaid was seated on a carpet of rich
colours, eating bread and dates, while the soldiers
were standing or sitting around. A black slave was
boiling water in a small brass tripod, while another
was polishing the brass tea-tray, and setting out the
little tea-glasses. The women-folk were seated apart,
carefully veiled, and the mules and horses were eating
the fresh green grass on the river banks. A lovely
picture they formed with the high mountains in the
background, the palm-trees overhead, and the fast-
flowing river of clean water at their feet. We
stopped and saluted them as we passed with a
" Good morning, peace be with you," and inquired of
each other our respective businesses and routes.

[8] Here it is, here it is, here it is.

All day, except for the last few hours, we were passing along the valley to the east of the Zaroun Mountains, steep wooded peaks, from out the dense forests of which peeped here and there romantically situated little walled towns and villages. We had got well ahead of our mules and found ourselves at a spot were two roads branched off. Our soldier took one, though Antonio, who was keeping up with us, had doubts as to its being the right one. Here a man who had accompanied us from Fez left us. He was a Shereef of Wazan, a cousin of the powerful potentate of that name, but not being of the elder branch, was delighted to accept our hospitality and share food and tent with our men for a little way on his road. He was a pleasant man, nearly a negro in colour, but with fine features, and I was quite sorry to see him leave us, and wave us adieu with his scanty luggage—a Shereef's battle-axe, with a saucepan and a bunch of feathers tied to the end. He was on his way to Tangier, as he spent his life wandering from place to place, begging alms by the way. Following our new road, we arrived at a duar, where we decided to pitch our camp about nightfall. Dismounting, we sat down to wait for our mules. The sun went down and darkness quickly set in, but no mules came. We knew they could not have taken the wrong road, as we had told some men we had passed on their way to Fez, which route we had chosen. Things were getting serious, and as the country we were in is so seldom travelled over by Europeans, and its inhabitants are so fanatical, I began to fear our caravan had been plundered, and to blame myself for having ridden on ahead. Finally, two hours of darkness having passed, I mounted my horse and set out into the blackness to try and dis-cover what had happened. A sharp tussle ensued between my horse and myself—he being of an ex-tremely nervous nature,—shivering with fright all over at the idea of the dark way. In time, by means of soft words and spurs, I persuaded him to proceed, and away we set off at a gallop. There was much mud and some few streams in the road, through which we floundered, as it was quite impossible to see a foot ahead, the moon and stars being hidden in dense clouds.

For half an hour or so I rode on, keeping my horse at a gallop, for the night was bitterly cold. At last I heard something ahead, so pulling up short, I cried out, "Who comes here?" I was delighted to hear in return a shout from the well-known voices of our men, and two minutes later I had found the caravan.

The soldier had chosen the wrong road, and nine of our mules had been immersed in the mud in one bad mud-hole. What language they used against Hadj Hamed, and no doubt he was very much to blame, as had he chosen the upper road, we should have reached our camping-ground without encoun-tering any mud or water at all; and they were furious also with him, too, for allowing me to ride out alone at night through country known to abound with lawless robbers.

Finally, I led the caravan to the village, and did my best to stop the curses the men hurled on the ancestors of our old soldier. I told them it was not curses we required, but the mules unloaded and the camp pitched.

We had to place our tents right amongst the "ghimas" of the Arab villagers, on account of the plundering propensities of the tribes around, and the result was—smells. We were pretty well inoculated by now with the perfumes of Araby, so did not suffer much ; but the noise our guards made during the night was terrible. One man, who had taken refuge under the flap of my tent, spent the whole night in repeating the Koran. By the rate he went on I hoped that at last he would have finished the whole book ; but no, or if he did, he started it off again without a pause. I tried every means of stopping him ; I cursed him, I begged him, I banged against the side of the tent, finally I took up the challenge and started off with "The Lady of the Lake." That made him stop for a time. At last, out of breath, I ceased, and away he went again, and at double speed, too, evidently to make up for lost time.

There is one advantage in the noise these guards make, that it keeps them awake. If once they fell asleep one could pull the whole camp down and steal the animals without waking them. I believe one could even put a dagger through their hearts and kill them on the spot, and they wouldn't wake. The next day we had a very heavy shower soon after leaving camp. The road was up and down over hills, but not at all interesting, the country being bare of trees and scarcely cultivated at all.

We saw more flocks of the pretty white ibises (egrets) here than we had seen anywhere. All through the country they are extremely common and very tame. It is a charming sight to see the

Arab ploughman driving his heavy wooden plough, while close around his footsteps hop these lovely birds picking up the insects the severed earth uncovers ; often, too, they settle on the backs of the kine and sheep, and no doubt make a good meal there, if Moorish kine resemble Moorish peasants. Like the storks, the natives do them no harm, but treat them with respect and almost reverence. This is a curious fact, as the ibis was a sacred bird in Egyptian mythology, nor is this the sole case in which the present Moors and the past Egyptians resemble one another, as the ape and the cat—especially the former—are also respected, as though some ancient tradition had been handed down from those ·early times.

In pouring rain we forded the Sebou, having passed shortly before the conspicuous tomb of Sidi Mahammed al Shleh. These white-domed marabouts are found all through the country, scattered here there and everywhere, adding much to the charm of the scenery, especially from the fact that all vegetation is considered as sacred in their immediate vicinity, and allowed free growth.

Morocco has been so despoiled of its trees that almost the only woods remaining, except in the actual mountains, are the cemeteries dedicated to some saint, whose remains in most cases lie buried within.

The passage of the Sebou at this spot is no easy task, as the stream in winter is very strong and fast, and none too shallow. However, we were lucky, and got safely across without wetting our luggage, which was piled up on the mules' backs. We, however, got

L

very much splashed ourselves in crossing; and even
when tucking up my legs well into my saddle, the
water was over my boots and knees.

Just across this ford is a curious pile. of rocks,
known as the Haja-al-Ouerkof. The rocks must be
a hundred or more feet in height, and from a distance
are not unlike a church steeple. The surrounding
country shows very little rocky formation, which adds
to the extraordinary appearance of this natural pile.
The height is deceptive, as from a distance the rocks
look much lower than in reality they are. It is only
when one approaches close to them, and compares
the height to a palm-tree growing close beside them
that one can gather the real altitude. Soon after
passing this spot the rain ceased, and the sun shone
gloriously once more.

We passed close to, and I dismounted and
examined, a salt-mine. The mine is entered by a
cavern in the side of the hill, at the end of which is a
deep hole. There appears to be an immense deposit
of salt at this spot, and the mine showed signs of
recent work.

We pitched our tents at a duar, on a gentle sloping
plain that forms the valley of the Ouergha, a large
tributary of the Sebou. The view was charming.
Looking over the great green plain with its winding
river, one could see beyond, into the mountains of
the Beni M'Sara and other tribes, range after range,
while on the far horizon were visible the snow peaks
of the Sheshouan and other ranges. Wazan's curious
double hill was plainly visible away to the north-
west. Our soldier had been complaining of feeling
ill all the road from Fez, and came this particular

evening to my tent to ask for medicine. As he
seemed to be suffering from headache, I lent him a
very strong ammonia salts bottle. He took out the
stopper and put the bottle close to his nose, and in-
haled it. The bottle dropped, and the soldier departed,
his eyes full of tears. I saw him a little later, and
he had not then recovered. However, it evidently
did him a world of good, as he never complained of
being ill or asked for medicine all the remainder of
the road.

The following morning we crossed the Ouergha,
about the banks of which we shot some fourteen brace
of partridges. The road was all the day pretty, and
the surrounding mountains varied the scene very
pleasantly. We saw nothing of great interest, though
our presence at a soko, sok al Arba, or Wednesday's
market, caused a great sensation. Hundreds of the
mountaineers gathered there, never having seen a
Christian before. Though thoroughly mobbed, we
suffered no inconvenience from the crowd, who behaved on the whole very well.

These sokos are great institutions in the mountains.
They take place usually at weekly intervals, one at
one particular place on the Monday, for instance,
while some village further on have theirs the following
day, so as to encourage the Jews and native traders
to journey from place to place and exhibit their
wares. They are not necessarily held at villages, as
often spots more convenient for the tribes round are
chosen. So at this sok-al-Arba there were no ves-
tiges of a village in the immediate neighbourhood
though we had passed one shortly before, whose level
green would have been a far more suitable spot than

the stony slopes of the mountain they had fixed upon.

It is a great place to study character. The tall mountaineers from the neighbouring tribes of the Beni M' Sara and others were here in large numbers, picturesque as ever, with their red gun-cases wound round their heads and their long guns, all ready for use, in their hands.

Men from the Gharb and plains were here also, in long, coarse haiks ; while amongst this medly throng were the Jews, with their low, cringing ways.

Oliver Wendall Holmes tells us that "Oriental manhood finds the greatest satisfaction in self-abase-ment," but compared to the Jews, the Moors of Morocco, are full of self-respect. At this very soko I sat on my horse and listened to a small-pox-marked whining son of Israel selling his goods.

"O, my Lords, the Mussulmans," he cries, "I am but à poor weak little man. I cannot fire a gun like you, my lords ; I cannot sit on a horse and gallop about as you do. You see me, what a miserable little specimen I am, unable to fight, powerless, an unbeliever on whom God has expended some of his wrath ; yet in spite of all this I can serve you, my lords, I can do the mean work your hands forbear to do, I can go down to the coast and bring up the merchandise you require. Come, my lords, and see the linens and calicoes I have brought from Tangier ; come and I will sell them to you at the same price as I bought, being proud to render a service for my lords, the Mussulmans."

Can anything be imagined more degrading. This self-abasement before people whom in reality the vendor both hates and despises, and, above all, fears. Yet he will degrade himself and his religion by speaking of himself as an "unbeliever," and by innumerable lies swindle the Moors on everything he sells them. And yet we talk about the persecution of the Jews in Morocco!

The goods are exposed for sale at the sokos, under little extemporized tents pitched in parallel rows. Everything from a split-pea to a mule—and often a slave—can be bought. It is also the slaughter-house of the district, and hanging by their hind-legs from scaffoldings of poles can be seen the corpses of many a sheep and goat.

We purchased some dry figs, dates, and raisins, also some bread, which was very excellent, though coarse ; and, after a pleasant half-hour of running questions and answers as to where we were going, what our clothes were made of, what was our nationality, how old we were, whether we were married, if we eat pork, &c., &c., I waived my adieux and galloped on. The road now turned more to the north, and followed the course of a small river. The valley was fertile to an extreme, even the sloping sides of the mountains being cultivated to some height up, though the east side less than the other. This east side is the boundary—or rather the stream is—of the lands of the powerful and fanatical tribe of the Beni M'Sara, of whom more anon. We had, therefore, to continue on the west bank of the little river, where we were perfectly secure, though to have crossed it would have been a proceeding fraught with danger.

We camped at the village of Sidi Mahammed Shereef, a nephew of Sidi Hadj Absalam, Shereef of

Wazan, and therefore a very sacred individual. He is reported to be exceedingly rich, and he treated us to his hospitality in a most courteous way. I went with our soldier to call upon him immediately on my arrival at his village. Passing through a gate, I entered a little courtyard. In the centre was a clear, deep tank, on which swam two geese. At the further end of the court was a kubbah, with three arches opening within. Two opened into a large room, the third, closed and bolted, evidently was a prayer-house or tomb.

Passing to one of the open arches, a striking scene met my eyes. The Shereef had not seen nor heard our approach—or pretended he had not—and was busily engaged in reading. Before he looked up I had ample time to take in all the details of the place.

Sidi Mahammed himself is a tall fair man, with auburn beard and large blue eyes, a very contrast to his uncle Sidi Hadj Absalam. He was sitting upon an exquisite old prayer-rug, his back against the wall. His clothes were all of white, while a large turban rested on his brow, over which the soft folds of his silk haik hung gracefully. The room was bare of ornament, except for a rich painted ceiling, a tiled floor with a few rugs scattered about, and some flowers in pots.

For a minute he did not move his eyes from the illuminated vellum manuscript.

Our soldier still maintained the same position, prostrate in the doorway, his forehead pressed against the doorstep. I remained standing without, hat in hand. Presently his Highness raised his great blue eyes and smiled.

"You are welcome," he said, "welcome to my lands ; all that you require ask for, and it shall be given you. All that I have is yours."

Of course it was a welcome in the exaggerated form of Eastern speech. We asked for nothing, but everything was brought us later on. I thanked his Highness, bowed, and left.

On the whole I was exceedingly pleased with our reception by one of the most fanatical and religious of Moorish potentates.

At nightfall tea was brought us : a tripod bearing a kettle, a large brass tray, a tea-caddy and sugar-box (both full), tiny cups and glasses, and silver spoons. Two slaves brewed tea for us.

As the process of making Moorish tea is one that all travellers in Morocco will probably witness at some time or other, and certainly will taste the result, I will give its recipe :—

Take a handful of green tea and put it in a tea-pot, fill the tea-pot entirely with sugar, and pour boiling water on the top. Allow the concoction to stand for a minute or two, then pour out half a glass (minute tumblers are more common than cups), and throw it away. This is supposed to remove any poison, copper, &c., which may be used in the coloration of the tea. Then pour out another half-glass, which the host or his tea-maker drinks with much gusto and noise, to show one that no poison lurks within. After that all is ready, and tea is poured out all round.

In drinking Moorish tea there are many rules of etiquette dependent upon the station of one's host. First, no matter where one is, it is a gross breach of etiquette not to drink three cups or glasses. The cups are very small, but the concoction—a kind of very sweet green tea syrup—proportionately strong.

That is the recipe for the brew for the first cup, the second generally has a sprig of mint in it, and sometimes also lemon verbena (though rarely), and often various other herbs ; the third brew much resembles the second, only there is more tea, and more herbs, used.

The result is very pleasant, and, unlike many Europeans, I not only drink my three prescribed cups, but often several more, which is not only allowed, but complimentary to one's host.

In high circles one sips one's tea as one does liquor in England ; but with the petty sheikhs, &c., one makes as much noise over one's cup as the proverbial alderman is supposed to do over '34 port.

Besides supplying us with tea, Sidi Mahammed was kind enough to send corn for our animals, and a goodly feed of kooskoosoo for our men. The following morning I bade him good-bye. He was again in his kiosk, where he seems to spend his days, though we had seen him the night before sauntering to his house some little distance off, attended only by his two geese, which followed him like dogs as far as his door, and then, doubtless recognizing fellow kind, turned and came cackling to my tent, where they eat from my fingers, and nearly swallowed them once or twice in their hungry endeavours to get bread.

Our ride into Wazan the following day was only of a few hours' duration. We still skirted the tribe of the Beni M'Sara, by one of whom, mounted on a white horse, all our movements were carefully watched. When we were proceeding through valleys, the form of the horseman could be seen on the hill-tops against the sky-line. When we were on the hills, he galloped around at a mile or so's distance, never losing sight of us. His presence disturbed our old wreck of a soldier, who hurried us on accordingly, though I myself do not believe the man meant evil, but was probably despatched by the head of the tribe to keep watch on our movements, and see we had no intentions of entering their country. The road till we reached the mountain of Wazan was uninteresting. All the way we were in full view of this two-peaked mountain ; but the town itself lies on the further, or eastern, side, so was not visible till we had rounded the southern corner and passed over the south-eastern slopes. Here the road was very rough, consisting, for the most part, of huge boulders of rock, in and out and over which our animals were obliged to climb. At last the furthest crest was passed, and a grand view met our eyes. We had been travelling through thick olive woods for the last half-hour, which had concealed the gradually-increasing scene till all at once it burst upon us. One is apt, after visiting a place, to exaggerate its glories ; but, though I had spent some days at Wazan before, I was as much struck, and even more, than I had been on first viewing it, at its splendid situation and grand surrounding. From our vantage-ground we looked down on the tiled gabled roofs of the town, close below us, from amongst which rises many a graceful mosque tower. Above us rose the mountain crag after crag, here wooded with olive and orange groves, here rugged and bare. In front range beyond range of mountains rise, one upon the other, till faint in the far distance one could see the snow on the Sheshouan peaks.

As a rule, in Morocco the views are not much varied.   Either the scenery is blocked up by mountains or the flat plains render it monotonous.   Another great defect, not to be found at Wazan, is the scarcity of trees.   Here the country was beautifully wooded, especially in the proximity of the town itself.   Nothing could be more varied than the scene that was stretched out before us.   Town, plains, valleys, woods, hills, mountains with crests of rock and snow, everything that is typical of Morocco, and a great deal that is not.   Of all the towns of Morocco I infinitely prefer Wazan.   It is cool, well supplied with delicious water, whilst Europeans who can claim friendship with Moulai Mahammed are treated with the greatest respect.   Nowhere all through the country have I been more pleasantly received by the natives than in Wazan, the most fanatical town that Europeans may visit.

I at once called upon Moulai Mahammed, and saw his secretary, Si Ali.   To my great surprise, on my presence being announced to the Shereef, not only would he not see me, but would not even give us a place to put up in, telling us, per his secretary, to camp in the soko, which meant " Get out of the place as soon as you can."   I immediately guessed at the reason, which afterwards turned out to be the case, that Si Ali, not wishing to have the trouble of getting a house put in order for us, never informed his Highness of my presence at all, merely stating that unknown Christians had arrived.   Moulai Mahammed, who had lately been shamefully treated by two Europeans, who not only suppressed their nationality, but passed themselves off as officers of another nation, and reported all his conversation and views, drawn out of him by the trick these low spies deigned to play, had closed his house, very wisely, to all strangers.

We pitched our camp forthwith in the soko, but it being market-day, we were much annoyed by the people, most of whom, coming from the mountains round, had never seen Christians before. However, they were decently polite, and did not curse us more than we were accustomed to, though their curiosity, which finally necessitated a "cordon" being placed round the camp, was objectionable. They watched us eat and drink, sketch and write, as though we were so many wild beasts. However, I would willingly have gone through all the inconvenience to overhear, as I did, the conversation of some small boys.

"What are they?" said one.

"Apes," replied another.

"Well," answered a third, "I have often seen apes before performing in the soko, but never without chains round their waists."

These boys were perfectly serious, nor would they have used the expression "apes" towards us if they had not been, for all the monkey kind are held in far greater respect than Christians.

As was only natural, we were much annoyed at the scant civility of the Shereef, but guessing he must be under some misapprehension, I despatched one of our men to him with a message, which I bade him deliver himself, and not through the secretary or any official. This was done, and the result was wonderful. Moulai Mahammed at once sent soldiers down to take me to his kubbah, while slaves and servants came to remove our tents, as a house was being prepared for us in the town.

I was at once ushered into his Highness's presence, and numerous were his apologies at the slight he had unwittingly paid us. I took the opportunity of telling him how uncomfortable we had been encamped in the soko, for which he again apologized.

I spent the whole morning with him, and in the afternoon brought all our party to tea. He was most pleasant, and regretted that we should have to leave the following day. On our bidding good-bye, he again apologized, and was gracious enough to present me with a handsome Smyrna rug, one of the yearly gifts sent him as a direct descendant of the prophet by that town. He exacted a promise from me on leaving that I would come on the first opportunity, and stay with him at Wazan for some time. This I promised to do, and a few weeks later did. I will not describe his Highness, or his principality here, as in my chapter on a visit to Wazan I shall treat at length on this most interesting subject.

I shall but tell very briefly of our return from Wazan to Tangier, as the same ground will be covered in the chapter I mentioned above. We reached Alcazar three days later, having shot by the way, and at one place, for two guns, obtained fifteen brace of partridges. At Alcazar we camped, as usual, just to the east of the town, on the top of a series of gigantic manure heaps. There is very little of interest in the town, though during this visit we

were lucky enough to witness a grand fête given by
a Sidi Mahammed, a cousin of Moulai Mahammed's,
in honour of the birth of a son.

Lab-al-baroud (powder play) on horseback and on
foot, were the principal items of the fête, both of
which were excellently performed. The mountaineers
were down in great numbers, and all armed, and the
governor of the city was fully expectant of trouble.
However, the day passed without any disturbance.

The Shereef was himself a splendid equestrian, and
his grey horse one of the finest I have seen in Morocco. The saddles on which the official body, which
turned out *en masse*, were mounted, were extremely
beautiful, in every shade of reds, mauves, and greens,
all richly embroidered in gold.

Rather an amusing incident happened to me in the
town. I had an idea that somewhere there was an
inn kept by a Jew, or rather that beer and refresh-
ments could be obtained at a certain Jew's house. I
asked the whereabouts of this imaginary establish-
ment, and, on being pointed out a certain house,
entered without knocking and walked upstairs. I
found a Spanish man and woman at breakfast.[1] I
immediately demanded some beer, which was given
me, and which I enjoyed immensely. Then I ordered
breakfast to be ready in an hour's time. I noticed
that the man and his wife looked surprised, but
nothing dawned upon me till the woman burst out
laughing, saying, in Spanish, " You have made a
mistake ; we do not keep an hotel ! " I apologized,

[1] There are some half-dozen Spanish inhabitants, for the most
part shopkeepers, in Alcazar.

offered money for the beer, which they refused, then fled as hard as I could.

A scene at Alcazar opened my eyes to the disadvantage of bigamy, for I saw two wives armed with broomsticks beating their poor husband in a most cruel way.   O ladies who demand franchise, how you would have enjoyed this disgusting sight!

Four days later our caravan arrived in Tangier, having been absent over seven weeks in the interior. The remainder of our party left in the course of a few days for England, while I remained behind, to start in a week or so once more for Wazan.

So ended, on the 23rd of February, our successful and most pleasant trip through Northern Morocco.

PART II.

A JOURNEY WITH H.B.M. SPECIAL MISSION TO THE COURT OF THE SULTAN AT MOROCCO CITY.

" Tandis que le progrès est la loi de l'existence des nations Chré-
tiennes, l'immobilité semble être celle des peuples mussulmans."—
M. MALEM.

CHAPTER I.

THE JOURNEY TO MOROCCO CITY.

WHAT a noise H.M.S. *Curlew* made, as she steamed into the quiet blue bay of Tangier on Thursday, April 7th, and saluted the Moorish flag with twenty-one guns! and what a din the twenty-one Moorish guns made in return, till they shook every window in the white rock-bound town, and threatened to knock even the houses down! All Tangier was on the *qui-vive*, for it is not often that her peace is disturbed by the thundering of salutes from men-of-war, a cargo steamer or two, or half a dozen feluccas from Spain, being usually the only craft to be seen lying at rest in the bay, except when the *Hassanieh*, an old tub—-the whole Moorish fleet—comes in like a great black whale, and disfigures the bay with her hideous form. But there was no disfigurement from the *Curlew*. Rather, the lovely view was enhanced by the pure white vessel, with her yellow funnel and scanty rigging, that lay at anchor a mile or two from the shore, and filled the air with the white smoke of her salutes.

M

We were all glad to see the *Curlew* arrive, for it meant no more waiting for us, but a speedy start. But where and why were we starting? We were going, through the kindness of Sir William Kirby-Green, with the British Mission to Morocco, and the man-of-war had come to take us to Mazagan, a port some little way down the west coast of Morocco, whence the journey overland was to commence.

Our party was a large one, and, as I shall have occasion hereafter to mention certain of its members by name, I shall commence by giving a list of those of whom the mission consisted. Firstly, his Excellency Sir William Kirby-Green, K.C.M.G.; Lady, Miss, and Mr. Jack Kirby-Green, and Miss Scudamore; Mr. Herbert E. White, H.M. Consul at Tangier; M. de Vismes de Ponthieu, Secretary and Vice-Consul; Surgeon-Major Charlesworth, Medical Attaché; Lieutenant Boulnois, Military Attaché; Mr. and Mrs. Caton Woodville, Mr. and Mrs. Treeby, and myself, who, with our servants and baggage for a couple of months, formed no small array. The day after the arrival of the *Curlew* being Good Friday, we did not start; for, if it is unlucky to begin a voyage on any ordinary Friday, how much more so would it be on this particular one! but Saturday dawned at last, and there was a rushing to and fro from the first peep of daylight, a slamming of boxes, a yelling at servants, a scramble for breakfast, and we were off.

It was a long procession we formed, as we trooped through the crowded streets of Tangier, jostled by the dirty water-carriers, now and again nearly knocked down by overloaded mules and bad smells, while half a dozen dusky Moors carried the lighter portions of our luggage in front of us, one item of which, and not the least important, was Marita, our monkey, joint-stock property, perched on the shoulders of Mahammed Rushti, Woodville's servant, who had his work well cut out for him in keeping off her small sharp teeth from his somewhat bulky neck. Down to the smelling Custom House, where the white-turbaned Moors sit cross-legged on their raised benches, counting their beads and gazing at one through their half-closed eyes as if there were no work in the world to be done, and, if there were, they were not the men to do it. On we trooped to the crowded wooden pier, till monkey, luggage, and all were bundled into a boat and rowed off to the man-of-war.

Our party was the first to get on board, and we had time to look round us at the admirable fittings of the *Curlew* before a salute of seventeen guns from port and starboard made us realize fully and in a jumpy way that the Minister had left the shore, and it was only a few minutes later that he stepped on board from the man-of-war's boat, in the stern of which flew the Union Jack, accompanied by their Excellencies the Italian and Spanish Ministers, who, after adieux and many kind wishes for a happy and successful voyage, returned on shore. Five minutes later the twin propellers began to turn, and we steamed gently out of Tangier Bay. Yet there was one episode in our parting that was amusing. Just

as we got under way, a shore-boat about two hundred
yards distant attracted our attention.   In the stern
stood an elderly Jewess, in native dress, waving an
enormous green umbrella ; in her we recognized one
of the most important members of the mission—our
laundress, for washing of any decency would be un-
procurable on the road.   The view was very charming as we sailed away ; not a ripple on the sea, not a
breath of wind to disturb the ship or ourselves.   As
we passed along the coast, and Tangier was hid from
sight behind its rocky promontory, we skirted the
hill known as the Mount, from the trees of which
peeped many a pretty house and garden, and here
and there figures could be seen enthusiastically
waving umbrellas and handkerchiefs.   Cape Spartel,
the north-west corner of Africa, was soon rounded,
the great bluff cliff, with its graceful lighthouse
perched high on a ledge of rock, and our course was
altered more to the south. Shoals of porpoises played
round and alongside the ship, throwing their great
bodies out of the water and plunging in again with a
splash ; while over the snow-white wake we left
behind us, gracefully skimmed the soft grey gulls.
A little later we passed Shaf-al-Akab, the scene of
many a boar hunt; and we could even see Awara,
where the camp is always pitched.   Arzeila and
Larache were left behind before dark, the latter too
far away to be distinctly seen.

Any one who knows the *Curlew* will recollect that
her accommodation is entirely insufficient for fourteen persons, with baggage and servants such as we
had ; but Captain Kingscock was kind enough to put

his cabin at the service of the ladies, and for us beds
were made up under awnings on deck. The quarter
deck was littered with almost innumerable packages ;
saddle-boxes and uniform-cases lay piled one above
the other, interspersed with portmanteaus of every
variety, over which gamboled Marita, the monkey.
Nothing could have been more enjoyable than our
afternoon on deck, especially when, at four o'clock,
tea, such as one seldom, if ever, gets out of England,
arrived. We did not dine off biscuit and salt junk,
as we believed one ought to do on board ship ; on
the contrary, we dined most excellently, and it was
late when we left our whiskies and sodas and turned
in.

Most of us slept on deck, but I preferred to rig
up my camp-bed in the ward-room, and was afterwards glad I did so, as there was a heavy fall of rain
in the night.

Soon after daylight next morning, draped figures,
some of them remarkable for the scantiness of their
drapery, could be seen pacing the deck, and gazing
anxiously at the indistinct shore, to try and discover
Mazagan, our port of destination ; but tide or current
had delayed us, and it was not till half-past ten, after
twenty hours at sea, that we dropped anchor in the
bay.

Mazagan from the sea, in fact from anywhere, is far
from interesting, though one day in the dim past it
must have been a strongly-fortified place, for it was
during many years in the possession of the Portuguese,
who built the high walls that still remain, though in
a more or less dilapidated condition. The town is

situated on a sandy, low promontory, which with the coast forms the bay, and a poor harbour enough it is, almost unprotected from the west, and entirely so from the north-west and north.   The great drawback to trade with Morocco is its insufficiency, almost its total want of ports, as those which offer any protection from the prevailing westerly winds are situated at the mouths of the rivers, which form bars, over which ships of any size are unable to pass.

No sooner was the anchor down than the *Curlew's* guns again roared forth a salute of twenty-one, answered by twenty-one from the fort on shore, as compliments to each other's flags; then seventeen from the *Curlew,* as Sir William Kirby-Green stepped over the ship's side, answered by seventeen as he landed at the jetty, accompanied by Mr. Redman, the British Vice-Consul, who had come off to receive him.

The town presented a brilliant spectacle as we landed, every one turning out to see the arrival.   On the jetty we were received by the Basha, or governor of the town , who was to escort us to the capital, and other Moors of more or less note.   On reaching the end of the pier, we were met by a couple of dozen soldiers ; and again, as we entered the town through a stone gateway, found the streets lined with regulars, in scarlet and blue, who saluted as we passed, while their band struck up some discordant music.

We lunched with Mr. and Mrs. Redman at the Vice-Consulate, where those who enjoyed any share in the ownership of the monkey were not quite at their ease, as every now and then a crash from the back garden made them realize that a monkey is an awkward animal to take on calls, especially where there is any attempt at horticultural decoration in the way of flower-pots. Nor was our happiness increased when, terrific shrieks being heard, we rushed to the window, and found Marita apparently actively engaged in devouring Mr. Redman's youngest son. However, he escaped without injury.

After a short walk in the small and uninteresting town, and a stroll round the ramparts, beneath one part of which is a curious native village, with its beehive-shaped huts of straw nestling amidst hedges of prickly pears and aloes, we visited the camp, which had been awaiting us some time. In all there were some fourteen large tents for our accommodation, and fifty or sixty for the escort, most of whom, by the way, slept in the open air. The camp was pitched on the sea-shore, and looked extremely well. Our tents were native ones, supplied by the Sultan for the journey. These Moorish tents are very comfortable, large, and high, and well adapted for hot weather, though they would be improved by having a double roof. Outside, they are of white canvas, with curiously-shaped patterns in dark blue cloth running in lines round the tents, parallel with the ground. In shape they are "bell" tents, an enormously heavy pole in the centre supporting the weighty roof; but they are lined inside in coloured cloths, on the ceiling in diverging stripes, and round the walls, which are some five feet in height, in the form of Moorish arches.

Our respective tents were pointed out to us, and, after a wash and a change, we dined to the sound of the sea dashing on the steep sandy shore a few yards off. Our escort's camp was a little way from ours, so that we were free from the noise of the braying mules and bubbling camels. As was only reasonable, we were anxious to discover with what class of riding animals the Sultan had supplied us, and, first thing the following morning, we went to see. Nor were we disappointed, for some of the horses were really very good, though not, as we had expected, slight barbs, but heavily built and thick-set animals, probably the descendants of the dray horses that George III. presented to one of the Sultans of Morocco of the beginning of this century.

It was Easter Monday, and it looked so, so great was the noise, so many the horses, and so varied the costumes. There was much to amuse and interest us : the constant flow of soldiers in and out of town ; Jews hanging around to make an honest—or, if they get the chance, a dishonest—penny ; half nude Moors saddling mules and horses ; Spaniards losing their tempers ; horses pawing the ground and fighting— in fact, a veritable circus. A last visit to the town, where we made a few purchases, and a bottle of beer at a kind of restaurant, which bore in large letters on its walls " Royal Victoria Hotel," completed our share of the morning's work, while his Excellency and the ladies paid a final visit at the Vice-Consulate, the latter afterwards visiting the harem of the Basha, where they spent a *mauvais quart-d'heure* in the clutches of half a dozen native ladies, who danced and sang to the music of a wheezy harmonium, while the guests were regaled with an oily kind of broth—

by the way, quite uneatable—and gallons of green tea. But though they did not drink the soup, they were not allowed to forget it, as one of the slaves cleverly succeeded in upsetting a plate of it over one of the ladies' riding-habits.

Soon after twelve o'clock we got away, and a more striking scene could scarcely be imagined. Before and behind us soldiers, a hundred and fifty mounted and a rabble on foot; while along the sides of the dusty road were stationed foot soldiers, in scarlet and blue, who saluted as we passed. In front of the procession rode a standard-bearer, carrying the Moorish red flag, while by Sir William's side were the Governor of the district and his brother; and the dress of these two needs description, for one scarcely, if ever, sees anything so perfect in colour. The Governor was mounted on a black horse, and wore a white haik—not unlike the Roman toga, and no doubt its descendant—of fine transparent web, and silk stripes, over which was thrown a dark-blue bernous or hooded cloak, while, to relieve this somewhat austere colouring, he rode on a huge saddle of an indescribable and lovely shade of salmon silk, his horse's head-trappings and reins being of the same colour, embroidered with gold. His brother was on a white horse, wearing a similar haik to the Governor, a pale torquoise-blue bernous, and using a crimson saddle and bridle.

After having been about an hour on the march, we stopped to see the troops at their Lab-el-baroud or powder play. From a dozen to twenty men would stand in a line on horseback at the end of an open

piece of ground ; at a given signal they would urge
their horses to a canter, salute with their long guns,
waving them round their turbaned heads, change from
a canter to a furious gallop, and crying out " Allah,
Allah," fire.   Nothing could surpass the picturesqueness of the tearing horses, the riders' flowing garments borne in the wind behind them, the gorgeous
trappings of the horses, the men's ease and grace in
the saddle.   Over and over again they repeated it,
till one's head was almost turned with the brilliant
sight and the quick volleying. Now and again a
man falls at this dangerous amusement ; but accidents
are rare, owing to the peculiar shape of the Moorish
saddle, made with a peak before and behind, which
prevents one from falling.   This is terribly heavy,
as no less than ten thick felt saddle-cloths are used
under the saddle, each of a different colour, while the
saddle itself is of gold or coloured embroidery. While
we were watching the Lab-el-baroud, the baggage-
mules and camels passed us, and we caught a glimpse
of Marita seated on the back of a mule, with a bland
smile of satisfaction at her elevated position, basking
in the mid-day sun. We had obtained another pet
that morning at Mazagan—a small kitten.   We
thought it would do to play with the monkey ; but,
on the contrary, the monkey played with it, and was
caught gently and with the utmost skill trying to
remove its great yellow eyes.   However, it was
rescued in time, and no damage was done. Our
other animals consist of two setters, an Irish and an
English, and two small Shetland ponies, part of the
present from the English Government to the Sultan.

Soon after resuming our journey, we came to the luncheon tent, which had been, as always was the case, sent on in the early morning, as the heat of the sun and the absence of trees rendered luncheon in the open an impossibility. Soon after our meal we were on our way again to the camp, pitched at a place called Dar-ben-Zahra, though a better spot might easily have been chosen, as the ground was hilly and stony. As could only have been expected, there was a good deal of confusion in camp after our arrival ; but with such numbers as we were, and with such a crowd of camp-followers, it could not be avoided. The tents were pitched in a row, and before the centre one the Union Jack was flying from a flag-staff.

The next morning we were up early, not so much from inclination as from the fact that the Bashador —a corruption of Ambassador—as the Moors called the Minister, ordered our tents to be struck at a certain hour, whether we would or no, on one occasion discovering a certain member of the mission gracefully decked in a pith helmet, which he evidently considered sufficient costume for the unabashed Moors. The scene on leaving one's tent in the early morning was a noisy one, and even if one had had the chance of lying in bed, it would have been no rest, so great was the row. In the midst of the camp were the camels being loaded with the heavier luggage, lying down at their masters' bidding, yet groaning meanwhile at their heavy loads, the mules braying to one another in anything but dulcet tones, and Moors quarrelling or laughing, shouting and yelling, in fact doing their very best to add to the confusion. There was a babel of tongues in camp; English, Arabic, French, Spanish, Italian, and Albanian were in constant use.

On leaving camp that morning we passed, as usual, between lines of mounted soldiers, who fell in directly behind us. The country continued flat and uninteresting, and, though well cultivated, the crops looked sadly in need of rain. At all the villages we passed—for the most part mere collections of mud or straw huts, with perhaps one tabbia house—the women would come out with red or yellow handkerchiefs tied to sticks for flags, and utter their shrill cry of welcome—a peculiar high note sounded with a tremolo, made by moving their tongues quickly between their lips. The Moorish countrywoman's dress, as one little known in England, is worth describing. A loose kind of skirt and body in one is worn hanging from the shoulders, caught there with two silver brooches, joined to each other by a silver chain that hangs across the chest. This garment is fastened at the waist with a coloured band, either of silk or cotton, generally the latter, while over all is worn a thick woollen haik, sometimes ornamented with coloured stripes. The costume of the town's-women is much more gorgeous, their garments being of silks and brocades, while they hang their ears and necks with silver and gold jewellery.

All the women are noticeable for their love of display, and the weight of their necklaces, earrings, and bracelets must be overpowering. The hair is worn in two long plaits, lengthened with interwoven black thread, while the eyes and cheeks are smothered in paint.

We lunched again in the tents sent on in the morning, and it was wonderful to see the way Moorish biscuits followed *paté de foie gras* down our hungry throats. Under the grateful shade of the tent we spent an hour or two, waiting for the cool of the day to ride into camp. We wandered from the tent to look at the country round, and saw many curious specimens of lizards in the stone walls. One of great size having attracted my attention, I made a grab at it, but, alas! only succeeded in capturing its tail. However, a few minutes later, an Arab brought me one of the same kind, which, with two others, I had hoped to have been able to bring back to England. They were some eighteen inches in length, and proportionately wide, being marked with alternate black and red stripes. Two hours' ride brought us into camp, where we found everything in better order than we had the night before. The site was the bottom of a dry valley, no doubt once flooded with water. The soldiers here mustered stronger than ever, and in all must have been some six hundred strong, foot and horse. On nearing the camp the greater part of our force galloped to right and left up the hill, drawing up in line on either side of the road. The movement was an exceedingly beautiful one, as not only were there greater numbers, but a much better show of horses, but still not pure barbs, but the heavy-necked breed we had seen all along. Every colour was used in saddles and trappings, and a black horse with yellow equipments and a rider in yellow bernous took our fancy immensely.

Our tents were all ready for us when we arrived in camp that evening. Perhaps the short description of the interior of one of our tents may not be out of place. The tents were, as I said before, of the shape known as " bell " tents, about twenty feet in diameter, and so allowing for more luxurious furniture than most tents. The ground was covered first with waterproof sheets, over which was spread native matting, and over that again rugs and carpets from the famous carpet-manufacturing town of Rabat, on the west coast of Morocco. A folding camp-bed with Moorish striped blankets, formed a most convenient lounge by day and bed by night. A square table, covered with a striped Moorish cloth, contained one's looking-glass and toilet things, while a couple of easy-chairs, a folding washhandstand, and a bath, completed the furniture.

The spot chosen for our camp that night was at Sok-el-Arba, where every Wednesday, as its name implies, the Moors hold their provincial soko or market. As the villages are so scattered, it is often impossible to hold the market at one particular spot, so a spot as near all as possible is chosen, where one day in the week the soko is held. A whole district often arranges its market-days succeeding one another ; for instance, Monday at one village, Tuesday at the next, and so on, allowing cattle-drivers, pedlars, and snake-charmers to wander from one to the other.

The next morning (Wednesday) while at breakfast, the sound of native music—the shrill pipe and the tomtom—was heard outside the tent, and we found some native jugglers in the middle of a performance.

Though far inferior to any ordinary English clown, the tricks that they did with their guns were very good, keeping the weapon continually spinning above their heads on two fingers.

On leaving camp, our escort went through their usual manœuvre of forming into lines, through which we passed. As had been promised us the night before, we began the day with a hunt with falcons and greyhounds. Leaving the road on our right, we verged off over corn-fields. The first sight of game that we had were two lesser bustard that we put up. The falcons, however, were not let fly—why, I do not know—but a stone curlew fell an easy prey a few minutes later. It was a sight worth seeing, the hawk suspended in the air on its quivering wings till with a swoop like a miniature thunder-bolt, it made short work of the poor bird. We next put up a hare, and a couple of greyhounds being slipped, had a most excellent run, killing in a fig-garden. The Moors are essentially sportsmen, and this was not the first coursing I had had in the country, as, when at Wazan earlier in the same year, the Shereef gave us an excellent day. The Moorish greyhounds are not nearly as swift as our English breed, or the hare, a poor animal compared with ours, would never stand a chance of escaping ; as it is, he often gets away. Again the falcons were let fly, this time at some lesser bustard ; but, unluckily, a plover was put up too, which, as being the less swift bird of flight, the hawk preferred and killed. We also got a few partridges. In the more southern parts, falcons are employed for hunting gazelle.

The love of sport amongst the Moors has its disadvantages as well as its advantages, for no sooner do they see one shoulder a gun, than they appear from every imaginable hole and corner and accompany one, shouting and yelling every time one hits anything, and going nearly frantic at a right and left. The Moors themselves with their clumsy but picturesque flint-locks seldom think of shooting a bird on the wing, but stalk a partridge with the same care as we do a stag. However, they are, as a rule, most excellent shots, considering the disadvantages they are under as to their guns, as many an old tusked boar has discovered to his loss as he has broken from covert, driven from his lair by the yelping hounds. Another method of sport in which they are skilled is the throwing of a curiously curved stick at game ; it is not unlike the boomerang, though it does not possess the almost miraculous power of returning to the thrower : with these sticks they are able to knock down running rabbits and partridges on the wing, so unerring are their eyes and hands.

During lunch that day we had Lab-el-baroud with the new soldiers, and much better done than any we had seen so far. Sometimes the rows of horsemen seemed as if they were charging straight at our tent, and, as it was, passed within a few feet of the ropes. Again and again they charged, saluted, fired, and stopped short, after making the horses rear till they seemed as though they must fall back with the cruel Moorish bit. Every now and then it was varied by a single man riding by himself and performing wonderful feats on horseback, his coloured kaftan only half-covered by his transparent haik, which flew behind him in the wind, his unwound turban showing his shaved shiny head, the wind blowing his temple locks out like horns, enhancing his ferocious appearance ; and, when his horse had reached its fastest pace, he would turn gracefully in his saddle and fire directly behind him.

Two hours' ride after lunch brought us into camp two hours over the wearying, dusty plain. The tents were pitched at Sok-el-T'lata, a large village, near which is a saint-house of some size, the burial-place of a marabout—not the white-domed building common all over the country, but a square stone house with a green-tiled roof.

On the road that afternoon we passed half a dozen lepers. Nothing more miserable than the appearance of these wretched people could be imagined. There, in the full glare of the sun, they sat on the scorching sand, wrapped up in their ragged jelabas, begging alms. They wore, as all lepers are obliged to do in this country, square straw hats, and had their faces bound up in linen, so that only the eyes were visible. What a life of horror, to be debarred from entering any village, or from holding any intercourse, almost, with the outer world. So great is the dread of lepers in this country, that they have a village set aside for them outside the walls of Morocco city, to which they are strictly confined. These poor beggars that we saw held wooden bowls for one to drop the coin into, for fear of contamination.

We were not off the next morning till about ten, as only three hours' march lay before us. The road was as flat and dusty as ever, but we saw the limit of that part of the plain in a range of low hills

N

straight before us. We often saw the mirage with wonderful clearness in crossing these plains. This day in particular it was very clear. In front of us, and apparently not far off, lay a great blue lake, skirted by trees that threw their shadows on the water below ; the lake looked beautifully cool in the burning sun, and the shade of the trees most tempting, but, alas ! as we approached we found it was all a myth, and lake, trees, and shade faded from view. One day, on the plains near Fez, we saw, not only the lake and the trees, but the sandy shore, women washing their clothes, and a white-domed house amongst the grove ; but all this, too, disappeared as we drew nearer, and left nothing behind it but a sandy waste and a few prickly pear bushes.

We lunched close to where our camp was to be pitched, and rested there three hours, so as to allow our tents to pass on and be all ready for us on our arrival. The site of the camp was prettier than any we had had as yet, just in the opening of a small valley, amongst the hills I mentioned as bordering the plain. Through the valley ran—or rather ought to have run, for it was dry—a small river, on the banks of which grew clumps of stately palms. In spite of the want of water, the valley was beautifully green, and a great relief after the yellow plains we had left behind us.

Two of us started, soon after our arrival in camp, to the top of a neighbouring hill in search of game, and to see the view ; and though we were disappointed as to the former, the latter amply repaid the steep climb, for we looked down upon the camp with its white tents, amongst which moved hundreds of men and horses, and there were the camels being driven out to graze by the half-naked Moors ; beyond, the plain stretched away as far as the eye could reach, dotted here and there by clumps of trees, or the tomb of some sanctified Moor. Altogether the sport had been disappointing on the road, especially as some of us had got such excellent sport in other parts of the country earlier in the year, only a few quail, sand-grouse, partridges, and lesser bustard having been bagged all the route.

We were off about half-past nine the next morning, and continued our journey through the valley. We passed several saint-houses and some tabbia ruins of great size, but what they were I was unable to dis-cover—probably the remains of some Moorish castle. About noon we passed into the Dukala district, and were met by a new escort, saying good-bye to our hand-some old Kaid and his showy men. The new escort was not nearly so gorgeous, but with our permanent troop of a hundred did not make at all a bad show. The reason of this falling off in appearance and numbers was that we had now entered a district less fertile and far less rich than that we had left, in fact, after this, all the way to Morocco we saw very little cultivation ; and yet another reason, not many years back, during a rebellion in this part of the country, the Sultan had marched through this district and destroyed the villages. The march of this potentate against any tribes is spoken of by the Moors as " the eating up," and a better expression could not be found, for the country had never recovered.

Three hours' ride in the morning, a rest for lunch, after which another hour's ride, and we were in camp

again.   On the road we passed a number of tholba
or scholars, who were begging by the roadside—a
sure sign that education is not far advanced in this
benighted country.   What an excellent idea for
undergraduates, after a bad week at Newmarket, to
replenish their empty pockets by standing in the
streets and begging in cap and gown.   Another
sign of the want of even the most elementary education was the fact that they had evidently never heard
of that most excellent proverb, " Cleanliness is next
to godliness ; " for a dirtier dozen men I never set
eyes on.   What little attempt at education does
exist is merely the drumming of half a dozen verses
of the Koran into little boys by means of a long
stick, and it is an amusing sight to stand at the
doors of the schools and watch the old thaleb seated
cross-legged, while a score of small urchins in their
shrill young voices shout after him verse after verse
from the Koran, the slightest mistake bringing down
upon their unlucky heads, or whatever portion of
their body is best within reach, a quick, smart blow
from his long stick.   The Moors possess no idea of
geography beyond this, that Morocco is the largest,
richest, best, and most fertile country in the world,
and that all the others are " in it " at all ; but they
are not the only people who think this of their fatherland.   Nor does there seem to be any likelihood of
an increase of education, and it is better so.   A
Moor will say, " My grandfather and father knew no
more, and they were good men, why should I bother
my head with learning ? "   When the day comes
that there are Board schools in the country, the
artistic life will die out, and the perfect dress of the

Moor will be changed for collars, broadcloth, and top-hats. Already the Jews in the coast town are wearing European costume ; but one can believe anything of a Morocco Jew. At present, no country can rival Morocco for picturesqueness ; but in a few years, it may be, trains will be tearing their hideous courses through the green, smiling valleys, and the gentle pipe of the shepherd-boy will be lost in the shriek of the railway-whistle. "This way for Fez, Morocco, and the Atlas ! " will cry the guard, while the pater-familias is blocking up the ticket-office with his numerous offspring, busily engaged in taking a weekly return ticket to Timbuctoo, "at reduced fares." Alas, alas !

Our camp that night was again in a valley, close to the remains of an old Moorish castle, surrounded by orange and olive groves. We spent the latter part of the afternoon in turning over stores, hunting for specimens. Our bag consisted of three snakes (alive in my bottle in my tent), seven scorpions of both the black and yellow varieties, and a great number of lizards and slow-worms. The latter I put in with my large lizards, but on hearing their great jaws scrunch-ing (is there such a word ?) the poor little reptiles I promptly separated them. Whether the snakes are venomous or not I do not know, for every one has refused my kind offer to try by letting them bite his fingers—what a selfish world it is ! As a long ride lay before us, we were up next day with the sun, and, after breakfast, set out. The weather was delicious in the early morning, but, even then, would have been too hot had it not been for a cool breeze blow-ing from the snows of the Atlas mountains. About an hour after leaving camp we obtained our first glimpse of the snow peaks rearing their heads far above the clouds that hovered round them. Like a great wall they stand, and seem in their foreboding silence to block all further way; as in reality they do, for beyond them lies the valley of the Sus, almost untrodden as yet by Christian feet, and beyond the Sus again, the great desert of the Sahara, over which lies the route to Timbuctoo and the Soudan.

We turned aside from the road during the morning to hunt gazelle, which are said to be common in that part. However, luck was against us, and though two of the party saw a herd of ten or twelve, the rest of us did not get even a sight, and those that were seen made off, after a long and tedious stalk, before a shot could be fired. Some great bustard, not uncommon in parts of Morocco, were also seen, but timid, as usual, kept well out of range. The plain was as wearying and uninteresting as ever, so it was a great relief, after three hours and a half in the saddle, to reach the luncheon-tent. Close to the village where it was pitched there was a curious fountain or water-tank, a long covered place, some thirty yards in length, and two in breadth, the ends left open, and descended by steps. This, we were told by Abu Beker, was a very old and celebrated fountain, as the water-supply is always good there, even in summer. After nearly three hours' rest, we rode into camp, a ride of about two hours' duration. The heat was intense, and much greater than any we had hitherto felt. It was curious to watch the small whirlwinds—"devils" they are proverbially called—lift the sand from the desert in circles, and send it twisting and turning over the plain, like a great pillar. One day, one of these whirlwinds caught my tent, and took out every peg that held the walls down. Luckily, however, some ropes held, as I was in the somewhat awkward position of bathing. Half an hour before our arrival in camp we were met by Carleton, who had preceded us to Morocco, and had already been some five weeks in the city awaiting the mission. He had ridden out that morning from the town, so that we began to feel that the end of our journey could not be so far away.

Our camp, which was pitched at the foot of a range of mountains lying not far north of Morocco, looked very well as we rode in, the tents of Carleton and his men adding to the effect ; and it looked better still a few minutes later, when we had changed our soiled and dust-stained clothes for clean flannels, and sat down to tea.

Here, as usual, the natives flocked to see the doctor, for surgery is at a very low ebb in Morocco, amputation being a matter of a knife, a saw, and a tub of boiling pitch. One man's complaint is worth mentioning.

"What is the matter with you?" asked the doctor.

"I cannot eat as much as I should like to," replied the patient, with a sigh.

Poor man, he could not stow away as much kooskoosoo as his companions, and came to the doctor for advice. Almost the only apology for doctors in Morocco are certain of the Jews, for the most part old hags, whose medicines are made of all the filth they can collect ; and the saints, whose curing is

" miraculous," but hardly successful. Charms are much resorted to, to avert illness and harm. By far the most common of these is the distended hand, a sure preventive from the effects of the evil eye. There is scarcely a house in the town that has not the hand painted on its doorposts or walls, so great is their superstition ; while the same emblem in silver or gold is worn round the neck. Salt, too, is a great preservative from the djins and evil spirits, and is often to be seen hanging in a small bag round the horse's, mule's, and camel's necks.

On Sunday, April 17th, we left our camp at eight o'clock, en route for El Kantara, the bridge that crosses the Tensift, the river of Morocco. Within an hour's ride of the city our road lay through a lonely mountain pass, on reaching the summit of which we got our first real view of the Atlas mountains, for the day before we had only seen the peaks. At our feet, as we stood on the summit of the pass, lay the great plain of Morocco, beyond it the mountains. In the centre of this plain, half hidden in groves—ay, forests —of palms, lay the city, only the great minaret of the Koutubia and one or two other mosques visible, just peeping above the feathery palms. Nothing could have been more lovely than the view in the bright April sunlight, the contrast of the green plain to the dark palms, and the dark palms to the white snow beyond. None of us were disappointed—no one could be ; it was as if some god had taken the Alps and set them down in the centre of a tropical plain. And yet there is this difference between the Atlas and the Alps, that the former are very little peaked, but run in a continuous line like a great wall ; and still another difference, that as yet the great Atlas are not overrun with tourists, and there are no railways to take one up to palaces of luxury like the Rigi Kulm.

We felt the heat a good deal before we reached the luncheon-tent at eleven o'clock. Soon after we had sat down, Kaid Maclean and his brother, Captain Alan Maclean, joined us, having ridden out from the city for that purpose. We admired their uniform very much, the mixture of Orientalism and civilization being admirably arranged. The Kaid was in white and gold, and his brother in soft grey, both wearing the tarboosh and turban. Their jackets were cut à la Zouave, and the trousers left loose to the knee, where they were gathered into top boots. Their horses also were very gorgeous, the Kaid's trapped in purple and gold, and his brother's in green. They lunched with us, and proceeded in the afternoon with us to our camp, the last before entering the city.

An hour's ride took us to the beginning of the palm groves, for which Morocco is so celebrated, and a few minutes more to our camp, pitched on the banks of the Tensift, amongst the palm-trees. The bridge El Kantara is really a fine one for Morocco, but sadly out of repair ; but bridges are almost unknown in the country, fording being the sole means of crossing the rivers, and this is often impossible in winter.

That night we had a glorious sunset, such as one seldom sees ; the sky a blaze of crimson and gold behind a foreground of palms, while the snow far away on the mountain tops shone like opals ; nor was it less lovely when the sun had set, and the crimson changed to mauve, and the gold to a pale lemon tint; and most lovely of all, when the sky became a rich torquoise blue, as the night began to throw her veil over the slumbering world and soften the outlines of the palm-trees to a delicate indistinctness.

CHAPTER II.

THE SULTAN.

> " Mislike me not because of my complexion,
> The shadow'd livery of the burnish'd sun,
> To whom I am a neighbour and near bred."
> *Merchant of Venice.*

ON Monday, April 18th, his Excellency the British

Lab-el-baroud—rider standing on saddle.

Minister made his official entry into the city of Morocco.

We were all up early in the morning, as our start

had to be made at eight on account of the heat and
dust.   At that hour we were all on horseback, looking
far more respectable than we had as yet, as collars and
white shirts were the order of the day.   As each one
entered the breakfast-tent, he was received with such
cries as, " By Jove, he's shaved," or " How long have
you been getting into those breeches ? " or some
remark equally insulting.   Immediately after breakfast we started with our escort of soldiers.   By far
the most gorgeous personage in the procession was
Costi, Sir William's Albanian servant, who appeared
in full war-paint, or, rather, an Albanian mountaineer's costume of white cloth, embroidered all over
in black and gold braid, and wearing enough weapons
for the whole garrison of Gibraltar.   The procession
was not long in getting into order.   First, after a few
kaids and the standard-bearer, rode Sir William and
Lady Kirby-Green, followed by the ladies and the
official members of the mission, and finally the "un-
officialities."   After having been on the road about
ten minutes, our way led us between lines of
mounted soldiers, who fell in as we passed along,
increasing the dust, which was already terrible, for in
spite of the early hour the heat was intense.   The
scene was a very grand one and thoroughly Oriental,
the procession headed by the vanguard, with the
standard-bearer in their midst carrying the Moorish
red flag, once the terror of European trading-ships.
A little further on the road was lined with infantry
in scarlet and blue, and here we were met by Kaid
Maclean, his brother, and the Basha of Morocco.   As
we passed the band of the regiment, they struck up.
What they played no one could say ; in fact, I think

they did not stick to one tune, but each composed a
little " morceau " of his own for the occasion.   As we
emerged from the palms into the open ground, the
sight increased in gorgeousness, as the foot as well as
the horsemen had fallen-in in our rear.   The hot dusty
road, with its soldiers in scarlet and blue, armed,
by the way, with Winchester repeaters, the sun
shining on the barrels and bayonets of the rifles, our
own party half hidden in the clouds of yellow dust,
the grey-walled town, with its minarets and palms,
all formed a picture never to be forgotten.   We
noticed the soldiers as we passed along ; a motley
throng indeed, but looking capable of good fighting.
They were arranged in no particular order, and their
variety of height and colour had a curious effect.
Next to a small, sallow Moor could be seen towering
above his companion, a great negro, his head as black
and shining as a block of coal.   Next to him, perhaps,
a half-breed of a coffee-coloured tint, in fact, every
variety of complexion was on view.

On every available mound stood gazers, while
behind the lines of soldiers, boys and men ran, keeping up with us.   Under the shade of some trees Kaid
Maclean pointed us out his wife and family, who had
ridden out in Moorish costume to see the procession
pass.   Hotter and dustier grew the road as we neared
the city, and we were heartily glad to pass through
the Bab Dukala, the remains of a once fine gateway,
and enter the town.   But, alas! we found no relief
there ; if anything it was hotter and dustier than
outside.   Here again were people on the housetops
and in the doorways to look at us.   Along the narrow
streets we rode, past the great tower of the Koutubia,

or mosque of the booksellers, raised by the same man who built the Giralda at Seville and the Beni Hassan tower at Rabat.   Sometimes we turned to the left, sometimes to the right, the road seemed interminable.

Hotter and hotter still it grew, until, just as we thought we could bear it no longer, we turned off through an archway into a most beautiful garden, planted with groves of oranges and lemons, pome-granates, and olives ; and this garden was to be our home during our stay at the capital.   About it was scattered the Maimounieh Palace—I say scattered advisedly, for the palace did not consist of one house, but of pavilions and kiosks here and there amongst the trees.   Looking down the principal avenue, one of great size, to one of the kiosks faced with Moorish arches was really a lovely sight.   The contrast of the cool shade and the sweet scent of the orange-blossom after the heat and glare of the long dusty road can scarcely be imagined.   From a desert to a paradise, and such a paradise !

Altogether our entry had taken about two hours and a half, and though very gorgeous, was a thing only to be seen but once, at least in such a heat as we experienced.   Every one was pleased, from the minister to the monkey, and from my live snakes in a glass bottle to the little black boys who sit on the backs of the mules and shout and laugh at their own jokes.   The gardens are full of birds, and as I sat that night and wrote my diary in my tent, the nightingales were singing in the trees above me, for some of us were living encamped, as, in spite of being housed in a palace, the accommodation was none too good.

Three days were granted us to settle down into our

palace and recover from the fatigues of our long, hot ride, before any business began ; and it was not till the Wednesday following our arrival at the capital that we were received by the Sultan. It had been announced to us immediately we reached the city that it would be his Majesty's pleasure that we should appear before him on that day, so that we had had the intervening Monday and Tuesday to prepare our varied uniforms and polish our swords and spurs. The two days passed pleasantly enough, spent for the most part in the enjoyable shade of the garden, in which we really lived, as not only did we pass our time under the trees, but even went so far as to take all our meals in the open air. But Wednesday came at last, and with it stir and bustle. We were all about early, as our reception was to take place at the somewhat incongruous hour of eight in the morning, so that we might escape the heat and glare of the mid-day sun. Before leaving for the Kubbah Sueira, in which the ceremony was to take place, we made a light breakfast, and about a quarter before eight mounted our steeds. The scene in our palace garden was a brilliant one, and the cool grey-green avenue of olives presented a very different scene from what it had during the last two days ; as, instead of being almost deserted, it was filled with gorgeously-equipped men, for not only had we donned our fullest war-paint, but the Moors who were there to escort us to the presence of the Emperor were arrayed in soft haiks of snowy whiteness, from the graceful folds of which peeped the brilliant scarlets, greens, and yellows of their kuftans, while the prancing, neighing horses added to the effect, each led by a soldier in scarlet and blue.

It was nearly eight o'clock before we started.   At
the gate of the Maimounieh we found a large escort
waiting for us, as we passed through which trumpeters
sounded a fanfare.   After a minute's halt we were
once more *en route,* our new escort having fallen-in
in the rear.   The road to the Sultan's palace was not
a long one, though it sufficed to give us a decent coat-
ing of dust before we reached our destination at the
Kubbah Sueira.   Passing through two rather fine
archways at each of which our approach was heralded
by a blast of trumpets, we entered the great square of
the Kasbah, into which the palace looks.   The square
we found full of troops ; on our right and in front
of us the infantry, on our left the cavalry, of which
each man was dismounted, standing at his horse's
head.   It seemed almost incredible to us that Morocco
could turn out so many soldiers, for we learned afterwards from the most authentic of sources, that there
were no less than twenty-two thousand men present.

In the centre of these troops was left an open space,
where already were the mules bearing the presents
from the British Government, in front of which stood
the small Shetland ponies, one led by Sir William's
Albanian servant, the other by a Moor.   In the centre
of this open space, we, having dismounted, took up
our position, while various Court officials rushed
about arranging minor details.   We were placed in
line, the Minister a few paces in front of us, bearing
his letters of credence wrapped in a gorgeous silk
cover.   In front of us, some hundred yards' distance
in the wall of the square, was the great green gateway that communicates with the palace, a fine example
of a Moorish arch, and boasting much finish and

decoration. Between us and this gateway, with their backs to us, and so facing the palace, stood a row of courtiers, some forty in all.

We had ample time to look around us before the ceremony of the day commenced, and this conclusion we all came to : Be the Moors in other respects what they may, they are unrivalled in arranging effects. The great square, with its curious turreted walls and fine gateways ; the thousands of troops all around us, the infantry in their scarlet and blue, the cavalry in white flowing haiks ; and the long-robed courtiers before us—all formed a wonderful picture. And if, then, we came to the conclusion that the Moors are perfect " showmen," how much more did we do so when a blast of trumpets announced the Emperor, and, the great gates being thrown open, the procession began to appear. First, led by black slaves, came four magnificent horses—a black, a grey, a bay, and a white—following which marched the Court-Marshall with a white wand, various officials, spear bearers, and others ; and, finally, the Sultan himself, mounted on a splendid horse, whose trappings of green and gold formed a strange contrast to the Emperor's plain white costume, which consisted of a jelab and haik, both of which were drawn over his turbaned head, no doubt as a protection from the sun, though this was scarcely needed, as high above him waved the Imperial umbrella, a marvellous structure of crimson and gold. On either side of his Majesty walked men whose duty it was to keep the flies off his sacred person by continually flapping the air with long white silk scarves. Following the Sultan were more officials, and finally a green and gold brougham.

O

As the procession entered the square, all the troops fell down, crying, " Long live the Sultan. Victory to the Sultan," and a wonderful cry it was from twenty-two thousand throats. As the Sultan approached the row of courtiers that I mentioned above as being between the palace and ourselves, they bowed themselves to the ground crying out, " It is the Sultan," then suddenly turned round and fled in every direction, as though even the sight of his august Majesty inspired fear. The front portion of the procession having diverged to right and left, the Emperor approached and addressed Sir William, who had already been announced by the State herald shouting in a stentorian voice, " The Ambassador from the Queen of England." To his Majesty's few words of welcome, the Minister made a complimentary reply, after which the Sultan remarked that " he hoped that the friendly relations that had always existed between the Courts of England and Morocco might long be continued."

An amusing story is related with regard to these words. At the close of the Spanish war of 1859, a representative from the Spanish Government was sent to the Sultan to arrange the indemnity and to demand Ceuta. This representative arrived at Court and was received just as we were received. Imagine his intense surprise when the Sultan said, " He hoped that the peace and good-will that had always existed between Spain and Morocco might long be continued," and the disastrous war scarcely over. I cannot vouch for the story being true.

On the termination of his Excellency's speech, the Sultan said he hoped we had had a pleasant journey, and had found everything satisfactory, whereupon he asked that the members of the mission should be presented. Each of us stepped forward in turn, bowing or saluting, as the case might be, while the Minister presented us. Our salutations were answered by a scarcely perceptible bow on the part of his Majesty, who, had it not been that he asked questions as to our uniforms and occupations, would have appeared totally unconscious of our presence. When all in turn had been presented, the ponies were brought forward, and much admired, such a breed being entirely unknown to the Moors, who were very naturally astonished at their diminutive size. The Sultan was very much interested in Costi's Albanian costume, the like of which he had never seen before, and asked questions as to his nationality ; then, bidding us adieu for the present, and the procession having once more formed into order, he retired to the palace. After a few minutes' conversation with some of the officials, we were joined by the ladies, who had witnessed the ceremony from a distance, and amidst a fanfare of trumpets retired once more to the cool shade of our garden at the Maimounieh Palace. And so ended our reception by the Sultan, and certainly it was the most gorgeous sight I have ever seen, and compensated us for having missed the Jubilee, which we spent in camp the day before arriving in Tangier on our return journey. But this was not all we were destined to see of the Sultan that day, for a message was brought to us on our arrival at the Maimounieh, requesting us to appear at Court again at twelve o'clock, to exhibit the remaining gifts, for, as I mentioned above, the ponies were presented at the same time as we were.

Shortly before the appointed hour, we left the Maimounieh, and again forming in procession, as in the early morning, rode to the palace, at the gate of which we dismounted.   Entering through a small archway, we found ourselves in a courtyard of no great size or pretensions, with a covered colonnade of Moorish horse-shoe arches across one side, under the shade of which some half-dozen slaves were busily engaged in unpacking the presents.   Here we were joined by Kaid Maclean, the Instructor-General of his Majesty's forces, and the Lord Chamberlain.

Suddenly a marshal announced the Sultan, who quickly entered, unattended.   The Lord Chamberlain fell on his knees and kissed the royal haik, while we bowed or saluted.   After a few words with the minister, his Majesty commenced examining the presents, which consisted for the most part of mechanical toys and firearms ; amongst the latter he was most pleased with a beautiful pair of Lancaster's four-barrelled pistols, in ivory and silver-gilt, which he was not satisfied in merely examining, but insisted on firing, nor did he seem to care much in which direction the bullets flew, as he merely aimed over the court-yard wall. An ambulance waggon took his fancy very much, though we afterwards heard a rumour that in-stead of putting it to its proper use, it was ridden by his wives when they took their afternoon turn in the " park." Altogether his Majesty was with us some time, and we had ample opportunity of noticing him. He is a tall man—a head taller than any one present at the time—of about forty-five years of age. In com-plexion he is very dark, black blood showing itself very plainly in his thick lips, though this does not prevent his being an exceedingly handsome man. His face is thin and looks worn. He wears a black beard and moustache, and dresses entirely in white, on this occasion the haik giving place to a long jelab of soft, rough texture. His hands are small and well shaped. His every movement is studied, and certainly he is most successful in appearing majestic.

Though the Minister had several audiences, we saw him only once more during our stay at the capital, when one morning we were summoned to bid him adieu. Hurrying into our uniforms, we rode fast to the palace, and were immediately shown into a richly decorated room in which, seated cross-legged on a Louis Quatorze sofa, was the Emperor. A minute or two's conversation, bows and salutes, and we were ushered away.

That afternoon we spent in seeing the Agidal Palace gardens, the great enclosed park of the Sultan. We rode there, and remained on horseback nearly the whole time, as the gardens are very extensive, and the heat was too great to walk in. The whole place is very fine, but badly kept and wild. Great avenues of olive-trees run in every direction, between which are wildernesses of oranges and lemons, palms, and pomegranates. There is very little attempt at cultivation. In the centre of the park, but inclosed with high walls, is the Agidal Palace, a new building erected by this Sultan, Moulai Hassan. It is a curious building from the outside, for, of course, we were not permitted to enter it, and almost resembles a mediæval castle, with its square towers and pointed roofs. At the foot of a grand flight of steps we dismounted, and ascending, gazed over the clear, calm

waters of the great tank—almost a lake—square, and
very deep.   Round the tank runs a paved pathway
shaded by lovely trees, and at one end, opposite the
flight of steps, is a picturesque kiosk and gateway.
Here we found the steam-launch awaiting us, in
which we went for a trip, though she is far from being
a fast or luxurious craft ; nor was our pleasure increased by the fact that we had to be constantly dis-
engaging the propeller of weeds, to prevent her stop-
ing altogether.   Near one side of the tank there has
lately been erected an enormous water-wheel, which
is, in some—at present—incomprehensible way, to
manufacture cartridges.   The wheel is of great size,
and was made to turn for our special benefit, greatly
to the delight and astonishment of the Moors, who
had never in all their lives seen such a prodigy.   I
wish it all success.   We spent some hours in the
garden, which, after all, from an English point of
view, was no finer, except in size, than ours at the
Maimounieh ; of this, as really belonging to the Sultan,
with whom and whose possessions this chapter is
supposed to deal, a description will not be out of
place.

The garden is enclosed by high walls, one of which
also formed the outer wall of the city, and is intersected by avenues of olives, which here reach a greater
size than I have seen elsewhere, and even rival English forest-trees in their dimensions.   Between these
avenues, as at the Agidal Palace, are groves of fruit-
trees, for the most part oranges and lemons, which at
the time we were there were not only in fruit, but also
in blossom.   Here and there, above the heads of the
oranges, rises a tall cypress, a pillar of stately dark

green. The avenues are laid down with a gravel, and bordered on each side by trellis-work of light cane, over which grow creeping plants.

At one end of the long avenue stands one of the houses that help to constitute the palace, a two-storeyed building of white concrete, and devoid of any external decoration. Passing by an archway under the house, the road turns off to right and left, the former to a private gate that connects with the country outside the city walls, the latter to another portion of the garden. Taking the right path, one passes on one's left the swimming-bath, a tank of some pretensions, with an asphalte terrace round it, and a small bathing-house. Adjoining the tank is another house, built, like all really Moorish houses, round a patio, the white pillars of which support the over-hanging roof. The floor is tiled all over, and in the centre gurgles a fountain, while in one wall there is another fountain of beautiful tilework, the water falling from the small pipes into a clear marble basin. Into the patio look rooms, large but more or less bare, and lighted only by the great doorways of brilliant-hued arabesque. At the opposite end of the avenue, and exactly in the centre of the garden, is a picturesque kiosk, faced with a colonnade of arches and pillars. Here we generally retired after dinner if the nights were chilly, as they not unusually were. Beyond this kiosk a fresh avenue led to the further wall of the garden, and served as our rifle-range. To add to the effect of the tout-ensemble, from amongst the thick orange-trees peeped our Moorish tents, for most of the men of the party preferred the tents to indoors, where the accommodation was none too great.

From the larger of our houses a staircase led to a turret, from which a lovely view of the city and its environs could be obtained. Below us, all around, except on the west, lay the city—in truth, a city of gardens—from amongst which peeped the houses of the rich, while a mass of white flat roofs, stretching as far as the eye could reach, represented the poorer and commercial quarters. To the south-east was the Sultan's palace, its green roofs glittering in the setting sun—for it was usually in the evening that we made use of this terrace—and beyond the palace, again, the Agidal gardens, the plains, and the gorgeous snow-capped mountains, tinged, like the diadem of some Eastern Queen, by the parting rays of daylight ; and even after the sun had set for us, the mountains retained their glorious colouring of crimson and gold. To the west lay the great plains, a forest of palm-trees, purple in the after-glow.

We dined every night on a slightly raised platform, leading off the principal avenue, under the shelter of Moorish canvas, prettily decorated with designs in dark blue ; while the walls of this dining-room were formed by high trellis-work, clustered with roses of all colours, that sheltered us from the cool breeze at night, and from the hot sun by day. The gardens were lovely at night, especially as we were lucky enough to have a gorgeous moon during the greater part of our stay, though it somewhat dimmed the effect of the fantastic Moorish lanterns strung across the avenue from tree to tree. But enough of our garden.

One day we were invited by the Sultan to a feast at the gardens of the M'nara, a palace situated about

half an hour's ride from the city walls. We left the
city by our private gate, and rode with an escort of
some twenty men to the M'nara, where we were
received as usual with military honours. Passing
through the gateway, we entered the garden, which
was in poor repair, and, riding along a drive, we dismounted near a kiosk, surrounded by a really pretty
garden, laid out in beds, almost the only one of the
kind we saw in the country. The kiosk itself is two
storeys high, the upper containing two rooms, joined
by a handsome doorway. The decoration of the
interior was very gorgeous, as also were the carpets.
Here we found the table laid ready for the dinner,
before which arrived we had ample time to look
around and admire. The windows of the larger of the
two rooms opened on to a semicircular balcony, which
overlooked a great tank, full of wild water-fowl.

The arrival of dinner called us within, and immediately below the windows passed a procession of cooks,
—led by an enormous black chef, who carried a wand,—
bearing dishes of enormous dimensions, a man to each
dish, and seventy-seven in all. One by one they
ascended the stairs and arranged the dishes in order
for our inspection. If cooking could be judged by
bulk, then our feast would have been magnificent ;
and even as it was, it was more or less enjoyable. Of
course we did not try all the seventy-seven dishes,
but selected some fourteen or fifteen, which appeared
the best. I began at the commencement of dinner
with a determination to taste everything, as I felt it
my duty to know as much about Moorish cooking as
possible ; and also with a determination to write down
the menu, which I succeeded in doing for about the

first half of dinner.   I think it is worth rewriting, so
give it here :—

Stewed pigeons, with oil and olives.
Roast mutton, with sugar, capers, and vegetable marrow.
Stewed chickens, with almonds and raisins
Kooskoosoo (semolina), with boiled mutton.
Roast chickens, pigeons, and mutton.
Pigeons and chickens, with oil and truffles, &c.

The dishes were of brown earthenware, each of
which stood on a gaily-painted table, with legs only
some few inches in height, and on to which fitted a
beehive-shaped cover of variegated straws, to keep
the dishes warm, which it most successfully did, for
the cooking was done some miles from the M'nara,
where we had our feast.   As I said before, some of
the food was quite delectable, though in every dish
they used the unpleasantly-strong oil that takes the
place of gravy.   To drink, there was only water, and
very poor stuff at that ; not only does the Sultan not
partake of spirituous liqueurs himself, but possesses
none.   The same cannot be said of all Moors of
position.   After dinner, which was served in the
middle of the day, came tea and coffee, both excellent, in charming little cups of crown Derby ; the
feast over, we took a walk through the shady
garden and had a little shooting on the tank, Carleton
succeeding in bagging three or four teal and a duck or
two.

Now, having treated of the residences and what we
saw of the Sultan, I will describe, as far as I am able,
his more private life.

To begin with, his titles are somewhat lofty, as a

man who is at one time a Sultan and an Emperor
deserves,—

His Imperial and Shereefian Majesty,
High and Mighty Prince,
Chosen of God,
Moulai Hassan,
Sultan, Emperor of Morocco and Fez, and the Kingdom of
Tafilet and the Sus, and King of the Algarves,
Is the son of Sidi Mahammed, the last Sultan, who departed
this life in a water-tank, and in hopes of something better
to come, in 1873.

There is another story of his death which runs
that one evening, as was his custom, he was
taking some half-dozen of his wives in a boat on
the tank, when they capsized. His shrieks for
help were heard by a couple of officers, who were
on guard in another part of the garden, who
immediately rushed to his succour and succeeded
in saving him, just alive and no more. In a minute
he recovered himself a little, and, turning to the
officers, said, "Where are my wives?" "Drowned,
your Majesty." "Did you see them drowned?"
"We did, your Majesty." Whereupon he exclaimed,
"You know the penalty for seeing the Sultan's wives;
give me your sword," and killed the two men. As
might have been expected, he died himself a day or
two later.

Moulai Hassan is the fourteenth Sultan of his
dynasty, who have held the throne some 250 years,
and who originally came from Tafilet. His position
as Sultan is not an enviable one, as some portion of
his kingdom is always in revolt; though perhaps it
is owing to this that his throne is as safe as it is, as it

detracts general attention from himself and gives his subjects something to think about.

The tale of the Sultans is a bloody tale—one long chapter of murder and sudden death, battles and poisonings, that, had the secrets ever leaked out, would fill volumes. What romances, what plots, have been hatched and accomplished within the painted walls of the palaces ! What love and what hate ! A despot is always all-powerful ; but the Sultan of Morocco is a despot of despots. A favourite one day, the next a carcase eaten by dogs at the city gate. A wife one day, robed in silks and jewels, the next a slave washing the feet of her who only a day before had waited on her. A governor, disturbed by rough soldiers at his meals or his sleep, may be dragged, loaded with chains, to the capital, and made to pay his uttermost farthing, or die under torture. And as the governors are squeezed by their rulers, so do the governors squeeze the lower officials, and the lower officials the people. A government and yet no government, the whole official life is a mass of bribery and corruption.

The nominal head of this evil government is Si Mahammed ben Larbi, an enormously fat man, with a senseless expression, yet not wanting in diplomatic skill. In selfishness and amassing wealth he is ably backed up by the other viziers. Nothing more rotten than the Moorish government can be imagined. The Sultan squeezes his viziers, the viziers squeeze the Bascha, the Bascha the Kaid, the Kaid the Calipha, and so on, till at last the peasant gains the enviable position of being squeezed and being able to squeeze no one in return. So doubtless has it been for generations.

And yet, in spite of all this, when we cast our eyes over what accounts we have of Moorish history, we cannot but be struck by the great names we find there, and the great monuments that have been left behind. Almanzor the Victorious, the most superb of the Emperors, who raised the Giralda at Seville, the Beni Hassan tower at Rabat, and the Koutubia at Morocco, and now lies forgotten in the cool shade of oranges, olives, and roses in the little ruined mosque at Shellah on the Booragrag river—one of the loveliest spots in the country. But it is not only the men whose names have been handed down to us by the monuments they left behind them that we ought to be thankful for—not only, I say, the men who reared palaces like the Alhambra, the Queen of Architecture, that has delighted the eyes of mankind for centuries—but such men as Averroes and Avenzoar, to whom, with many of their contemporary Moors, we owe not a little of our medical, scientific, and astronomical knowledge. And yet throughout all Moorish history there is an undercurrent of murder and bloodshed. How was it Almanzor was in a position to build his palaces and his towers? By carefully removing every obstacle in his way by wholesale murder and dark assassinations.

When we gaze upon the wondrous architecture of the Moors, the question comes before us—Who are these Moors? whence did they spring? No one knows. Every one has a theory which he asserts is right. I have no theory, therefore I cannot be wrong. Doubtless they are the sons of a wandering tribe, who, after toiling over the deserts, intermarried with the half-savage natives, and gradually settled to an agricultural life, though till the time when they reached their highest pitch of civilization and artistic merit they never forgot what they had inherited from their fathers of the desert—endurance and gallantry. They, like all other dynasties, have risen and fallen ; and, though their fall was not as the fall of Egypt, Assyria, Greece, or Rome, yet it was to themselves as disastrous as any ; for, though they were not exterminated, they had to fly back to their wild African soil, where, year by year, they are sinking deeper into ignorance and bigotry. They have lost their activity, these Moors of to-day. Instead of leading his soldiers into battle, their Sultan sits in splendid halls, passing his life in indolence, save when, now and again, on the march from one capital to another, he deigns to chastise some erring tribe with fire and with sword. The Moors, whose ancestors once conquered in almost every war they undertook, sit and sigh, and sing quaint ballads to Granada, their mountain-home in the Sierra Nevada, and weep now and again over the keys of the houses that their ancestors possessed in Spain.

But to return to Morocco of to-day. Though the Sultan is only allowed by the Koran four legal wives, no restriction is laid down as to the numbers contained in his harem ; and rumour, which often speaks the truth, asserts that it contains some fifteen hundred ladies. Probably his Majesty is in as great a state of ignorance as to his wives as the general public, for not only is he constantly getting new ones, but is at the same time selling off the old stock in the slave-markets of Morocco, where, if she is not over-passé, she may realize a " fiver." It is the keeping of these women that renders the interiors ot the palaces invisible except to the Emperor himself and the eunuchs who guard the harem ; but I doubt not that if one could penetrate into the palaces at Morocco, Mequinez, and Fez, one would see architecture that might rival the very Alhambra itself, with which many of the palaces are coeval.

There is a story worth relating, though its truth cannot be vouched for, with regard to the treatment that the wives receive at the hands of their imperial husband.

Not many years ago the French government presented to the Sultan a number of bicycles as an official gift. Now there is a proverb and a belief in Morocco which states that the Emperor can do successfully all that he attempts. His Majesty therefore never attempted to ride the bicycles, but used them for another purpose, that of punishing his wives. Whenever there was a row in the harem, the delinquents were brought forth and according to their sins sentenced to ride till they had fallen a certain number of times. One can imagine the Sultan addressing them ; to one he says, " You are an old offender, I have told you over and over again, that if you fought with the others and scratched and pulled their hair, you would be seriously punished ; you shall now ride the bicycle till you have fallen twenty-five times ;" to the other perhaps he remarks, " This is your first offence, ten falls will suffice for you ;" and away they go, while the Sultan sits and looks on with peals of laughter. However, I cannot vouch for the story.

The Sultan but a short time ago discovered that one of his viziers was becoming too powerful. He

summoned him therefore to tea and complimented
the man on his great wealth.   The vizier becoming
vain, boasted of the number of his houses, horses,
wives, and slaves.   Thereupon the Sultan rebuked him,
telling him he was too rich, and thought a great deal
too much of himself.   To show him exactly what
he was worth, his Majesty had him taken by soldiers
to the slave-market, where he was put up for sale,
some one bidding 8*d.*—the only bid—for him.   He
was then brought back before the Sultan, who remarked, "Now you know your proper value—8*d.*
Go home and ponder over it."   However, when he got
home he found his houses had been taken, with all
his property, by order of the Emperor, merely one
small residence, one wife, one horse, and one slave
being left him.   His Majesty is seemingly fond of a
small joke !

The following anecdote illustrates the existing
state of ignorance and credulity amongst the court.
The Sultan was engaged in conversation with a
European, and was discussing the Sultan of Turkey.

"He has a wonderful executioner," said the
Emperor.

"Indeed, your Majesty, I have not heard of him."

"I will tell you, then," said his Majesty; "he is a man
worth having.   The last executioner having died, the
Sultan of Turkey sent for another.   Several men
presented themselves for the post, which was to be
decided by a contest.

"The victims, three in number, were brought out
and made to kneel down.   The first candidate then
took a sword and at one blow cut the man's head off,
the head rolling away.   The second did the same

with a backhanded blow. The third was so skilful that though he cut the neck through, the head remained where it was. Then taking a pinch of snuff in his fingers the executioner put it to the nose of the victim, who sneezed, the exertion of which caused his head to fly off to a spot some yards distant. A 'malem,'[9] indeed, that executioner."

And the Sultan thoroughly believed the tale he was telling!

Life at court, at least amongst the lower classes, such as slaves, &c., is not altogether comfortable, to judge by a remark made by a small boy, a servant of Captain Alan Maclean's, who was overheard speaking to a black slave who had brought a message from the palace.

"No," said the boy, "you must not come in, we don't allow lice and dirt here ; this is not the Sultan's palace, please understand."

Nor do the viziers' families seem to be altogether free from such objectionable belongings, as on one occasion, a European lady having asked the wife of a celebrated vizier what presents she would like sent on her (the European's) return to civilized countries, she answered, as she fondly clasped the lady in her arms, "there is only one thing I beg, small combs, for our heads are full of animals," and she commenced to take down her hair to exhibit her live stock. Tableau.

The Sultan lives a very simple life. He rises early, before sunrise, and prays regularly seven times a day. His food is simple—there is very little variety at any time in Moorish cooking—and each dish is tasted by

[9] Malem—expert.

an official taster, a post of great honour at court, as a guarantee against poison. Though now and again his ministers eat in the same room with him, they never taste the same dish. His Majesty, like all Moors, scorns knives and forks, and eats from the dish direct with his fingers. Though this seems, to our civilized senses, a disgusting modus operandi, it is really nothing of the sort, for to so great a dexterity has practice brought them, that they scarcely make their fingers sticky, and the practice of washing before and after meals does away with after-effects, that, should it be one's duty to shake hands with one of them, would otherwise prove unpleasant. In religion the Sultan is very strict, in fact the religion of Morocco is far stricter than that of any Mahommedan country, except, perhaps, a few of the sacred cities of Arabia. For example, no Christian can enter a mosque in any part of the country of Morocco, not even in civilized Tangier. The Ramadan, or fast of thirty days, is strictly kept by the Sultan, even when on the march, when the prophet states it is allowable to break it. His Majesty seldom appears in public, taking his exercise in the enormous gardens of the Agidal and his other palaces. When on the march, no tent is allowed to be pitched before he is safely ensconced in his. As the Sultan was preparing for his journey from Morocco to Fez when we were at the capital, we had an opportunity of seeing his tents. That for his personal use is an enormous marquee, crowned by brass balls, while around stand four or five smaller tents for the women who accompany him, the whole being surrounded by a wall of canvas ten feet in height.

He is said to be a good business-man, and to know far more of his affairs of State than any of his Ministers, in fact, much of the official work of the country passes through his hands. Though we can gather pretty much what kind of a life he leads, it is only very seldom that we can hear anything of the life led by his wives, except that it must be a tragic one, for the favourite, for the time being, lolls on cushions of velvet and gold in dimly-lit rooms full of the odours of incense and flowers, and attended by slaves, any one of whom, should she find favour in the sight of her lord and master, would usurp the place of the Sultana, who would sink to the degradation of slavery ; and no doubt this is often the case.

The succession of the Sultan is not exactly hereditary. The monarch on his death-bed has the right of naming his successor, who must be a relation, but not necessarily a son, though generally the aspirant to the throne who has the most money succeeds. The custom has its disadvantages, as there always arise many pretenders who generally end their lives in prison, by poison, or on the scaffold. This idea of succession is general through the whole country, and gave rise to a curious circumstance and a piece of skilful diplomacy on the death of the father of the present head of the Wazan family. The son he wished to succeed him was a little boy, who had always been his favourite. " I nominate as my successor," he said, " my little boy, whom you find playing with my walking-stick," which his Highness had given the child shortly before. A slave of the Shereef's, passing his door, overheard these words, and she herself having a son by him, ran to the children's apartment, and taking the stick from the

right child, gave it to her own son, who was discovered
sucking its ivory handle a few minutes later, and this
lucky brat with the clever mamma is the present Grand
Shereef of Wazan, Sidi Hadj Absalam.

Shortly before we left Morocco City, the Emperor
started on an expedition against the tribe of N'Tifa,
whose taxes had not been forthcoming for some time
past.

The last news we had of his Majesty before we
left was from one who accompanied the army, and
was therefore in a position to give authentic news, for,
as a rule, truth is an article not much in " demand "
in Morocco, though I must say the " supply " is still
smaller. He wrote that the Emperor had arrived
safely in the province, and had been received with a
propitiatory dinner of 4000 dishes, each carried by
one or more tribesmen ; but, in spite of this noble
repast, the Sultan punished the tribe by burning its
houses and its trees, though he little thinks what
damage he is indirectly doing himself by destroying
the woods and forests, and thereby lessening the
supply of rain over the whole country. It is not
stated whether this wholesale destruction of property
was due to royal indigestion following the dinner.

Though his army is large, there are many parts of
his enormous possessions in which his power is only
nominal, if that. For instance, in the upper valleys
of the Atlas Mountains ; in the forest of Mamora,
situated in the centre of his possessions, near Rabat,
and inhabited by the fierce Zimmour tribe ; and in the
northern mountain districts known as the Rif. These
wild tribes, when attacked, retire to their mountain
fastnesses, and leave the Sultan and his men to burn

and plunder their villages at will, which, on the departure of the attacking force, they rebuild, and continue refusing to pay their taxes.

The royal cities are Fez, Morocco, Mequinez, and Rabat, though the latter two are not much visited by royalty, while at Saffi, which was once a favourite coast resort, the palace, a huge building, containing some beautiful architecture and arabesques, has been allowed to fall to ruins. The royal journey between Morocco and Fez takes some six months, and as his Majesty is usually accompanied by from thirty to forty thousand troops and countless camp-followers, his march is of far more import than It might seem to be to us Europeans, especially as the commissariat department is by no means in perfect working order.

The Moorish Navy is easily dealt with, she is one. However ungrammatical that may be, it is a fact ; and the old coal-hulk of a Hassanieh represents the country on the seas. I believe she carries no guns ; but of that I am not very certain.

Altogether, the existing state of things in Morocco is not satisfactory ; but as they are, so have they been for generations ; and so they will be, till some European Power makes a " coup " and conquers the land ; yet, though it would benefit to have the country taken, both itself and extraneous trade, one almost hopes to see it for a time as it is now ; for in these days of ultra-realism it is pleasant to see a country in which there remains, both in the court life and in the country, some vestige of romance, a mixture of barbaric splendour and barbaric squalor. Burmah has fallen, and the jewels that once decorated its palaces are gazed on by the bustling crowds of

London ; and by its fall there is one the less from
the small number of Oriental countries that exist.
Perhaps it is better so.   Civilization must go on,
though in its wild rush it does not stop to think what
will become of civilization when all the world is
civilized.   But it is in this steady, half-suicidal stride
of civilization that Morocco must pass away, the last
of the independent States of northern Africa.   But
whatever will be its future, we who have seen it now
have this to be thankful for, that we have seen it in
its old state, as it has been for centuries ; we have
seen it before the refining hand of the European well-
wisher has built his factories and his mines : we
have seen it before the Moors have taken to European
dress and are regular attendants at church, and before
English-speaking guides personally conduct one
through the palaces, where now the greatest of Mahommedan potentates, the true descendant of the
Prophet, a Sultan and an Emperor, languishes
amongst his women, listening to the soft splash of the
fountain in a marble and mosaic paved court, and the
softer music of the musicians in the garden without ;
we have seen it in a time when the Sultan is all
powerful, and not, as is likely to be the case in the
future, the mere tool in the hands of some European
Power.

CHAPTER III.

DURING a residence of some three weeks at the
capital, I had ample opportunity of exploring all the
ins and outs of the great city of Morocco. In size,
Morocco is estimated as equal to Paris, though, of
course, its population is vastly less ; nor is one able
to arrive at any idea as to how great it is, owing to
the absence of any system of registration.

In position, Morocco is one of the finest cities in
the country. It lies in the midst of a plain to the
north of the Atlas Mountains, which rise sheer from
the fields at their base to a height of some 13,0c0 or
more feet. To the north of the city, some fifteen
miles distant, runs a parallel range of mountains,
none of which reach an altitude of much over 4500
feet. This plain is drained by the Wad Tensift and
its tributaries, on the junction of one of which with
the main stream the city is situated, in the centre of
a palm grove of enormous extent, which adds greatly
to the whole picturesque effect, and which, together
with the numerous enclosed plantations in the city,
has gained for it the title of " The City of Gardens."

Morocco, like nearly all oriental towns, is walled
by high stone walls, and defended by towers errected
at intervals along them. Outside the city one enters

directly upon the country, there being no suburbs, unless the village of lepers can be called one, and a gruesome place it is !

Within the walls the houses are low and the streets narrow; on every side one sees desolation and ruin, very different from the more flourishing northern capital of Fez ; nor, as in Fez, does one see, except few and far between, little pieces of exquisite wood or arabesque work in plaster. The south-westerly part of the town, as in London, is the fashionable quarter, and there are the palaces and gardens of the Sultan, his ministers, and of most of the rich Moors ; while to the north and east lies the commercial quarter—a dense maze of narrow, dirty streets and booths. Not far from our palace was a small sôk, or market-place, on to which Kaid Maclean's house looked, and here we often went in the hope of picking up curiosities ; but, except for a few curious pieces of pottery, we got nothing there. Far finer was the Sok-el-Khemis, or Friday market, held outside the Bab Dukala. Here one could see every variety of native, selling every variety of native manufacture. In one corner would be sitting a group of fierce-looking mountaineers, selling silver daggers, and long, inlaid guns ; in another a group of women with a gorgeous-tinted carpet, worked in some country village and brought in for sale. Here straw baskets lay piled one on the top of the other in great heaps, and there bright kuftans were causing a little crowd of admirers. Under the shade of a tent the barber was bleeding a Moor, while, next to him, another was having his head shaved. In the centre of the circle a performing ape was going through its varied tricks,

whilst the harsh-sounding pipes bespoke the presence
of a snake-charmer. Everywhere something new and
something noisy ; for the Moors are shouting and
gesticulating, fighting and laughing, just as if the
success of the whole market depended upon the
noise they made, added to which was the constant
jingle of the water-carrier's bell and his shrill cry of
"alma" (water). Near this market, and on the same
day, was carried on the horse and animal sale, where
long-robed Moors were galloping the sturdy little
barb horses up and down the long open space to show
their paces, and where the wild Berber from the
mountains, noticeable anywhere from his scarcity of
raiment, was trying to sell a couple of small Moorish
donkeys. Camels, mules, horses, donkeys, goats,
sheep, oxen—all kinds and varieties of animals—
could be bought there. Nor were the streets less
interesting than the markets, though one did not see
such variety all at once, as usually all the shops in one
street sell only one kind of merchandise, so that if one
wants to buy shoes one goes to the street of shoes to
get them, and there one has endless varieties to choose
from. Many shops, however, have arrived at the
civilized state of selling more than one article, and in
them one can see exposed to view many English and
French manufactures. In fact, the sight that most
surprises one on arriving in these Eastern cities is the
immense quantity of imports exposed for sale. Linen,
coloured handkerchiefs, matches, scented soaps, perfumes, looking-glass, candles, and beads, are perhaps
the most common, while the whole of the tea of the
country—and the Moors drink scarcely anything else
—is imported from Europe.

The scene in the streets is always a bright and gay one, and always a noisy one. I never knew such a shouting people as the Moors, it is their normal condition to be yelling at each other or oneself. We used to enjoy in the cool of the evening riding through the crowded thoroughfares, under the covered bazaars, amongst the jostling crowd of men, women, and children, mules, horses, and camels, though at times these proved inconvenient. There are whole streets of eating-shops, where a grave, turbaned Moor sits and frizzles small scraps of liver and such-like over a dull charcoal fire ; nor is the smell of the savoury "kabobs" refreshing on a warm afternoon. Another street, which we as often visited as we avoided the latter, was where the workers of leather had their abode ; and here we used to stop and watch the skilful way in which the gorgeous coloured silks and gold threads were embroidered on bags, saddles, and horse-trappings. The workers of bernouses and jelabas, too, were always interesting to watch, especially when sewing on the brilliantly hued braid, which was done by a small boy at a distance holding on each of his fingers a long thread of the different coloured silks, which, by moving his hands, he changed in such a way that by crossing and recrossing his needle the workmen could make first one colour and then the other appear. The jewellers were not such favourites with us, as, being Jews, they lived in their quarter—the " Mellah "—which is unrivalled, I think, by anything I have ever seen for dirt. They are, however, skilful workers in silver and gold and brass. So much has been written and said about the persecution of the Jews by the Moors that a word or

two on the subject may not be out of place. No
doubt the Jews have been, and are still, to a small
extent persecuted ; but it is not in the least to be
wondered at, for they swindle, on every possible
opportunity, the slow, thick-headed Moors, who borrow money from them without the least understanding
at what interest they are repaying it, which is generally something like fifty per cent. per month. When
one arrives in the country of Morocco, just as when
one first sees the Jews in Russia, one is apt to pity ;
but experience of a few days teaches one differently,
and one learns that, after all, it is more their fault
than that of the Moors, whom they despise, and make
the victims of their hard-hearted usury. I do not at
all mean to say that all the Jews in the country are
the same. I am speaking now of towns like Morocco
and Fez, where they are in the same state of civilization as the Moors themselves, only dirtier. A distinctive
dress is worn by the Jews, the jelab being of dark blue
embroidered cloth, and a small black cap ; for none
are allowed to wear the red fez. In many of the
cities they are strictly confined to their " mellah,"
though allowed to walk in the other parts of the town
barefooted. One sees them taking off their shoes as
they pass through the gate which divides the Moorish
quarter from their own. The Jewesses are sometimes
pretty, and always vain, and, when they get the
chance, dress in European costume, which often comes
from Paris. A place that was a constant and almost
daily resort was the " kesseriah," or auction-market—a
long, wide, covered bazaar, with shops down either side.
Here, about four o'clock in the afternoon, Morocco
gathers together to do its business. The auctions are

managed on very different plans to ours in England, as the auctioneers—there are a number of them—rush about amongst the people carrying the articles for sale, and shouting out the latest bid. Of course this gives a great opening for fictitious bids, especially when Europeans are present. The scene is a purely Eastern one, and equally charming. In the half gloom of the bazaar are crowds of Moors, some in the fine white haik, which betokens wealth and position ; some in little more than the historical string of beads. Here we bought many curiosities, daggers and carpets, haiks and leather work, in fact all varieties of native produce. Every day or so some incongruous article would be put up for sale ; one day it was a small parasol of a light buff colour, and trimmed with lace—almost a doll's parasol, so small it was. It was sold for about a sovereign to the fiercest-looking of our warriors, who used it to shade himself all the journey back to Tangier, much to our amusement, though he saw no joke in it, and gave himself terrible airs on its account.

The scenes in the streets would often be varied by a wedding, the gay procession passing by to the music of some score of tomtoms and pipes, the bride shut up in a box on the back of a mule, or even a donkey. Funerals, too, were constantly occurring, as I suppose they are all over the world. Of the two, I preferred the funerals, as the music was much softer and more sweet, and one of the two death-chants they sing really beautiful. As in other parts of the Oriental world, the relatives of the deceased pay people to attend the funerals, and mourners are hired at so much a dozen —a gross at an enormous reduction.

We often visited the slave-market, which is, I think, quite the most interesting sight in Morocco. We had all of us read the fearful accounts, which the press of Tangier is so fond of repeating, of the terrible doings of slavery in Morrocco, and, I must confess, were most pleasantly surprised. We went very often to the market, but never saw such sights as children separated from their parents, though we saw both sold together in the "lot." Nor did we see many other things of which we had read ; in fact, the slaves wore a wonderfully contented, even cheerful, expression while the sale was proceeding. We were much amused at watching one young lady—who, by the way, was rather handsome—alter her expression from sullenness when an old Moor was looking at her, to cheerfulness when a handsome young man began his inspection. So there is coyness even in the wild deserts from which these slaves come ; in fact, far from being a painful sight—for by the accounts we have of those who have seen it before, they all left " with our eyes full of tears "—we found it rather amusing than otherwise, and I do not know that we are more hard-hearted than the generality of mankind. This I will say, that I would far rather be a slave in Morocco than a peasant. From what, too, I saw of slaves out of the market, they appear not to have such a bad time of it, and in many of the houses enjoy more liberty than the paid servants. Of course there is truth in many of the fearful stories we hear of ill-treatment ; but, again, I know an old Moor on whose death all the property goes by will to his slaves. It is not slavery that is so bad, it is the kidnapping that slavery necessitates, and the terrible long journey over the

scorching desert ; but, of course, to put down kidnapping we must aim at slavery direct. The market
is mostly supplied from the Soudan—not the " Soudan " as we call Nubia, but the Soudan that lies south
of the Sahara and east of Senegambia, an enormous
district of sand—but it is not at all an uncommon
sight to see white slaves in the market—Moors and
Arabs. The prices average about 3*l.* to 5*l.* a head for
all varieties, though we saw one elderly female
knocked down for about 22*s.*, much to her own
disgust.

Of the mosques in Morocco one can say little, as
they are strictly guarded against the entrance of
Christians, though this does not prevent one, as one
passes by, from gazing in at the long aisles, dimly
lit by strange-coloured lamps, while a blaze of sun-
shine falls on the centre court, with its marble and
coloured columns and gay tile-work, and on the
bubbling white fountain in the centre. A delicious
scent of incense pervades the mosque doors, the
smoke of which gives a soft grey appearance to
the interior that makes one long to enter and pace
those long corridors with their softly matted or
carpeted floors. But, though we saw no more than
this of the interior, there is no difficulty about seeing
the exteriors, which, as a rule, are not fine, though
some boast graceful minarets, the finest of which, by
far, is that of Koutubia, or mosque of the booksellers,
a minaret 250 feet in height and 50 feet square from
base to summit. It is the sister tower to the Giralda,
at Seville, and the unfinished tower at Beni Hassan,
at Rabat, but is finer than either, as the Giralda has
undergone restoration and change at the hands of the

Spaniards, whereas the Koutubia remains in its pristine glory. The minaret is of stone, richly inlaid with tiles, for the most part green, many of which, however, have tumbled out. The summit is domed. To ascend the tower there are no stairs, but a sloping way, up which one could ride—so it is said—on horseback. No doubt the origin of this was to take the beasts of burden as near the working level as possible. This minaret, as it raises its head far above the low-lying town and the forests of palms, forms the landmark of Morocco. It was the first we saw of the city on our approach ; it was the last we saw on our departure. The adjoining mosque is said to contain a fine library, the books of which, no doubt, are mouldering away, uncared for and untouched, just as the mosque itself is. The whole edifice was raised by Almanzor, in the twelfth century.

Of the other buildings in Morocco there is not much to say, as I have described elsewhere the Maimounieh Palace, in which we were quartered, and the palaces of the Sultan.

As I said before, Morocco has only one suburb— the leper city. We went several times to see this almost unique village—a village of lepers. The place itself is not large, and is situated near the Bab Dukala, immediately outside the city walls. The houses are much the same as those of the poorer classes within the city—one-storeyed dwellings. We saw, of course, numberless lepers, who go about their business as long as they are able, like other folk, and then, when the disease in its steady strides renders them incapable, take to begging. I was surpised to see no leper children, nor have I ever seen any but one, but he was enough to make up for a hundred. Apparently, from what inquiries we could make, the leprosy does not show itself till the victim is about fourteen years of age. These lepers intermarry, but whether the children of lepers are necessarily lepers themselves I was unable to ascertain. The poor wretches are obliged by law to wear a distinctive dress, and are never allowed to enter the city, at the gates of which they sit begging. Here one could see specimens of the disease in every stage, from the man who had a patch on his face or chest to the legless, armless lump of humanity that crouches huddled up in a corner.

We had two feasts to go to before we left Morocco, neither of which, though each in its way was good, came up in magnitude to that of the Sultan, though at Abu Beker's I believe—for I was not there myself —the cooking was superior. There, too, wine was supplied, the only place in Morocco at which it was. After dinner dancing-girls performed to the music of a string-band ; the *première danseuse* balancing a tray of tea-things on her head very successfully. Abu Beker's house is one of the finest in Morocco, and I much regret having missed seeing it ; but some of us were away in the Atlas Mountains at the time. At the other feast, at Sidi Garnêt's, the Foreign Minister, there was a great display of cooked meats ; but the weather was terribly hot, and a band seated at the door of our dining-room kept up such an infernal din, that conversation was out of the question. The ladies visited the harem, and reported that the wives were very stout and not exactly beautiful, according to our ideas. As we were at dinner, we noticed a peculiar haze over the courtyard, into which our room looked, which, we discovered was the commencement of a sandstorm. As soon as we left Garnêt's house, it began to blow with a vengeance, the small red sand nearly blinding us as it came in great clouds down the street. We tore the puggerees off our helmets and bound up our faces in them, and again pushed on our way. We were on horseback, and so exposed to the whole force of the storm. Everything was hidden by the dust, and it was only now and again that we could catch a glimpse of the road ahead of us. For some two or three hours it blew, and covered everything with sand. We saw no one about ; every man, woman, and child had sought refuge in their houses, and the city seemed deserted and dead. We reached the Maimounieh in safety, but nearly blinded by the force of the gale. In the country districts, where there is no protection, the Arabs have to imitate the example of their Eastern brethren, and lie down, man and beast, till the storm has passed over.

It was amusing riding through the streets to hear the curses which little boys, and sometimes even grown men, used to heap upon our heads. " May Allah burn your grandfather and grandmother," they used to say ; but somehow we thought that these reiterated prayers to Allah for this purpose could not have much effect, so we used only to laugh at them. Now and then, though, a Moor got his ears well boxed for it by our soldiers, and on one occasion by one of us, when a strong young European might have been seen seated on the prostrate body of a shereef, and saying in perfect Arabic, " You burn my parents, will you ? "—bang. " You'll call me ' haloof ' " (wild boar)—bang. " I'll teach you to speak to Christians

like that "—bang. I don't think that Moor would
have breath enough left in him tò curse again for
many a long day. This, however, was not in Morocco,
but in a town on the coast.

One class of building that forms a prominent feature in Morocco are the fountains, some of which
appertain to the mosque, while others are separate
buildings of themselves ; and it is in these fountains
that one finds almost the only beautiful remains of
Moorish architecture in the city of Morocco. Along
the bottom of the fountain runs a large basin or trough,
in which the Moors wash. The whole structure is in
the form of an archway, no doubt so that the water
by being shaded from the sun may keep cool and
fresh. Many of them possess exquisite wood-carving,
and the colouring of the walls is often equally lovely.
Every type of design—but all pure Moorish—are
found on these many fountains, and as one stands
and gazes one can almost imagine that one is in
some old palace, till one turns and sees the squalor
and dirt of the street and the people around one.

One is much struck in Morocco city by the tame-
ness of all the birds and animals ; and sparrows are
constant visitors on the dinner-tables, whither they
come in search of food. They seem literally to have
no fear. These sparrows are not like our English
birds, but larger, and with blue-grey heads. We found
the snakes, too, as tame as the birds, though this was
not as pleasant. One huge snake, seven feet long,
once calmly swallowed a rat within a couple of yards
of our luncheon-table, in the open roadway of our
garden. It was, however, shot. One word as to
history. The founding of Morocco is wrapped in

more or less uncertainty, though probably the town is not more than eight hundred years old, as it was founded by Yusuf ben Tisfeen, whose date, even, is doubtful. From the kasbah, of which it originally consisted, it grew to be a city of great importance and size, and at one time, according to Leo Africanus —almost the only authority of Morocco of the Middle Ages—contained upwards of a hundred thousand buildings. However, it has fallen again, and now is no more than a great straggling, half-ruined town.

CHAPTER IV.

THE GREAT ATLAS MOUNTAINS.

IT had been during the whole trip the desire of some of us to try and obtain some sport in the Atlas Mountains, and great was our delight when, through the kindness of Sir William Kirby-Green, a letter arrived from the Sultan, couched in the following terms :—

"We give permission, by the help of God, to the four Englishmen who are bearers of this letter to travel in all parts of our Empire in which there is no present danger. But in parts where there is danger, or where the inhabitants are in rebellion, they must not go, either in the plains or mountains. And to those whose business it is, I give this command, to the Kaids and Caliphas, that they take care of them and pay all attention to their wants; that they accompany them, and supply a fitting escort ; and that they point out to them the dangerous places, and advise them not to enter them. Moulai Hassan."

Without such a letter as this it would have been impossible for us to have visited the mountains, as no sooner would we have arrived at their base than we should have been arrested and " returned " to Morocco for the Sultan to do what he pleased with us, as the mountains are forbidden land to the traveller. This rendered them all the more interesting to us, as we knew that only a very few had been before us in most places, and in some none at all.

Everything having been arranged for our mountain expedition, we started early one morning (Thursday, May 5th), leaving the Maimounieh between six and seven o'clock. Our party consisted of four—Woodville, Treeby, Boulnois, and myself—with an escort of an interpreter, two European servants, a Kaid, and four soldiers, three soldier-servants, and two tent-pitchers who also were army-men. We took a large tent for ourselves, a tent for the Kaid, and two small tents for our men; four horses for our own use, and six mules to carry our baggage; a mule for our interpreter, and three horses for the Kaid and two of the soldiers; while the remaining part of the men walked, or took it in turns to ride on our baggage beasts. The sun was already hot when we bade adieu to the rest of our party at the Maimounieh, who were kind enough to appear to wish us " goodspeed" in a diversity of toilets, and set out along the narrow, dusty road toward the Babel-el-Hamar, a rather fine, though modern, archway. On leaving the city we struck away to the right, skirting the walls of the Agidal Palace garden, the enormous park of the Sultan.

The country was very dried up, and the stones rendered our travelling anything but quick or pleasant. We crossed a strip of desert-like ground, which extended some eight or ten miles, and then entered the fertile plain that lies along the base of the Atlas Mountains and is watered by their

numerous streams.   These streams—some the merest
rivulets—seem to rush in every direction, and we
were pleasantly surprised at the general fertility, so
different from what we had seen on the road from
Mazagan to the capital, nor are the inhabitants
ignorant of their good-fortune in possessing this
constant water-supply, as everywhere are to be seen
little banked canals joining the small streams, and
used for flooding the fields.   Here, too, we saw the
finest crops of wheat that we had ever seen, making
one fully realize that the Romans were no fools when
they made Mauritania their corn-market.   At one
place we passed a very curious aqueduct, if such it
can be called, through which the water passed under
the road, finding its level again on the opposite
side.

The mountains looked very fine as we approached,
and what had seemed to us from Morocco mere
hillocks compared with the central range, began to
appear, as they really are, great mountains.   As the
country changed its aspect in the way of fertility, so
the villages began to take another form, and instead
of the everlasting beehive-shaped hovels, there were
houses of stone and plaster, with overhanging roofs,
the whole village usually enclosed with a tabbia wall
of some height and strength, and guarded with
flanking towers, as a defence in time of rebellion and
war.   Some of these little towns are exceedingly
picturesque, nestling in groves of palms and olives,
and surrounded by the vivid green fields.

About five in the afternoon we entered a grove of
olives, fine large trees, under which the sward was
like an English lawn, while here, there, and in every

direction ran little brooks whose banks were glorious
with oleanders. For two hours our road continued
the same, until, in fact, we reached Ourika, our first
resting-place. The little town is perched on the
side of the steep hill high above the river of the
same name. We never could quite find out the name
of the place; it seemed to have many, and every
native we asked would answer: "This town? Oh!
Ourika, of course;" while his companion contradicted
him, and said "Achliz;" so we called it "Achliz-
Ourika," and had we had any letters to write would
have headed them so. The river must be a grand
one in winter, as even in this dry season it was fairly
full of water. The village resembled a fort more
than a village, the houses being built tier above tier
up the precipice, and entirely devoid of windows on
the outside, though many of them boasted a verandah-
like arrangement. We had left the Moors now and
were in the country of the Berbers, or wild mountain
tribes, who speak Berebba or Shleh, a strange language
almost unknown to Europeans; and the fortified
state of these villages clearly showed that they were
ready for all exigences, for in this land fighting is
almost as common as peace. The building *par excellence* of Achliz is a curious fort, the walls of which
must be some thirty feet in height, and which is
flanked with towers; the whole building, being larger
at the base than the summit, has a strong resemblance
to an ancient Egyptian temple. Close to this fort
we found our camp awaiting us, for we had lingered
on the way, so as to allow the tents to be pitched
before our arrival, which created no small stir in the
neighbourhood, as Europeans are *rara· avis* there.

The view from our tents, as we looked down on to
the valley and plains below, for we were up some
height, was a truly lovely one. Far below us the
river rushed over its stony bed, its banks covered
with olives and pomegranates, vines and palms ;
away over the plains we could see the palm-forests
of Morocco, and the glistening summit of the Koutubia ; up the valley the scenery was wilder, for
there, though the lower parts of the mountains were
wooded, rocks formed the chief object, such rocks as
one sees in Switzerland or Norway, precipices
thousands of feet in height, and away beyond them
again the glistening snow. After a bathe we set to
work to cook, and really, for amateurs, managed
very well, though perhaps, after all, to make a decent
Irish stew is no great task. Almost before the moon
had risen over the mountain-tops we were sound
asleep ; but we were up again before the sun appeared,
and bitterly cold it was.

At sunrise the Calipha visited us, as he had done
the night before, but, in spite of the great deference
he paid our passport from the Sultan — for whenever
he got a sight of it he tried to kiss it—he put every
possible difficulty in our way to prevent us pene-
trating further into the mountains. However, we
were stern and relentless, and at eight sharp set off,
the wretched Calipha having to accompany us, as
the Sultan's letter directed. It is always the same ;
one has the greatest difficulty in going one's own
way and not that of the local governor or Kaid, which
is never the direct one.

As the Sultan's guests, food was supplied to us
all along the road, which it would have been an

insult to offer to pay for; and the very first night
we found our Kaid Absalom—an old thief and a
robber—calmly selling the presents that had come
for us. As these valleys in the Atlas are not connected with one another, but run into the mountains
parallel with each other, it was our intention to
strike across the spur between Ourika and the
valley of Hasni, and so to reach the latter place.
On telling the Calipha this, he asserted it was impossible. "If there were a road," he vehemently
ejaculated, on our saying there was one, and that he
did not wish to show it to us, "God knows I would
show it you, and even come myself with you to
Hasni." However, we did not believe him, and it
turned out we were right, though our discovery came
too late. "Anyhow," we said, "we insist on going
up this valley as far as possible;" so we all went off
together, leaving directions with our men to push on
by the foot of the mountains as near as possible to
Hasni. The road was very bad in some places, quite
impassable for baggage animals, so we found we had
done well in sending our mules by the longer route.
We followed the river-bed for some time, then,
crossing to the right bank, we passed under a curious
cone-shaped hill that stands in the centre of the
valley, where the oleanders were gorgeous in blossom.
We saw many mountain villages all built more or
less like forts, and mostly perched high above the
river. On reaching a large village, the name of which,
as far as we could gather, was Asneen, we found the
road went no further; but the Calipha told us that
we could, by continuing on the river-bed, get a mile
or two further up the valley. However, as we had

already been two hours on the way, and had been
unsuccessful in finding the desired track, we decided
to retrace our footsteps and overtake our baggage
animals.   The people in the villages seemed well
disposed, and very much astonished at our presence ;
but one and all wished us a hearty "salaama" as we
passed.   The people are darker and more negro-
looking than in Morocco city, though here and there
we passed fair men.   Jews, too, we saw in great
numbers.   I believe that this small corner of Morocco
is the only place in the world in which agricultural
Jews are to be found ; for here they themselves work
in the fields, ploughing and reaping.   Two hours
sufficed to take us back to Achliz, and from there we
set off towards Tahanout, a town at the foot of the
mountains, *en route* for Hasni.   We were now again
almost in the plains, and the road continued uninteresting the whole way.   After four hours and a
half more in the saddle, making eight and a half
hours since the morning, a long stretch in the hot
weather, we reached Tahanout, a place of some importance on the River Hasni.   The town much
resembled the others we had seen in the mountains,
but was more pretentious.   Here we overtook our
baggage animals, which had been unsaddled for rest ;
ten minutes later we were on our way again up the
valley, finally pitching our tents in an olive grove
near Tassilunt, after nine hours and a half hot riding
on an abominable road.   This valley of Hasni is
equally fine as that of Ourika, except that perhaps it
lacks a little of its grandeur.   We bathed in the river,
and returned to the tents to dine.   Here we found
again that Kaid Absalom was robbing us, having

asked the Kaid at Tahanout, whose duty it was to supply us with provisions, to give him money instead, which was done, so that we only got a few chickens that night, and our poor beasts got nothing but a very little corn.

Our road the next morning was very lovely and grand, especially at one place where we passed, wading our horses through the stream, between two perpendicular walls of rock, the lower levels of which were covered with masses of maidenhair fern. About half-past twelve we reached Hasni, and called on the Kaid, who had come out to the town gate to meet us, a kind old man, very decrepit, but who seemed much more educated than most Moors, and discussed European politics with much zest, though, from the topics he spoke on, I should say he had just heard of the Crimean War. Our camping-ground was charming, in a shady grove of trees near the town wall, and surrounded on three sides by a swift stream. The Kaid, Calipha, and Sheikh called in the afternoon and took tea with us in state, and quite a pleasant little party we had in our tent. The old man told us, greatly to our disappointment, that our further passage up the valley was impossible, owing to the rebellion of the tribes there. We had heard so much of these rebellions that we rather doubted it, till we found from other sources that he spoke the truth, for a wonder. This was a great disappointment, as it was from Arround (or Arūm, the Moors call it, though Hooker gives us the former spelling) that Sir Joseph Hooker and his party ascended the Tagherot Pass. I cannot say how much we are indebted to Sir Joseph Hooker's book on the Atlas, for we found it in-

valuable in all our excursions, and the map most
useful. The Berbers were delighted with our firearms,
and we had enough of them, and their surprise at the
shooting we did with our Winchesters, carbines, and
revolvers made us almost feel heroes from Wimble-
don. In the evening we went for a walk round the
town, which we found small, dirty, but curious. The
houses have no windows in the exterior, but all look
into courtyards in the centre, into which, too, the
sewers seem to empty themselves. Altogether, they
are most uncomfortable-looking places, and are
built in the roughest possible way. We had a thun-
derstorm that evening, but by sunset it was clear
again. The night was lovely, and we sat outside the
tent and silently watched the moon rise through the
gently murmuring trèes, till every mountain stood out
clearly as by daylight. Near us the town walls
formed a dark line against the sky. As we watched,
we saw the form of the muezzin on the little mosque,
and heard his clear voice ring out the call to prayer,
and the echo from the wall of rock behind took it up,
then another and another, till it died away in the still
night ; but it was loud enough to wake a nightingale
in the pomegranates, who began his song and kept
it up all night—at least, 1 suppose he did, for I was
too sleepy to sit up and listen.

We were guests next day at a great hunt after
muflon and boar, but were not very successful. We
arrived about sundown at our camp, and a little later
paid another visit to the town, where we managed to
pick up some curiosities in the way of silver ornaments,
rings, necklaces, and charms.

The following morning we were off again, with as

bad and as beautiful a road before us as usual. The first hour or two we spent toiling up a fearful path to the summit of a higher plateau, the top of which was richly cultivated. After riding for about an hour and a half on the plateau, we came to a village of some size, which literally overhung a precipice thousands of feet in depth. All the views we saw in Morocco, almost all the views I have seen in my life, were surpassed by what lay before us then. Below us lay the great plain of Morocco, almost at our feet it seemed, a rolling desert of stones and sand, except where some river wound its course and irrigated the soil. As far as the eye could reach, hillock after hillock of yellow earth, varied here and there by an oasis of palms or a little white village. The whole thing looked so near in the clear atmosphere that it resembled a ploughed field, yet every furrow represented a valley, and every line of upturned earth a range of hills. At our feet, seeming as though it merely wanted one step to reach it, lay Agregoreh, nestling in dense groves of trees, a charming little town, with a couple of mosques and an old gateway or two. Far away to the north a dark line in the plain represented the palm-forests of Morocco ; and, yes ! there was the Koutubia again. Away beyond the city, in the distance, we recognized the mountains we had crossed two days before reaching Morocco.

Down a zigzag path in the face of the precipice we descended. It was almost the worst road I had ever seen, as the ground was of smooth, slippery rock, sloping down towards the edge of the precipice. We passed through a village half-way down, which, like that at the summit, clung to the edge of the precipice ;—

> Like an eagle's nest hangs on the crest
> Of purple—

Well, it was not "Apennine" this time, but purple
Atlas; but that doesn't seem to rhyme somehow.

At last we reached the bottom of the precipice,
where we gave ourselves and our beasts a rest under
a delightful pomegranate grove, in the cool shade of
which we were supplied with tea in crown-Derby cups
by the neighbouring Kaid. We had already been
four hours on the road, and the heat was intense, but
after an hour's rest we had to push on again. We
passed many villages, but none of any size except
Largan, where there seemed to be the usual number
of Jews. Some of us bathed here, and bought some
fish from a Jew, who was most delighted with the
franc we gave him for a couple of dozen small fry,
and tried his best to go through the horrid performance of kissing our boots, though he got kicked
for it. We reached Amsmiz, our resting-plaee, in
another three hours and a half, and pitched our tents
near the river of the same name. Amsmiz is a place
of some size and importance, and boasts a "mellah,"
or Jews' quarter, separated from the walled town, of
which latter the mosques and gateway are fine.
Altogether it is a most picturesque place, situated in
the opening of a large valley. We received a letter
sent by special courier on our arrival, stating that
his Excellency Sir William Kirby-Green, and the
"Bashadorial" party would arrive on the following
Friday, four days thence.

We spent our first morning in Amsmiz in the sôk
or market, but found no curios. The poor Basch of
the town was terrified when he heard where we had

gone, as he said the place was full of wild, fanatical hillsmen, and not at all safe for unprotected Europeans. In the " mellah," or Jews' quarter, we succeeded in picking up a few more curiosities. I also bought a curious camels'-hair bournous of black material, a hooded cloak which is so finely woven as to be impervious to water. As the negro from whom I bought it looked as though he might possess belongings whose acquaintance might prove of annoyance to me, on my arrival in camp I sallied down to the river to wash my new purchase. Following the example of the Moors, I pulled off my shoes and stockings and washed with my feet. While in this somewhat degrading position the Kaid of the escort espied me ; for a moment he stood dumbfounded, then shrieked to me to return. He could not understand how anyone could do anything so degrading as to wash one's own clothes, especially any one travelling, as we were, with an autograph letter of the Sultan, and belonging to the " Bashadorial " party. On my refusing to comply with his vociferated request, he sent half a dozen soldiers down to me, so that, at all events, I might have some appearance of respectability. As usual, the trees round our camp were full of nightingales; to tell the truth, nightingales were getting rather too common, and when we heard an owl at night we would sit and listen, and say, " What a delightful change ! "

The next day we ascended a mountain near Amsmiz. We rode some way up, and dismounted at a spot where the mountain-side became very steep. Though at no place was it difficult climbing, it was rough, hot work ; yet on the summit we obtained a

cooler breeze than we had experienced for a long
time. We were disappointed at finding no snow on
the peak, as we could see it on a level, and even
below us, on the mountains near ; however, from there
was a view that made up for everything. To the
north and west we looked over the great plains that
stretched away far as the eye could reach ; to the
south lay a dark valley narrowly winding its tortuous
way between enormous precipices, one of the few
routes into the Sous valley. Amsmiz itself is in the
Sous, but not the Sous known to explorers, which
ought properly to be designated by the term "Sus
Valley." The summit of the mountain was a veritable
peak, not more than fifteen feet in diameter. Our
barometer registered 9600 feet, though, allowing for a
correction, the peak was probably some 300 feet less
in height. We got back in camp about sundown,
after an enjoyable though tiring day.

Early next morning we started off up the valley,
keeping to the right-hand side. The path, the
merest track in the side of the precipice, was not a
good one, as it was in no place more than two feet to
three feet wide, and proportionately slippery. Riding
along such roads as these is not over-pleasant work,
especially when, hundreds of feet below one, rushes a
turbulent river, into which one would ultimately
alight—at least, portions of one would—should the
horse make one false step. However, after some two
hours and a half of more or less holding one's breath,
we emerged into a valley running at right angles to
the one we were in. The scenery all along the road
was very grand ; far below boiled and bubbled the
river, its banks green, vividly green, with narrow

strips of corn-fields and groves of walnut-trees, while a line of crimson oleanders marked out the river's edge. The valley we entered was very lovely. At the end, which opens into the great valley, stands a village of some size, by name Imminteli, close under the walls of which runs a swift, clear, deep river, whose bed is cut out in the solid rock. On each side of the river is a lawn of green grass, the whole shaded by gigantic walnut-trees. We crossed the river some few hundred yards up to where it issues from the solid rock, a most curious spot, for there is no cave, simply a pool of water at the foot of the precipice—a clear, deep pool, from the centre of which, far down in its transparent depths, issues the stream.

There is a curious old fable relating to this place which we heard from the Moors. They call it the well of the Christians, for once, so the story goes, how long ago no one seems to know, the Christians had their great treasure-house here. (It is a necessary qualification to state that the Moors call all the former inhabitants of their country Christians.) It is supposed that this treasure-house was built in such a way that there were two connected doors ; when that leading to the treasure-house was shut, the river flowed through the other. Naturally the belief at present is that whoever can shut the door of the stream will open that of the treasure-house, so our movements were very closely watched as we peered into the pool of water. We saw many pretty rock-squirrels playing about, which the Berbers consider very efficacious for medicinal purposes.

That there had been former inhabitants at this

R

spot one cannot for a moment doubt, as blocks of
stone lying in disorder by the banks of the river
show very clearly the signs of having been cut and
squared by the hand of mortal man, and that man
certainly not of the Berber tribe, who build, and
always, so far as we know, have built, with tabbia.
We returned to camp by the opposite side of the
great valley to that by which we had ascended it,
where we found the road far better, and not so
perilously dangerous as the other had been.

Mturga Haha.

The next day the Minister and party arrived, and
we were back once more in our luxurious camp,
which was pitched above the little town on an open
piece of ground, near the sôk, or market. The
following day we spent hunting, ascending the mountains to the right of the valley, and returning as we
had done on our former trip up the gorge. Though
several muflon were seen, we were unsuccessful in
obtaining any.

The day following our hunt we left Amsmiz, and
proceeded once more on our road towards the coast.

We continued along the foot of the Atlas mountains passing through M'Jot, Mturga, and the Haha, a wild district, with deep valleys full of wild olives, and with here and there great castles on the hills, the homes of semi-independent Kaids.

Close to Aïn Tarsil we visited some curious Troglodyte caves, which, as I believe we were the first Europeans to enter, I will describe.

Though seen by Balanza and afterwards by Hooker, neither seem to place much importance in the existence of these strange dwellings, as the former merely passes over the subject with a mention that they do exist in this part, and the latter, owing to difficulties put in his way by his men, did not explore in the few places where exploration is possible, but merely mentions having seen them from below, quotes the " Periplus " of Hanno, speculates a little as to the means of entrance and exit practised by the strange dead race, then turns again to botany.

The Kaid at Aïn Tarsil, the village at one end of the valley in which the caves are situated, did his level best to prevent our visiting the spot, by misleading us on our road. However, this was discovered —a discovery that led to bad language and an immediate return.

The scenery at Aïn Tarsil undergoes a complete change. Instead of the dreary plain that we had been passing over for two days, the country is split up into deep ravines, not unlike miniature cañons of California—yet not so miniature for all that—and it is in one of these strange valleys that the caves are situated. The gorge is a narrow one, the cliffs on either side rising almost perpendicularly from the bottom of the deep valley to a great height, through which trickles a diminutive stream, owing its existence to a hole in the rock.

After progressing some little way through this valley we came in sight of the first batch of caves, situated in the right-hand cliff, at a great distance from the ground and cut in the solid rock. They are in some places in single tier, in others in two or three tiers, one situated directly above the others.

The entrances are small, varying from three and a half to four and a half feet in height, and about three feet in width. In places where the rock has fallen away the entrances are faced with masonry of a neat type, and in one or two cases where the natural formation of the rock necessitated exceptionally large entrances this masonry served also the purpose of dividing the door into two parts, one of which, no doubt, served as a window.

How the original inhabitants succeeded in gaining entrance to these caves is a puzzler, but I doubt not they made use of ropes and ladders, which would serve as a protection from man and beast, as they could be drawn up from above.

Only in very few cases were we able to enter the caves. We found them for the most part much resembling each other, though one or two were more after the style of houses, and contained several rooms.

The low pitch of the roof makes one believe the people were a minute race, though Hanno in the " Periplus," speaking of Southern Morocco, does not say so. He states that in the interior lived a race whose homes were in the rocks, who were swift as horses, with a language more resembling shrieks than speaking, and that they eat snakes. I never like to contradict any one, for fear I should be found out to be wrong, but Hanno has been dead some years, so I think no one can very well prove his statements, for I think, by the careful way in which these caves are excavated, that his description is a false one, and that this dead race must have been far more civilized than he leads one to believe. There are some hundreds of caves altogether. On the road to Sheshouan, and again beyond Wanan, I discovered fresh evidence of Troglodyte cave cities.

We arrived at Mogador on May 24th, and two days later started on our long journey up the coast to Tangier, a distance of 400 miles.

I will not describe in detail this journey, but will give a general description of the coast towns, and the places of interest passed on the road.

CHAPTER V.

THE COAST TOWNS.

ABOUT Mogador there is not much to tell, yet it is not at all an unattractive place. The name of the city has arisen in a curious way, though, like most of the Moorish coast towns, it is known by two names, being commonly called by the Moors "Sueira," *i.e.* the picture.

Buried palace and Berber village, near Mogador.

The origin of the name Mogador is as follows :—

In the fourteenth or fifteenth centuries, a ship was wrecked on the spit of sand on which Mogador of to-day is situated. At that time, however, there was no city, merely the Berber village that still remains standing only a few miles away existed then.

The sole survivor of this wreck was a Scotchman, McDougal, who succeeded in reaching the shore, and making friends with the natives, amongst whom he lived for many years, teaching the tribes many useful arts, such as working in metals, &c. To such an extent did they come to venerate his superior knowledge, that on his death they raised a monument over his tomb, known and worshipped to this day by the natives, as Sidi Mogdul—a very slight change from his original Scotch name of McDougal. The story is no doubt true, as Mogdul is a name unknown elsewhere amongst the Moors and Arabs, while the fact that he is also reverenced by the Jews—a not very distinguished honour—renders more clear that his origin was neither Jewish nor Moorish. From Mogdul, the

The Islands, Mogador Bay.

town has taken its name, being corrupted by the Europeans into Mogador.

The town is situated on the extremity of a spit of sand, jutting out into the Atlantic Ocean, which seems all through the year to attract cool breezes, rendering Mogador one of the healthiest spots in all Morocco. In climate, it far surpasses Tangier, from which it is distant about four hundred miles, though the want of accommodation renders it unsuitable for

invalids.   The harbour is by far the best on the whole
of the Moorish coast, being sheltered to some extent
by islands.   The town itself is clean, built rather on a
European than a Moorish plan, and several European
families, as well as a British Consul, reside there.
From Mr. Consul Payton and his wife I have always
received the kindest hospitality, and as he is a man
whose knowledge of Morocco and the Moors is very
wide, I have gathered much information from many
pleasant conversations with him.   To readers of the
Field, he is well known, under the name of "Sar-
selle," as one of the most enthusiastic and successful
of sea fishermen, and our knowledge of what sea fish
pertain to the shores of Morocco is entirely owing to
his untiring exertions.

Not far from Mogador on the sea-beach are the
ruins of an ancient Sultan's palace, now half buried
by the drifting sands which separate—almost isolate
—Mogador from the surrounding country.   The
palace is a building of no great pretensions, though
covering a large space of ground.   The whole is surrounded by a high wall, forming an immense courtyard, at each corner of which are houses, of two
stories, and containing very large rooms.   The north-
west corner house is fitted up into a species of what
the Portuguese would call a "Morante," or summer-
house, and, with its flooring of rich tiles, its painted
doors and picturesque windows, is very charming.   It
was near here we managed to enter the palace, for the
doors are locked, and, even if not closed, would be useless, as they are entirely buried in sand.

In the centre of the courtyard is a large building
one story in height, with a tall, green-tiled pointed
roof, terminating in a sort of gilt lightning-conductor.

This building is flanked by white marble columns, with Corinthian capitals, forming an arcade on each side, while the corners of this central palace are plain, each being a room of no mean size. The centre forms a huge chamber, evidently at one time an audience-hall. This room we found it very difficult to enter, owing to the sand having drifted up against the gorgeously-painted doors, preventing them from

Old palace buried in sand, Mogador.

being moved. However, after hard work in scraping away the piled-up sand, I managed to make a small hole, through which I slid, and very quickly too, as I had entered from the level of the top of the immense doors. I fell, however, on to soft sand, and soon recovered my feet. A few bats I could hear flapping about, but the darkness prevented my seeing anything. Striking a match, I lit a candle.

High above my head rose the domed roof, richly painted in designs in red and gold. Round the upper part of the walls ran Arabesque in white plaster, bearing in graceful designs verses from the Koran. The walls were of plain, slightly-tinted plaster and the floor of tiles. At the further side was an alcove, evidently the seat of some former Sultan.

A difficult climb up the doors and a crawl on all fours through our sand tunnel, and I was once more in the open air, half-blinded with the mid-day sun, after the cool darkness. The whole building is an exceedingly interesting place, and well worth a visit, though it is seldom the drifted sand lies thick enough to allow one to climb over the high wall, and so enter the court. On our return, we visited the small Berber village that exists close by, though·it has long since fallen to rack and ruin, the shells alone remaining of a few old houses, in which the Berbers have built up their huts and spread their tents.

Mogador is—with the exception of Morocco city— the best place for picking up curious objects from the Soudan and the Sous, especially guns and daggers ; while the Jews there are skilled workers in metals. The Mellah and its inhabitants are as dirty as elsewhere ; Spanish is spoken principally among the Jews of the coast.

Two days' journey north of Mogador is situated Saffi. The country between the two is hilly and well wooded ; for the first part of the way the Argan tree grows in great luxuriance, and is a source of wealth to the natives from the oil they draw therefrom. The fruit is long and yellow, not unlike the mango from a distance, but exceedingly bitter to the taste. I once bit one in curiosity, but did not lose the acid flavour for some days. The tree itself, peculiar to this part of Morocco, and unknown elsewhere throughout the whole world, is thick in trunk, with low, distended branches. The leaves are hard and shining, of a dark green colour, and the branches are covered with long thorns. So thickly do these branches grow and at such uniform height from the ground that it is a common sight to see goats in the branches, a sight I have seen nowhere else, except in the country in Malta, in the few trees that exist there. Though the Argan does not reach any great altitude, it is far-spreading, which gives rise to many exaggerated accounts of its size. On the road from Morocco city to Mogador, before we had come across any specimens of the Argan, I was told by one of our kaids that we should see a tree capable of giving shelter to a hundred men on horseback. In time we arrived at the tree—certainly a large specimen—under which twenty men, certainly *not* on horseback, might find shelter. I told the kaid that he had exaggerated, and laughed at him, but he still stuck to his statement, allowing, however, that they must be "small men and small horses." Lizards mounted on rabbits might, perhaps, be a fairer test to judge by.

Between Mogador and Saffi one has to ford the Wad Tensift, the river that drains the elevated plains of Morocco and flows close to the city of that name. The ford is a wide and, in the rainy season a deep, one. Near the ford stands the ruins of some ancient town, though it is difficult to say to what period the remains belong. They are not unlike the ruins of ancient Tangier, two miles from the modern town along the beach, but are of greater extent and in better preservation. Saffi is approached from the

south by high ground, along the cliffs, one part of
which, known as the " Jews' Cliff," being a narrow
path cut in the precipice.   Its name is derived from
its being the spot where a party of Moors bundled
some Jews, who had swindled them, over the edge on
to the rocks far below.   The town of Saffi—or Asfi, as
it is called by the Moors—is situated on the side of a
steep hill, crowned by the ruins of the ancient palace,
one of the most magnificent remains in the whole
country, though fast falling into decay.

I have twice explored this ancient castle, and have
been each time more impressed with what its grandeur
must once have been.   It was built either by Moulai
Ismail or Moulai Sliman, and probably by both.   From
the outside it presents nothing more than immensely
high walls crowned with towers and turrets, but these
walls are filled with delightful little courts and balconies.   One small court, with its pointed arches, tiled
floor, and marble lion fountain, the rooms leading
into it richly tiled and with gorgeous ceilings, must in
its day have been almost as fine as anything in the
Alhambra itself, nor is it much less beautiful to-day
when wild roses have crept over everything, and
flowers, weeds, and shrubs forced their way between
the tiles and inlaid marble.

A court containing a miniature mosque, with its
green-tiled pointed roofs, its tiny arcades of pillars,
and rich ceilings, is in almost perfect repair ; a very
little expense would suffice to realize its former
beauties.   Nor are the shady balconies, unsafe to walk
upon now, with balustrades of musheribeyah work,
that surround on two stories a small deep court, less
lovely, especially as the windows look far out over the
town, hundreds of feet below on the side of the

hill, away to the great blue ocean, for ever rolling its breakers on the open coast.

A curious breech-loading gun of great age can be seen lying rusty and half buried on one of the battlements of the palace. However, the last half-dozen Sultans have not cared for Saffi, and day by day the old palace is crumbling away, tired, perhaps, of never being seen, aweary of its glories worn for nought.

The place is always kept locked up, and it is generally extremely difficult to obtain permission to view it, though I myself had no difficulty, as on one occasion I was on the " Mission" with Sir William Kirby-Green, and the second time obtained entrance by the fact of my former visit, and the additional help that the Basha of the town personally remembered me.

The next town reached on a journey up the coast is Mazagan, called by the natives Jedida—*i.e.* the " new "—though it scarcely deserves that name now. As I have elsewhere described all that is to be seen and done in that far from interesting place, I will pass on to another city—Azimour—situated only three or four hours' ride from Mazagan. This city is an extremely fanatical one, nor are any Christians allowed to reside there. It is situated on the south bank of the river Ribeah on a high cliff. The town is large and uninteresting, but very sacred on account of the tomb of Sidi Moulai Bushai. On passing through this place on our return from visiting the Sultan, Mr. White, H.B.M. Consul at Tangier, took several photographs ; the natives were quite unconscious of what was going on, so that some good groups were obtained. As a rule, the Moors object most strongly to being photographed, on account of portraiture being contrary to the Koran, and their entire ignorance at this spot of the objects of a camera was a great help to the photographers. The passage of the river Ribeah is carried out in large flat-bottomed barges, on which horses, men, and baggage are safely—generally—conveyed across.

The next town on the coast is perhaps the most important of all, Casablanca, or Dar-al-baida, both of which names mean the same, "The White House."

It is a town of but little interest and, comparatively modern; like all the other coast towns in Morocco, it is walled. Its importance is owing principally to the fact that there are many Europeans there, engaged in trade. There is little to see in the place, which is clean, nicely laid out, and half European in appearance. There is no harbour, as at Mazagan and Saffi, the ships lying in the open roadstead. The principal trade of Dar-al-baida is the exportation of wool. Many small steamers and sailing-vessels call here for cargo, besides the regular forward line boats which visit the coast ports—up and down—about once every three weeks. It is a very pleasant way of spending a week or two, especially in the summer, when there is every chance of fine weather, by taking a passage on one of these steamers and visiting the coast towns, the same boat bringing one back to Tangier in about a fortnight. One usually steams at night, while the days are spent ashore, one day at each port, except Mogador, where two or three are generally passed.

Outside Casablanca are large private gardens, prettily laid out, some belonging to natives and a few to Europeans. There are one or two native *café* gardens there, where one can sit under the trees and enjoy Moorish tea—if one can—and coffee.

About sixty miles north of Casablanca are the two towns of Rabat and Sallee, situated respectively on the south and north banks of the river Booragrag.

These two towns are by far the most interesting on the whole Moorish coast, not only on account of their romantic situation, but also from the historical facts connected with them.

Every reader of Robinson Crusoe knows how he was taken by the famous—or rather infamous—Sallee rovers and carried into slavery, but everybody does not know that it was only a comparatively very few years ago that the British Government ceased to pay a sum of money to the Sultan of Morocco against the attack of these pirates on British vessels. Even to-day Sallee is a most fanatical town, and within the last few months there have been hostile demonstrations against the few Europeans who reside in Rabat, for in Sallee none are allowed to live.

To the north of Sallee without the walls of the city is a fine aqueduct, built by Almanzor the Magnificent, and it is a specimen of building worthy of its great originator.

The road passes under the high arches of this aqueduct, and reminds one very much of the road from Lisbon to Cintra. Within the city there is little to see. The streets are narrow, but not so dirty as in many towns. When there with the British Minister, the Bascha of Sallee, a venerable man of extreme age, called upon us in our camp, and told us many interesting things about the place, amongst others, that in his youth he remembered having European slaves, sailors kidnapped by the " Rovers." The river between Sallee and Rabat must have formed a safe harbour of refuge for these pirates, though the surf on the bar prevents boats of any size from entering, otherwise the wide river would form an entirely land-locked harbour.

To pass from Sallee to Rabat and back one has to make use, as at Azimour and Laraiche, of great flat-bottomed barges, over the high gunwales of which one's horses and mules must leap in and out.

Between Sallee and the river is a large space of sand, where one can camp, though the natives do not like one doing so there.

I remember once having arrived at Rabat from Fez and Mequinez, not having seen a single European except our own party for weeks and weeks. We called upon our Vice-Consul in the afternoon, and proceeded towards sundown to our camp. Seated there at tea our eyes were suddenly nearly struck blind by a wonderful sight. Not fifty yards from our camp sauntered past an Englishman. He was dressed in tall yellow leather boots, with a shine like varnish, very neat breeches, a large check coat, and waistcoat and collar. "Collars" isn't the word for it—there is no way to fully express the broad snow-white expanse of linen, two or three inches high, at least, that encircled his neck. His moustache was neatly curled and he was beautifully shaved. Over one arm he carried a gun.

Oh, British respectability! Our hearts sank when we saw this young man dressed in fine raiment. Our clothes were old and travel-worn, and I had always to be sitting down for fear any one should see the hole in my breeches.

He never looked at us; he had not been intro-

duced. That was the first time I saw Captain S——
of the —— Hussars.

Next day the ice was broken—we were introduced.
No Englishmen may ever be allowed to speak to one

Captain S——.

another, even though hundreds of miles away from
everywhere, without being introduced.

Introduction led to calling, calling to friendship,
and all the way to Tangier our camp rejoiced in S——
and his collars. He was travelling with a large green

s

bath, at least he said so, though to this day I believe
it was his collar-box.

The "side" I put on all that journey! As the
Moors stared at me, I returned their gaze with one
which clearly said, "Yes, I may be in rags, and my
pony is not a beauty, I acknowledge ; my boots are
full of holes and my saddle patched with red and
yellow shoe-leather, but you must not ·gather the
importance of our caravan from me. There is one
coming along the road soon, whom you will see anon,
who has a white neck as long as a stork. What matters it if rags go on ahead, respectability comes anon."

Captain S—— had a camp-bed, the best ever invented, he said. It consisted of poles of every length
from about an inch to a foot and a half, which had to
be put in such a way as to fit. No puzzle I ever saw
came up to that bed. As soon as we arrived in camp,
before the tents were up even, S—— got to work.
After an hour or so the poles were all fitted, but he
had forgotten to string the canvas on ; it all had to
come to pieces again, an operation of say an hour and
a half. In S——'s hurry and worry he would forget to
arrange the separated poles in order on the ground,
with a result that having arranged the canvas he
could not find the right poles. Sometimes when we
got up in the morning he was still at work fitting up
his bed. One night he managed to tie it with a piece
of string. I waited till he was asleep, then cut the
string ; down came the bed. S—— said—no I cannot
—rather I dare not—write what S—— said, but he
contented himself by sleeping on the floor.

As he dozed off he still murmured, " It is the best
camp-bed ever invented."

Rabat is situated on the south bank of the river, and is certainly one of the most picturesque spots in Morocco. The rocky promontory that forms the southern bank is crowned with an old kasbah, or fortress, battlements and towers rising tier above tier, the whole covered with clustering creepers and shrubs.

Under the shelter of this promontory lie native feluccas, and perhaps a small Spanish or Portuguese sailing-ship.

Within the walls of Rabat there is but little to see. The street of the dyers forms, perhaps, the most picturesque spot of all. It is a steep slope ; on each side are the dyeing-houses, from in and out the doors of which fly pigeons, while hung on long jutting pieces of wood, almost crossing the street, are skein upon skein of bright wools, reds, greens, yellows, every colour is represented. Here, there, and everywhere can be seen the dyers themselves, swarthy Moors, with their bare arms stained with colour. In the Kasbah there is a fine old gate, though the centre arch has been built in, and it is now used as a prison. The streets are covered from the sun by matting which gives the place a cool look, though by forming an impediment to ventilation, doubtless it adds much to fever, for which Rabat is so well known.

Above the town the river widens out, and on a high steep cliff at this spot is situated the famous Beni-Hassan tower, and the ruins of the ancient mosque that Almanzor intended to be the largest in the world. This tower forms one of the famous three, the Giralda at Seville, the Koutubia at Morocco city, being the other two. The Beni-Hassan, however, was never completed, owing to the death of Almanzor, and his successor never cared to carry on the work, doubtless preferring to raise palaces and mosques of his own.

This tower, like that at Morocco, is fifty feet square. It originally possessed a door, but the Moors have built it up, so that the only means of ingress is by a narrow window some thirty feet from the ground, to which one has to climb. I did so once, but will never attempt it again, as there is only an inch or two for foot and hand to hold on by, and the descent is even worse than the ascent. At one place one has to pass along a ledge of window-frame merely hanging by one's hands, with no place to put one's feet, and so crawl on hand over hand. Within the tower is not ascended by steps, but by a sloping way, as in the Mosque of St. Sophia at Constantinople, no doubt originally intended as a means of bringing masonry to the summit on the backs of pack animals.

Close to the tower stand a great number of pillars, surrounded by orchards and thick brushwood, and covered with vines. These pillars are of great size, though it is difficult to judge the elevation at which they would eventually have supported the roof, as they are sunk to some extent in the ground. Surrounding them are the remains of an ancient wall and the foundations of the mosque.

. The view from this spot is charming, as the valley widens out here, and one can see the river turning and twisting in serpentine coils far away to the east, while to the west are Rabat, Sallee, and the ocean. The banks of the river are low and marshy, and swarming with water-fowl, which are very difficult to approach, as the marsh is too deep to walk in, and the rushes too thick to allow the passage of a boat.

To the north-east one can see the hill-lands of the fanatical Zimmouri tribes, whose territory stretches from here almost to Mequinez, consisting of the range of hills that skirts the southern edge of the Beni Hassan plain.

On one occasion, coming from Mequinez to Rabat with Mr. and Mrs. T., we let our soldier lag behind and rode on, knowing we were only some few hours' ride from the latter town.

We, however, missed the road, and before we knew where we were, found ourselves assailed in a thick wood by three fierce-looking natives, who pointed their long guns at us. It was no good trying to ride for it, as if one had been wounded the other two would have been obliged to return. Curiously enough, as we were that day going to enter a town, none of us were wearing revolvers—a lucky coincidence, I think. There was nothing to do but to face the men, and T. quietly rode up to them, Mrs. T. and I following.

People often talk in a silly way of women losing their heads and that sort of bosh. If anybody could have seen the calmness with which the lady who was with us faced the danger, for no doubt we were in great danger, they would never speak in that way again.

The men still held their guns pointed at us ; then spoke a few words amongst themselves, and asked us where we were going. At that time I spoke only a very few words of their language, but could just explain we were on our way to Rabat. From that

moment all our fears died away, and the very men
who had seemed a minute or two before desirous of
shooting us, themselves took us to our right road.

I fancy they must have been outposts of the Zimmouris, in whose country we were, and who at that
time were at war with the Beni-Hassanis. Had we
ridden on I feel sure they would have fired, as they
would have suspected that we wished to enter the
country, closed entirely to Europeans.

However, all's well that ends well, and we said
good-bye to our now smiling assailants on the Rabat
road an hour or so later, and galloped on to the town,
distant some three or four hours.

A few miles up the river from Rabat stand the interesting remains of Shellah, ruins both Roman and
Moorish. Though the former from their antiquity are
perhaps the most interesting, yet it is the Moorish
remains that render Shellah one of the most lovely
spots in the country. The thickly-wooded hills slope
down to the river's edge, completely concealing the
ancient town in the dense foliage. Passing through
some orange-groves, one comes suddenly upon the
ruins, for the most part delicate mosques and tombs
scattered about amongst the trees. Some of the
stone arabesque work is exceedingly beautiful, and
the highly-coloured and polished tiles on the minarets add a charm to the scene peculiar to Morocco.

Within a little mosque lies the marble tomb of the
great Almanzor, covered with writing telling of his
prowess and magnificence. Many other sultans, too,
are buried here, but the graves are allowed to lie
untended, the roofs of the mosques have fallen in, the
towers are crumbling away, in fact Shellah is a decay-
ing ruin ; yet how much more beautiful in its ruined

state than it must have been in the days of its magni-ficence. The Roman remains are nearly invisible owing to the earth having by time been piled above them, though some baths can be made out ; of course the Moorish officials allow of no excavation.

The walls are covered with maiden-hair fern, while tiny fountains splash on every side.

Above is a large open space, walled in, many acres in extent, the site of the ancient town, of which not one vestige now remains. At the southern side of the wall is a fine buttressed gate, which gives the appearance of having been designed, if not erected, by Portuguese architects.

The delightful shade and the romantic situation and history of Shellah render it a charming spot, and several times have I been rowed up the Booragrag River and picnicked under the walls of the little mosque that contains the deserted remains of the greatest of Moorish sultans.

Farther up the river are two islands, and again a few miles beyond them some troglodyte caves in the face of the steep cliffs.

The road to Rabat from Mequinez is not an in-teresting one, as it passes nearly the whole way over flat plains, the scene varied only by the circular tent villages of Beni-Hassan Arabs.

From Rabat to Laraiche is a journey of two and a half or three days. The whole way, with but little exception, one passes by marshy lakes visited by great quantities of water-fowl.

Some hours to the north of Rabat, and situated on the road to Laraiche, is Mehedia, a small walled town on the banks of the River Sebou, the river of Fez. There is little within the walls of Mehedia, the immense solidity of which gives a look of importance to the miserable collection of mud-huts and brown tents far from being deserved.

The river is very wide at this spot and is crossed by a ferry, the same species of rickety old barge being used as at Azimour and Rabat. Were it not for the shallow bar at the mouth of the river, Mehedïa might have become a harbour of importance.

I will not again describe Laraiche or Arzeila. They have both appeared already in "A Journey through Northern Morocco."

A few words on the coast in general. Travellers camping through the country I advise to keep away from the coast as much as possible, as, except for Rabat and Saffi, there is very little of interest, and the roads between the various towns are dreary and dull. However, there are spots where one must travel by the coast as the interior is unsafe.

To the south of Magador little is known of the country with the exception of the road to Agadir, a curious, almost deserted town, situated on the summit of a high hill, slightly to the north of the mouth of the River Sous. Beyond the Sous is the Wad Nun, a district as yet almost unexplored, and beyond that again the great desert of the Sahara, which an enterprising Scotchman wishes to turn into a sea, though he has discovered that the British public do not yet recognize in him a new creator.

On my various travels on the Moorish coast I have met with nothing but kindness from the European inhabitants, who do everything in their power to render one's stay in the towns cheery and pleasant, and in this they thoroughly succeed.

PART III.

A VISIT TO WAZAN—MY RIDE TO SHESHOUAN.

" I have been in countries," said an Irishman, " where the hand of man never yet set foot."

CHAPTER I.

BAD weather prevented my starting on my promised visit to Moulai Mahommed at Wazan, till ten days after my return to Tangier from our journey through Northern Morocco.

At last, in desperation, I decided to start—rain or no rain—and accordingly on a Saturday early in March set off.

I had with me but a small caravan, for being the sole European I was able to arrange myself and my affairs exactly according to my own tastes, and rough it accordingly. By roughing it I do not mean to say that I attempted to commit suicide by not taking a sufficient quantity of things ; *au contraire*, I was well supplied ; but with my former experience knew exactly what was useful and necessary, and what was not. The result was that I found two mules ample for my baggage, while my black steed bore me. Selim, of course, accompanied me, and I took also Gil Ali, the best hand at putting up tents that I ever saw, and a strong, good natured fellow withal, though inclined to be lazy, and Abdurrahman, the sweet-tempered, classical-looking youth, quiet, but with a decided vein of humour when he did speak, and in every way a gentleman.

Although Morocco is ruled by one of the most

despotic and all-powerful of Sultans, yet the country is a democracy by nature. Caste and hereditary position have but little power, except in cases of the Sultans themselves, and such mighty shereefs as those of Wazan and Tedla. My servant Abdurrahman held property at Tangier of great value, which had belonged to his family from generation to generation, yet it was no disgrace for him to come and work for me and earn a franc a day.

Quite the contrary this to the caste-degree in India, where one caste performs only a special kind of work. Another example of this democracy is the fact that sons of slaves are eligible for all appointments in the state ; and again another, the sons of Sidi Torres, Minister of Foreign Affairs at Tangier, one of the most powerful and important of the viziers, keep respectively a boot and shoe, and a sweet shop in Tetuan.

One more man completed my party, a strange, uncouth fellow from the Gharb, by name, Larbi. Two tents were sufficient, one for my men and the kitchen, the other for myself. Selim worked as cook, and turned out to be first-rate at it, as he is at most things, some of his savoury dishes of " kabobs," &c., being worthy of a London dinner-table.

The rain came down in torrents as my mules left my diggings at Tangier and passed along the sea-beach. Here, however, we suffered no trouble, as the sand quickly dried ; but as soon as we had emerged into the crooked lanes that intersect the gardens that skirt the beach, we found mud. You, who call the slight covering of damp dust in the London streets, mud, have no idea of Morocco in a rainy season !

Every step the mules took they sank knee-deep in the soft clay, and were it not that we were continually urging them on, I doubt not our caravan would be fossilizing there still. Four hours and a half through rain and mud, but the men and mules worked well, so that on reaching the village of Ain Dallieh Sorehr, I determined to pitch my camp there, as I saw both were thoroughly tired out.

It was not long before the tents were up and Selim presiding over his fire, while Abdurrahman had gone off to the well for water and Gil Ali to buy provisions and corn.

The charcoal fire soon warmed the tent within, and half an hour or so later we all sat merrily drinking our Moorish green tea from little glass tumblers. The sheikh of the village, an old friend, called upon me, and as night came on Selim brought forth his gimbri, and merry music and songs might have been heard within the walls of our little tent, to the accompaniment of pouring rain beating on the canvas.

The following day being as wet as ever, I did not strike camp, as I heard that the rivers were so swollen as to render it impossible to proceed. The day in camp passed pleasantly enough, though a gloom was cast over the village by the unexpected appearance of a soldier from the Bascha of Tangier demanding ten men to be sent immediately to the Anjera coast to prevent the rumoured laying of a second cable from Gibraltar to Tangier, and again demanding money to pay for the " mona," or provisions, to be supplied to the French and Portuguese Ministers on their approaching visits to the court at Fez.

That and the breaking loose of one of our pack

mules were the only events of the day. The mule galloped away, delighted to be free, and we all set off in pursuit. Nothing, however, we could do allowed us to get near enough to catch him, till at last Larbi, whose duty it was to look after the animals, lost his temper, and after calling her every name under the sun, ended up by a string of oaths. "May the Almighty burn your parents and your grandparents . . . unbeliever of a mule, dog of a Christian." I then lost *my* temper, and turning to Larbi enlightened his dull mind a bit about using epithets which were uncomplimentary to me, and showed him clearly, with Selim and Gil Ali's aid, that even though a Christian might be (to him) a dog, yet he was superior to a dirty native from the Gharb, and meant to be master, at all events in my camp. I never had reason after this to fall out with Larbi.

A bright morning on Monday cheered us up, and soon after eight our caravan was once more *en route*. We ascended the hill at the back of Ain Dallieh, and passing down the other side entered a morass. An hour or more it took us to pass through some few hundred yards of it. The river we crossed tolerably easily, nothing getting wet, and once on the ascent of the Akbah-al-hamra matters improved, for here the muddy soil changed to rock and sand. On descending again on the farther side we found too much water in the river to allow us to ford it, so pitched our camp at N'sala-Akbah-al-hamra-Ain-Dallieh, a sufficiently long name for a few mud and thatch huts.

I soon made the acquaintance of the sheikh, whom I found to be a most charming man. He spent the evening in our tents amidst great tea-drinkings and music.

A village donkey caused us much amusement by eating our corn. On trying to drive him away he stood his ground well, and merely let fly with his heels. However, the owner of the donkey was sent for, and in return for the amount of corn the donkey had devoured supplied us with milk. Exchange is no robbery, though on this occasion the donkey-man got the best of it.

Another fine day lowered the water in the river, and after some trouble and anxiety we passed across, and wading through a mile of mud entered the sandy slopes of the Gharbia. The recent rains had improved the look of the country very much here, the more so in our eyes as it looked dry, the sandy soil having absorbed the water very quickly. Everything was beautifully green, and it was easy to see spring had set in in earnest. Gorgeous beds of purple irises covered the slopes of the hills, while a dwarf variety of the same flower grew all over the roads, the "blue" daisy was in full bloom, and on all sides were the hoopoes, goldfinches, and storks, basking and flying around in the bright sunlight. We skirted the hill of N'sala Boreian, leaving the large village on the right. Near the sacred grove of the tomb of Sidi Mahommed Ben Ali were gathered all the world and his wife, hundreds and thousands of Moors, men and women. Some had ridden in, most had walked, all the country round had collected there. It was the anniversary of the birth or death (no one seemed to know which) of the saint, and they were keeping his Amara, or saint's day.

Rich and poor were collected in an extraordinary medley; guns were being fired, tea brewed, music played and sung; and as evening came on, I was told

by my men, the revels became an orgy, and the dark
shade of the wood the scene of riot and debauch.

We camped at a small tent-duar, by name Ghareefa,
where we found the people very pleasant.   This day's
journey had taken us some eight and a half hours to
accomplish, though in fine weather, or rather over dry
roads, one could easily do it in six hours.

The following day another eight hours' journey
brought us to Alcazar.   We were obliged to deviate
from the road several times in order to cross a river,
the Wad Waroor, which we did some miles from the
ordinary ford.

Alcazar.

Alcazar looked very picturesque as we approached
it from the north.   The town lies in the centre of a
flat plain, and is surrounded by dense groves of trees,
above which rise the mosque towers and the palms,
the latter enhancing the scene very much.   But the
town within the walls is filthy.   There is no other
town in Morocco that can compare to it for dirt.
Through the soko runs, or rather crawls, a small, dank,
green river, covered with bubbles and full of drainage.
The soko itself is a small sea of mud ; yet in spite of
these drawbacks it is not unpicturesque, the gate lead-

ing into the dimly lit bazaars being a good specimen of Arabesque, while the dull red tiles on the houses, crowned with storks' nests, give a curious effect. Little extemporized tents can be seen about, under which sit the dusky Moors selling oranges, fish, and vegetables, while the water-carriers are in full force, rushing everywhere with their cry of " Elma, elma." The sight, *par excellence*, of Alcazar is the tomb of Sidi Ali-bu-Rhaleh, a most decorative building, half-tomb, half-mosque, with emerald-green tiles, and shady colonnades, surrounded by horse-shoe arches. Of course no Christian is allowed to enter the sacred precincts, but one can gain a very satisfactory view of the place from without. It stands outside the city walls to the north of the town, surrounded by groves of trees.

"Ah Sidi Ali-bu-Rhaleh, Assalama Sidi Ali-bu-Rhaleh, salaam alikum," cried our men as we passed the tomb. I took in a few provisions at Alcazar, renewed our stock of charcoal, had one mule re-shod, and left the next day for a small village on the confines of the Shereef's country, only some two hours' ride from the town. Before leaving I sent a messenger on to Wazan, announcing my intended arrival to his Highness the Shereef.

Soon after leaving the town we forded the Koos, a large river, with steep, muddy banks. The Koos ford is quite one of the sights of Morocco, as there is always a crowd of camels, mules, donkeys, men, women, and children pushing their way through the wide, fast-flowing stream. I have seen many a comic accident there ; once it was a bucking mule that kicked its comfortable, fat, and well-dressed rider into the

T

water; another time a whole line of women were crossing, holding each others' hands for safety, when the middle one fell down, dragging all the others after her. As the water generally reaches the waists and often the shoulders of the men and women, I doubt not serious accidents are common. We, happily, got across safely, and without getting the baggage wet. The road after the ford proceeds over the plain for some way, crossing a bridge over a marshy stream, where I have shot duck. Then turning to the left near some orange-groves the path to Wazan branches off from the main Fez road, which I had been following since leaving Tangier. Ascending some hills, I pitched my camp at a village of the Shereef's, and as the day was yet young, spent the afternoon in shooting, and bagged five and a half brace to my own gun.

We were off early the following morning, as a long ride lay before us to Wazan.

I had taken the precaution of writing on to Moulai Mahommed, as I was travelling without a soldier, and I knew he would send to meet me before I entered the mountain tribes amongst which Wazan is situated; nor was I disappointed, for not long after leaving camp half a dozen guards armed with European rifles rode up and saluted me. I had dressed with great care that morning, donning a pair of clean white riding-breeches, my yellow boots all polish and shine, and a grey felt hat with clean white puggaree; but, vanity of vanities, we had not progressed far before one of our mules fell in the mud. In a second I was off my horse and together with the men knee-deep in black clay, unloading the struggling beast. All my hopes of making an impression by cleanliness failed, so I had to fall back upon Moorish customs and ideas, and remain dirty.

We passed through the lovely mountain-gorge of Abdullah Malek, in the tribe of M'mzoda, with its steep rocky crags on either side high above my head, each peak crowned with a little group of mountaineers, who gazed on the Christian passing through their lands, though they did nothing more than gaze.

A little stream runs through the gorge, finally tumbling over the rocks, clustered with maiden-hair fern, in a lovely cascade. Here meet the women to draw water, and, unless they do not resemble all the womenkind I have ever met with, to talk scandal and the latest Alcazar fashions. In the centre of the valley is a clearing in the dense wood where stands a small village, built as if on terraces, one house being raised above another on the side of the steep hill. On account of the romantic scenery and the dense woods, this, to me, is one of the most delightful spots in Morocco, though it is not renowned for the good name of its inhabitants, who are wild, lawless hunts-men, and a little given at times to plunder and violence. Having ascended the gorge the road con-tinues along the top of the mountains for some little way, till suddenly turning a corner, the plains below and the mountain-range opposite, on the crest of a ridge of which one can see the outskirts of Wazan, come into view. Two hours and a half across the plains brought us to the commencement of the town, here more a ruin than aught else. Winding lanes with high hedges of pricky pear, aloe, and bamboo hid the view often from sight, but still the peeps of the surrounding woodland were very beautiful. One

emerges quite suddenly from these lanes into a wide
open street, in a part of the town without the walls,
which leads one into the soko.   At the upper corner
of this soko one passes through the gate and enters
the town.   Here I was met by Si Ali, the Shereef's
secretary, and several officials, who welcomed me
with all the accustomed show of pleasure, and probably
with a certain amount of indifference.   However, they
concealed it very well, and from their many words
of welcome one was almost inclined to think them
genuine.   This superficial show, however, was only on
the part of the officials of the Shereef, as with his Highness himself I have a sincere friendship, of which he
takes every opportunity to show me, not only in words,
but in inconveniencing himself to please me, and in
giving me handsome presents of rugs, &c.

I was escorted to the house put at my service by his
Highness, the same kubbah as we had occupied a few
weeks before, on our return journey from Fez, though
on this occasion the house boasted some furniture,
divans having been erected along the walls, and rugs
being scattered about in profusion.   I immediately
changed, and after having rested for half an hour or
so, was summoned to appear before the Shereef.

Passing out of my garden I entered the street near
the mosque, then turning sharp to the right descended
a narrow precipitous path, a *cul de sac.*   At the lower
end of this alley-way is a small open space surrounded
by high walls, in one of which is a small wooden
gate, and before it were seated half a dozen soldiers
and slaves.   They rose on my approach and opened
the door; I passed in.   Within there is a chamber
with seats all round it, a sort of rough waiting-room

for those seeking audience with his Highness. Passing through this room we left it by a second gate, and descending a few steps entered a small walled garden, full of exquisite flowers and curious trees. The walls of the garden are very high; here and there decorated with designs in paint and stucco, and covered with roses and other creepers. At one end is a small tank, into which tumbles a fountain. The whole garden is laid out in oblong beds, the paths between being narrow and covered with sand. At the end of the garden, facing one as one enters, is the kubbah or day-house of Moulai Mahommed. It is a building of no great size, but exceedingly pretty, faced with a façade of lovely arches of varied design. The flooring of the façade is marble and tiles. The whole exterior is painted white, and nothing can be imagined more Eastern than the brilliant one-storied building with its arches half-covered with blooming roses, a foreground of flowers, and the blue sky above.

Large double-folding doors of cedar-wood and brass fittings give entrance into the rooms within.

At this door I was met by several black slaves, dressed in white, who bowing conducted me within.

One enters a long room—sixty or seventy feet in length, by about twelve or fifteen wide,—running at right angles left and right of the door. On entering it gives the appearance of a room each side of one, as curtains and portières divide it into various lengths. The centre part is tiled, and possesses a fountain, a curious structure of wood and brass, which forms candlesticks as well. When the fountain is playing the effect is charming, as each jet of water falls amongst dozens of lighted candles, and yet touches

none.   Round the walls run divans, mattresses
covered with silk and velvet, while on the floor lie exquisite carpets from all parts of the East.

Exactly opposite the door is an archway leading
on to a large raised divan, around the whole of which
runs a passage, opening into the divan by arches.
These arches are covered with portières, while the
whole divan floor is strewn with rugs, and surrounded
with mattresses and soft pillows.

It is a charming spot, as seated here and drawing
aside the portières of the arches one can see in every
direction.   In front is the gate into the garden, and
the effect of sitting in the cool dark room and gazing
into the gorgeous garden with its myriads of flowers
and brilliant sunlight is charming ; while if one turns
the other way one can see through the windows of the
passage the ranges of mountains, range beyond range,
stretching far away into the East.   Here I found
Moulai Mahommed, reclining on pillows of dark-blue
and white cloth.

He is a man of some thirty years of age, of dark
complexion, fine features, and with a black beard and
moustache.   His face is sensual, but not sufficiently
so to detract from his good looks.   Black blood
shows itself in the slightly heavy lips.   His eyes are
dark ; the lids slightly overhanging give him a curious
look of lassitude.

He was wearing as usual soft woollen and silk
clothes, a bernous of very fine woven wool covering his
silk haik, which was only visible over his head.   I kicked
my slippers off and ascended the divan.   His Highness
smiled very pleasantly, rose, and shook hands with me,
bidding me welcome and asking many questions as to
my health, and thanking me for returning so soon.

I, of course, paid him all the Moorish compliments I could think of, and then tea arrived, brought on a silver tray. Si Ali, the secretary, turned up at tea-time, and approaching his Highness bowed and kissed the hem of his garment, then seating himself on the edge of the divan made tea for us. Conversation went on swimmingly, now and then interrupted by some member of his Highness's household, who would enter, and bowing down kiss the hem of his garment, as Si Ali had done, and perhaps delivering a message or note.

We discussed all manner of European affairs—with which Moulai Mahommed is well acquainted—nor did Moorish politics escape discussion, and in my various conversations during my fortnight's stay at Wazan I learnt much from his lips as to the state of Morocco, its Sultan, &c. He spoke always without reserve, though he was careful to regulate his expressions so as not to offend either myself as an Englishman, or to speak anything but praise about his Sultan, with whom he is on terms of great friendship.

At nightfall the kubbah was illuminated, the Shereef being particularly (and justly) proud of his new fountain-candelabra, which he told me had been made from his own design. Large brass candlesticks, three or four feet in height, were stood about the place, some bearing one light, some half a dozen or more. The effect was very beautiful, and what with the tea and a delicious pervading scent of incense it did not require much to make one believe oneself to be in the land of the Arabian Nights. About seven I rose and made adieu to my host for the night. He was most friendly, and again thanked me for coming to see him.

On my return to my kubbah, to which I was escorted by slaves bearing lanterns, I found dinner

awaiting me, sent up already cooked from his Highness's kitchen. He had apologized during my visit that
afternoon for his cooks, telling me he had no cook
who understood European cooking. However,
dinner was very excellent, especially some devilled
fowl, with a hot sauce. Tea succeeded dinner, the
tray, tea-things, etcetera, being sent direct from the
palace. Slaves brought me in each dish, and, waiting till it was finished, or I had eaten enough, carried
it away again. Dinner finished, a large bouquet of
lovely flowers, Neapolitan violets and orange blos-
soms, was brought me in a vase, and placed beside
my divan, set in a slightly raised archway at one end
of the kubbah.

I then asked the slaves to enter, and some half-
dozen turned up, bringing gimbris with them ; a
second brew of tea was quickly made, more candles
lit, and we passed a very pleasant musical evening.
From the slaves I learned many interesting facts
about the tribes near Wazan and about the life of
the Shereef himself.

The following morning I again spent two or three
hours with the Shereef, and he was kind enough to
tell me that he was organizing a hunt for me for the
following day, at which he himself promised to be
present ; so early next morning we were off a-hunting.
It was a glorious day, and the long file of hunters,
guards, soldiers, and courtiers, formed a striking
picture. We "met" in the soko, and it was only then
that I heard that the Shereef himself was too ill to
accompany me. He had been suffering from cold,
which had increased during the night. However, the
whole of his household and several of his relations,

gorgeously equipped and mounted, came out. We
passed through the valley below the town, and soon
emerged into the open country. Here the greyhounds and other dogs of all degree were let go, and
the beaters—some two hundred—spread out in line.
Two or three good runs after hares were succeeded
by a magnificent galop after a jackal, during which
I got a nasty fall into a nullah, which I had not seen,
as the thick brushwood completely concealed it. At
first I was very much stunned, as the horse in his
struggles had kicked me on the head and arm. There
was general consternation amongst the huntsmen,
and a Shereef, the leader of the hunt, a cousin of
Moulai Mahommed's, was quickly on the spot. I was
still lying on the ground, dizzy, when he arrived.
He dismounted, and seizing my hand, said, "You are
not killed? you are not badly hurt?" I just found
breath enough to answer, "What, in the holy city
of Wazan—impossible!" This made a great impression on the crowd around me. I was quickly
mounted once more, and at my express wish the
hunt was continued. We soon entered the tribe-lands
of the Beni M'Sara, and after leaving Wizan about
four hours reached Ain Zorah, a large village of that
tribe. Near the village are some ruins, probably the
remains of an ancient Shereef's palace. At this spot,
too, there is a stream of beautiful clear water, rising
from a spring, which flows through and irrigates
some very fine gardens, the property of the house of
Wazan. Our sport was very good all the time, and
even close to the village we obtained several hares,
and a run or two after jackal. Turning more to the
north, we passed out of the Beni M'Sara tribe and

entered Zoua, a small unimportant tribe, and passing
over a corner of their lands, entered Ghruneh, where
we had tea at a large village, situated at the summit
of some strange volcanic hills. The sheikh and
people were very kind, and told me that I was the
first European who had visited this stronghold of
theirs. This led me to ask the reason why Christians
—or rather Europeans—are not allowed to visit their
country. They told me that it was not because of
the difference of religion, as is generally believed, but
because they feared that every Christian who entered
the country would return some day with an army at
his back.

Four hours' ride brought us to Wazan about nightfall. I was at once ushered in before the Shereef,
who told me he had spent a miserable morning, as
he had heard by messenger of my accident. However,
I again said that I was scarcely hurt at all, and that
any dangerous effects would be warded off by the
sanctity of the holy ground I was on. My head had
a lump like a turnip on one side, and was extremely
sore ; however, with cold-water bandages, &c., I
managed to reduce the swelling and so lessen the
pain. My left arm too was rather cut and bruised,
but a few days later I was quite recovered.

I spent the following morning with his Highness,
who had summoned two sheikhs from the Beni M'Sara,
to meet me. I never saw such a look of surprise
as these men gave when on my entrance Moulai
Mahommed rose and shook hands with me. They
expected, I think, to see me go down on my knees,
as the Moors themselves do, and kiss the hem of his
garment. We then talked over my proposed visit to

the Beni M'Sara, and these two sheikhs of the tribe promised to protect me with their lives. This trip came off a few days later, and I visited many villages in their country; but, as I saw nothing of great interest, I do not think it worth while to give a detailed account of it.

A few words, however, on the tribe itself.

The Beni M'Sara are tall men, for the most part very fair, blue eyes and yellow beards being the general rule. They have a pleasant way of speaking, and in all my dealings with them I found them most kind and hospitable, infinitely preferable to the town or plain Moors. In stature, too, they far surpass any of the lowland tribes, being perfectly built and of wonderful presence. I have seen ideal Lohengrins amongst the wild hillsmen. In habits they are much cleaner than their brethren of the towns, bathing in the rivers, and most particular about their dress, which is very picturesque. It consists of a brown jelaba, or cloak, richly embroidered in coloured silk, while an embroidered leather strap covered with silk tassels is slung over one shoulder, supporting a carved wooden or painted leather powder-flask, or a brass powder-horn, as well as a dagger: In their hands they carry long-barrelled, flint-lock guns, while round their closely-clipped heads they wind their scarlet and gold, or blue and gold cloth gun-cases. By profession they are robbers, not the class that shoot from behind hedges, but who organize bands and steal the cattle and women of the neighbouring tribes.

This women-stealing often leads to pitched battles between the tribes. All the mountaineers live more or less debauched lives, and, not paying taxes, are richer, and therefore work less than most of the Moors. The result is that they have more time to waste and spend with their women. They seldom marry, as robber-bands are continually stealing women from the tribes round, who are put up for sale and bought by the highest bidder. They are then trained to dance, and wonderful nautches are performed of an evening in the long-rooms of the mountaineers' houses. I have on several occasions been present at these festivities, nor are they in any way unwholesome. The women are dressed in gorgeous clothing, principally noticeable for gold embroidery, while strings of beads hang round their necks, and bracelets and anklets bedeck their wrists and feet respectively. Their hair is worn in long plaits, and bound over the forehead with silk scarves and chains of coins. Were the dance a little more graceful, nothing could be imagined more charming than these mountain ballets. The women keep their faces unveiled before the assembled men, nor when I was present was any attempt made to conceal their beauty from my eyes. They are far better treated than the wives of the town Moors, and though never married to the men, they continue to live with one man only, who zealously guards them from all evil. They never seem to regret being kidnapped from their native haunts, and no doubt they are far better looked after amongst the new tribe, where, instead of drudgery, they spend their time idly, and under no great restraint, having the best of everything. The great sign that clearly shows that this system is not one that materially degrades or injures the tribe is the

fact that of all the Moors they are the most trust-
worthy, the most hospitable to friends, the bravest in
battle, the finest built, and most healthy. Nor does
their moral nature seem to have suffered, for in conversation they are discreet, and the usual topics might
be freely spoken in an English drawing-room, which
cannot be said of the town Moors.

I did not return to Wazan till after nightfall, but
I was in time to witness a curious ceremony only
practised, I believe, now in very remote parts of the
country.

Moulai Larbi, a brother of Moulai Mahommed,
was lying seriously ill in his house at Wazan. The
people therefore gathered together about ten o'clock
with lanterns and music, and forming into procession
at the top of the town proceeded to his house. All
the road they kept forming into circles, in which they
would remain some minutes, all crying out, " Allah,
Allah, Allah."[1] Then the circle would be broken up,
and once more they would make a move towards the
house. On reaching the garden they took up their
stand there, and all night long cried in this way to
God to preserve their great saint. An unpleasant
and noisy cure.

The following day I spent in exploring the town.
There is not a great deal to see, though the gate and
tower of the mosque are fine. There are, of course,
no Europeans in Wazan, but a certain amount of
Jews reside there, amongst whom there reigns supreme
their deity "dirt."

The bazaars are of no great extent, though the
jelabs and haiks manufactured on the looms of

[1] " God, God, God."

Wazan are renowned for softness and fineness throughout the whole country.

I often visited these looms, and was struck by
their resemblance to the hand-looms of North Ire-
land ; in fact, they are almost identical. In the
bazaars I managed to pick up some curios. Articles
of mountaineers' dress, daggers, and a beautiful
Hispano-Moorish sword, with a blade by Andrea
Farara. This I purchased for three dollars (12s.).

I have spoken already of the surroundings of
Wazan, so that I need only mention here that with
the exception of Sheshouan I have seen no town in
all Morocco more romantically situated.

An amusing incident happened at court that afternoon. A man was being received in audience by his
Highness, but as the Shereef was engaged in talking
to me the man had to stand waiting for an hour or
more. At last the Shereef spoke to him, and kept
him in conversation some time. All the while the
man seemed to be in a desperate hurry to be gone.
At last Moulai Mahommed noticed this, and asked
him the reason.

" Ah, my lord," said the man, falling on his knees,
" before I left my home I put my supper on the fire
to cook, and now, alas! I have been over an hour,
and it will be all burnt up."

The Shereef laughed heartily at the man's distress,
but at the same time commanded a dinner to be sent
him from the palace kitchens.

A hunt had been ordered for the following day,
but the huntsmen arrived too late to make a start.
I was with Moulai Mahommed when at length they
turned up.

"You are late," he said.

"Sidi,"[2] commenced the spokesman ; but Moulai Mahommed interrupted him. Turning to his slaves he said,—

"We will hunt to-morrow instead. Put the huntsmen and hounds in prison. We will thus make sure of their being in time."

His order was immediately carried out.

I visited the market the following morning, with an escort of the Shereef's men, not for fear of danger, but as his guest I was surrounded with stringent rules of etiquette. Though the Soko was not five minutes' walk from my house I was told to ride, as it would be *infra dig.* to appear on foot.

I made a few purchases in the soko, but there was not much worth buying. I was treated with the greatest respect by the hordes of mountaineers, to whom a European was a novelty. This respect, however, was but reflected glory, as it was only on account of my being a guest of their great saint that the usual curses—or, perhaps, rougher treatment— were not showered upon me.

To such an extent did my friendship with Moulai Mahommed increase that this very morning he took me to see his wife's garden—strictly private, and not even visited by any of the court.

The garden is small, enclosed by high walls, but beautifully laid out. On every side are water-tanks, while roses bloom in great luxuriance.

At the end of this garden is his house, a curious irregular building of some size. So afraid was he that I might catch a glimpse of his wife, that heavy rugs

[2] "My Lord."

were hung over all the windows on the outside, though I saw one gently pushed aside, so as to leave a chink large enough to peep through. Though, of course, I did not see the lady, yet I doubt not she saw me.

O Eastern exaggeration ! At a meeting of the court one day a travelled Moor—he had served on a Spanish man-of-war to learn navigation—was telling stories of his travels. He had been to the West Indies, and had there visited three islands—Ceylon, Herat, and Smyrna ! He had also ascended the rock of Gibraltar, and gazing through the telescope there had distinguished—he acknowledged in the far distance—Paris, Tangier, and America. Being Friday there was a large assemblage at the court, all the functionaries being present. I arrived early, and was told to sit next to the Shereef on the blue and white cushions at the end of the divan. About ten o'clock the levée began ; the various members of his household, &c., on entering, bowed to his Highness, then, approaching with lowered head, dropped on their knees, and kissed his cloak. He took no notice whatever of the people, continuing his conversation with me, or with others, as though no new arrival was doing him homage. Some twenty Moors having assembled, they seated themselves on the various divans, and conversation became general.

Black slaves, all dressed in white, then entered, some bearing the tea-tray, cups, &c., while one carried a covered silver brazier of fine workmanship, in which burned incense. This was handed round, each in his turn holding out his flowing robes over the sweet-scented fumes. The incense burned in Morocco is exceedingly nice ; it is called by the Moors " oud," and is not a manufactured article, but the fragrant wood of some tree, though no doubt it passes through some process before being ready for burning.

After the incense long-necked silver bottles were brought round, from which scent was squirted all over us, rose and orange water, according to desire. The next item in the programme was tea.

I was the principal topic of conversation, and his Highness, on introducing me to the various Moors, was most flattering. Court lasted for two hours or so, and then broke up. In the afternoon I visited the garden of Sidi Hadj Absalam, the father of Moulai Mahommed, containing a beautiful tank, full of clear water, which swarms with gold-fish. When I had visited this spot two years before there had been a fountain of marble and tiles in the centre of the pond. This I noticed had now disappeared. I asked the reason of one of the guards who accompanied me, and he told me that on Sidi Hadj Absalam's visit a year before he had brought a clockwork model steamboat, which had damaged itself by knocking up against the fountain, whereupon his Highness had ordered it to be removed. At one end of the tank is a pretty bathing-house, flanked with Moorish horseshoe arches, with tiled floor and painted doors. In another part of the garden grew the most wonderful violets of all varieties, collected by the Shereefa, the English wife of Sidi Hadj Absalam, from various countries. Never have I seen such a wonderful display of blossom in violets, for

U

the cool shade and plentiful supply of water rendered the spot a most suitable one for their luxuriant growth. The garden is of great extent, or rather the park adjoining it is, and beautifully wooded with olives and orange-trees.

Having by this time been at Wazan ten days, I proposed to the Shereef that I ought to be leaving. He would not hear of it, and laughingly ordered his soldiers to imprison me if I attempted to go. On his pressing me, I decided to stay a few days longer.

The day I left he gave a great hunt. We started from Wazan before sunrise, and after two or three hours' ride, through groves of trees and over mountains, we breakfasted on the summit of a high hill overlooking Ajin, a town of Ghruneh. The ride out was delightful. The trees were not sufficiently far apart to allow our party to keep together, with the result that whichever way one looked the glades were filled with men on horse and on foot, some leading greyhounds, some armed with guns.

I rode with the Shereef, surrounded by his foot body-guard, armed with a diversity of European rifles. His Highness, not yet having quite recovered his health, was mounted on a mule, while his horse was led behind him, in case he desired to change. The harness of the mule, as is customary all through Morocco, was simple in the extreme; but the horse was bedecked with gold and crimson, the heavily embroidered breastplate being fastened to the saddle by a buckle of beautiful workmanship, studded with emeralds. The trappings of their horses are almost the only show the Moors allow, as any personal decoration is considered unorthodox.

After breakfast, which had been cooked on the spot by men sent on for the purpose, we visited the town of Ajin, killing a dozen or so hares *en route*. Ajin is the town at which all the Jews who die in Wazan are buried, as their unholy bodies are not allowed to pollute such sacred ground.

The whole town turned out to welcome his High-ness, and we visited the Shereef's gardens, groves of oranges, in which our camp was pitched. In the afternoon hunting was continued, and we had one or two grand gallops after jackal. On our return I dis-mounted and shot, killing several hares, and a few brace of partridges. His Highness's professional shot was out, a handsome young mountaineer, who, with a gun, the barrel alone of which was five feet two inches in length, scarcely missed a partridge, bringing down the driven birds in beautiful style. Altogether the hunt was a great success, as indeed it ought to have been, as we had some 300 beaters, as well as several hundred men on horseback. What the bag was I do not know, but twenty-seven hares were brought into camp, and I think as many again must have been killed, which were either torn to pieces by the hounds, or concealed by the Moors.

His Highness gave me an opportunity of witness-ing his splendid shooting with a small-bore rifle. As we were resting for lunch, under the shade of the tent, he ordered a man to stand up at about thirty paces, and to hold up flat, round, Moorish loaves of bread—about six inches in diameter. This the man did, and his Highness, without a trace of nervous-ness, at the risk of hitting the man's hand, put bullet after bullet through the bread. Nor did the man who held the bread appear nervous, probably he had often done it before, and knew the certainty of the Shereef's aim.

That evening I parted from his Highness. I rode towards Wazan with him for half an hour or so on his road, then, as the sun was setting, and I was some way from my camp, which I had forwarded on, I dismounted, and, giving my horse to a slave, walked towards the Shereef. He was most kind and friendly, holding my hand, and begging me to come back again whenever I could.

"You will be always welcome," he said. "Let me know when you are coming, and I will have everything prepared for you. Good-bye, and may the peace of God be with you !"

I thanked him as best I could, and stood while he rode on. Ten yards away he turned to and called out,—

"Good-bye, and remember when you are in far-away lands you have a friend in Wazan."

He then turned his mule's head towards his home. For some minutes I stood watching him with feelings of regret at parting from a Moor so different to the usual specimens one comes across, and who had been so kind to me, not only in his hospitality, but in the handsome rugs he had insisted on my accepting.

I mounted my horse and galloped to my camp with an escort of ten soldiers, who were told off to see me safely to my tents.

On arriving at the village in which they were pitched, I was met by the Makaddan of the place, who welcomed me, bringing me food for myself, my men and beasts.

The Shereefs of Wazan are probably by far the most direct descendants of the Prophet Mahommed in the world, tracing their genealogy, without one hitch, from father to son as far as Idrees, who was the grandson of Mahommed. The power that these potentates possess, not only in Morocco, but in Oran, Algiers, and even Tunis and Tripoli, in the Great Sahara as far as Timbuctoo, and amongst the wild Berber tribes of the mountains of North Africa, is immense. In fact, in the neighbourhood of Wazan, and amongst all the mountaineers, their power is far greater than that of the Sultan himself. The Beni M'Sara, amongst whom the Shereef's word is law, never acknowledge the Sultan at all, all their devotion being centred in the princely house of Wazan.

As is the case with the Sultans of Morocco, no authentic history remains of the House of Wazan, though one name stands pre-eminently before all others, that of Moulai Abdullah Shereef, who beautified, almost founded, the city of Wazan, and whose holy and charitable life renders him the patron saint of that place; so much so, in fact, that a Wazani never does anything without mentioning his name. If one knows the name Moulai Abdullah Shereef, it is almost all the Arabic one requires in Wazan. The town contains his shrine, which of course I have not seen, though I was hard pressed by one of my men to visit it in disguise, as it is one of the most magnificently decorated shrines in Morocco. However, I would not do so, as, possessing such a kind friend in Moulai Mahommed, I would do nothing that would wound his feelings, as such a visit doubtless would do were rumours of it brought to his ears.

The later history of the house of Wazan, and of its present head, Sidi Hadj Absalam, father of Moulai Mahommed, is a strange one. His Highness fell in love with and married an English lady. There can be no doubt that the act on the part of the lady in question was a rash one, but I believe most fully that she was in love with him at the time. He must then, though of very dark complexion, have been an exceedingly handsome man, and, allowing for the romance of the affair, and the influential position of the Shereef, I can quite understand the lady marrying him. The ceremony was performed at the British Legation by the then Minister, Sir John Drummond-Hay. Many severe criticisms have been passed upon the lady since that day, and I think her marriage was strange enough to justify criticism, but her life since she allied herself with the Prince has been one of hard work, of unselfishness, of patience, and latterly, I regret to say, of sorrow. Far be it from me to enter into private details, but it is just possible that a few words may render more clear the whole case, and do away with prejudices and misunderstandings that have been circulated by some of our newspapers.

That Miss Keene loved her husband there can be no doubt, and the first few years of her married life passed happily. Everything seemed to be going smoothly ; two sons were born to her, but in some way Sidi Hadj Absalam came under bad influence, and ever since then has been on the downward road. He separated from his wife and took to drink. He became low and degraded in his tastes, but it is only lately that affairs came to a climax, when, in spite of deeds signed to the contrary, he publicly married a

native girl of low position. How the Shereefa bore
these years of hardship, no pen of mine can describe.
While receiving ill-treatment from her husband, her
every act watched by spies, fearing even poison in her
food, she was visiting the sick, nursing patients with
small-pox, and vaccinating members of households
where inmates were already dying of the disease.
Nor did she confine her good works to Tangier.
Wazan knows and loves her. In the impenetrable
regions of the Riff her name is reverenced, and in
Oran and Tlemcen the natives are her staunch friends.
Her two step-sons, Moulai Larbi and Moulai Mahommed, at Wazan, are on the most friendly terms
with her, and her conduct in not attempting to influence her husband toward her own sons in preference
to her step-sons, is clearly shown by the fondness they
bear her.

Her position in Tangier of late can be imagined,
especially when the Shereef publicly, with great re-
joicing, took to himself another wife. Her funds were
stopped by her husband, and, with a body worn out
with anxiety and sorrow, she left Tangier, to take up
her abode in Oran, where the Moors take her part
against that of her husband, and where her noble
and self-sacrificing life is better appreciated than in
Tangier.

Should these words meet the eye of Madame de
Wazan, I am sure she will forgive my writing them,
when I tell her I do so out of regard for her, and in
justification of a noble woman who has been sadly
misunderstood and maligned. That her sons will
inherit her character and moral strength is one of the
few hopes that exist for a future for Morocco.

There is no character better known, or more despised, amongst the Europeans at Tangier than Sidi Hadj Absalam, whose excesses have reached such a pitch as to render his presence, except in his official position, impossible at the various Legations. Very different he is from his religious and kindly son, Moulai Mahommed, whom I number among my best friends in Morocco.

The day after leaving Wazan I went only a short march, as my horse was tired with the previous day's hunting, I therefore pitched my camp just beyond the mountain gorge of M'Mzoda, in an olive grove near the house of Kaid Abdul Malek. The woods were full of mountaineers, Beni M'Sara and Gruneh men, who were paying an official visit to the Kaid. The presence of these fine fellows gave the place a still more picturesque look, and in the evening we all sat round a great bonfire, strumming the gimbri and telling tales. They asked me about railways, never of course having seen such a thing ; and when I explained that they might accomplish the journey from Fez to Tangier (160 miles) in four hours, instead of as many or more days, one said,—

"Yes, but that is by telegraph, not by train."

I did not start early the next day, as I wished to see the last of my mountaineer friends, so made another short march, camping at a village about two hours the Wazan side of Alcazar, where I shot, obtaining several brace of partridges. The following day I passed through Alcazar, then, instead of keeping to the main road, turned to the left and made my way to Tangier viâ Gibel Habib. Nothing, however, of interest happened during my journey back to that town, which I accomplished in three days' good travelling over now dry roads from the first village I stopped at after Alcazar, where I had heard the startling news of a British naval demonstration in Tangier bay. One Arab advised me to return to Wazan. " You are safe there," he said, " with the Shereef, but in Tangier you will be killed ; for the Moors of Audjera have swum out in the night, with their guns in their mouths, and captured eleven of your men-of-war and killed the admiral." However, I doubted the news, and continued my journey. I had spent a most pleasant four weeks in my tour, and shall ever look back with pleasure to my visit to Moulai Mahommed at Wazan, a visit I mean to repeat upon the first available opportunity.

CHAPTER II.

MY RIDE TO SHESHOUAN.[1]

I DO not know whether it was merely from love of
adventure, or from curiosity to see a place that, as

Sheshouan.

far as is known, has been only once before looked
upon by Christian eyes, that I made up my mind to

[1] A considerable part of this chapter is republished from
Blackwood's Magazine through the kindness of Mr. William
Blackwood.

attempt to reach Sheshouan, a fanatical Berber city situated in the mountainous district of Northern Morocco, between the large tribe-lands of Beni-Hassan and the Riff. But whatever was my first impulse, this helped to bring me to a decision, the very fact that there existed within thirty hours' ride of Tangier a city into which it was considered an utter impossibility for a Christian to enter. That such a place can exist, seems almost incredible to those whose sole experience of Morocco is based on the luxurious Tangier hotels, and the more than semi-civilization of that town.

My mind once made up, it did not take long to prepare myself for my journey ; and on a Friday of July in last year (1888) I might have been seen purchasing in the native Tangier shops the articles of clothing that were needed for my disguise, for any attempt to proceed thither in European dress must prove unsuccessful. The costume that I chose consisted of the white long shirt and baggy trousers of the Moors, a small crimson silk sleeveless jacket, the tarboosh or fez, and a jelaba or white-hooded cloak that envelops one from one's knees to one's head. Having successfully purchased these articles, my next business was to send for a boy, by name Selim, who lived in Tangier, but who was a native of Sheshouan and had previously been my servant. An hour later he came, looking very thin and down on his luck ; I told him of my idea, and found him, much to my surprise, ready for a comparatively small sum of money to accompany me, and act as guide. I forthwith sent him into town, where he hired two mules with burdas or Moorish pack-saddles, which were to be at my

hotel at two o'clock the following morning. I then
packed my luggage, a not very tedious proceeding, as
it consisted merely of a small red leather native bag,
which I wore slung over my shoulder, containing a
toothbrush, a revolver, twenty-five rounds of cartridges,
a few sheets of writing-paper, a pencil, and fifty
cigarettes. Beyond this I only took a blanket, which
was spread over the rough pack-saddle.

About three the next morning we left, and arrived
at Tetuan, our first stage, distant from Tangier some
forty-five miles, in about ten hours.

The journey from Tangier to Tetuan cannot be
called one of extreme interest, though the latter part
of the way, where the road leads one between the
great mountains, swathed in forest and torn by
torrents, is very fine. In fact all through Morocco,
except the road I pursued the following day, and the
valley of the Atlas mountains, there is not much that
can surpass the Tetuan valley in grandeur of scenery.
For the first half of the way the road is dull and uninteresting, passing over low, undulating hills, destitute
of trees, nor is it until one reaches the slopes of the
hill on the summit of which is situated the well-known
Fondak, which forms the half-way resting-place for
caravans, that things improve. The view from this
spot is fine.

Here one always makes a halt for luncheon if one
is making the through journey in one day, and for
the night, if one is spreading it out over two. I have
often pitched my tents at this romantic spot, and a
fine camping-ground it made too, as there was abundance of wood for a camp fire, and the wild cries of
the jackal at night added to the romance of the scene,

making me, as I lay in my tent, almost think that I was back on the Ghauts of India again. The path after leaving the Fondak proceeds along the pass, and finally descends steeply to the level of the river below. This descent usually takes an hour more to accomplish, and rough work it is, as on all sides the path is blocked by great boulders of rock and stone.

Descended to the level of the river, the road improves, and, until one reaches Tetuan, is in good condition. In summer, and even in spring, nothing is more beautiful than the view here, the river with its banks crimson with gay oleanders, the cool shaded mountains, and the white town of Tetuan itself, half blocking one end of the valley, and beyond that the blue Mediterranean.

My first journey to Tetuan I shall never forget. We left Tangier about mid-day on the 1st of January, 1887. Our party consisted of Mr. and Mrs. T. Ingram, Jack Green and myself. We had sent our camp on ahead the day before, under orders to pitch at the Fondak, distant from Tangier only some five hours' ride.

It was a blazing hot day and accordingly we were all arrayed in the lightest of costumes.

We had not proceeded very far when T. discovered that his spaniel was missing, and rode back to fetch it, saying he would overtake us anon. Shortly before dark, between five and six, we began the ascent of the Fondak hill, all rather tired with the exertion of packing our camp off the day before, and the usual worry of a departure, besides which we had been shooting along the road, a tiring process under the hot sun. The idea of reaching the camp in a few minutes was

most cheering, but when we arrived at the level
ground no tents were to be seen. Meanwhile darkness set in.

We proceeded to the Fondak, and inquired of the
Arabs if they had seen our camp. "Yes," they said,
"it has gone on to Tetuan."

Here we were in pitch darkness in the wild mountain pass, half starved, and to add to our discomfiture,
the thermometer fell suddenly and a frost set in. T.
was nowhere to be seen, evidently he had lost his way.
We took a few moments to consider matters, and came
to the conclusion that at all costs we must push on.

Luckily there was a moon, but even with its aid the
path down the boulder-strewn mountain side was
anything but pleasant.

For hours we toiled on. The moon had set, we
had no lights, and the cold was so intense that we
were obliged to walk and lead our horses to keep any
warmth in our bodies. About half-past ten, after ten
and a half hours in broiling sun and frost, we came
upon our camp, not in Tetuan certainly, but still no
great distance from it. We found dinner ready, and
our men in a state of terror, as it is not at all safe to
travel over the Tetuan road by night.

Still T. did not turn up. We hoped that he had
remained in Tangier, but though we spoke lightly of
it, we were all very anxious.

About four in the morning he arrived, having been
all the time on the road. He had lost his way, but
finally found a guide, who led him across the country
to the Fondak, in pitch darkness, and brought him
safely into camp, with his horse dead lame. Our men
caught it well for their disobedience in pitching our

camp in the wrong place, and a few days later we parted with Larbi, the headman, who was to blame for this and many other misdemeanours, and gave the charge of the whole camp into Antonio's hands, a decided improvement. Nor had we any trouble for the rest of the journey, which lasted two months.

Tetuan itself is a picturesque town, though, like most

Scene at Tetuan.

Moorish cities, there is not much to be seen therein. Probably its inhabitants number some twenty-five to thirty thousand. In this city are found the finest houses in Morocco, as it was here that many of the Moors driven from Andalusia took up their residence, building themselves palaces according to their own hearts.

These houses are built round a square patio, and are

generally two storeys in height, the upper storey possessing a balcony, on to which the rooms open. The patios are paved in marbles and tiles, and possess beautiful fountains, from which water is ever gushing. Palm and orange trees grow within, rendering the whole more a garden than a courtyard.

The city was taken by the Spaniards under Marshal O'Donnell in 1859, after a severe struggle with the brave natives, who, badly armed as they were, held it and the surrounding country against the invading foes for some months.

However, it fell at last, and Ceuta was added to Spain, while an indemnity of four millions of pounds was paid them. This indemnity has probably been one of the best strokes of luck the Sultan ever had, as the Spaniards, knowing that otherwise it would probably never be paid, seized the custom-houses, levying a ten per cent. ad valorem duty on exports and imports. This succeeded well, and a few years ago the four millions were realized. The Sultan, however, keeps on the duty, himself drawing the ten per cent. now, and so enriching himself to the extent of some hundreds of thousands a year.

To return to "my ride to Sheshouan," on my arrival in Tetuan I put up at a small native fondak, or caravanserai, full of mules, camels and vermin, where I spent the night in my disguise.

The following morning we were up before dawn, and, fording the river near Tetuan, proceeded on our way. As soon as it was daylight, we began to pass Moors coming into town with vegetables and wood, laden on donkeys ; and I was pleased to find that my disguise was sufficiently satisfactory as to lead them to

assume that I was an Arab, and to salute me with
the salutation, never offered to a Christian—"Salaam
'alikûm." After about two hours on the road, we
passed through the village of Zenat, perched high on
the mountain side, a pretty, picturesque little place,
half hidden in its groves of olives and oleanders, with
tiny streams and miniature waterfalls in every direction, and rocks clustered with maidenhair fern. When
we had left the village behind, the road led us along
the mountain-side at a great distance above the valley
beneath, till, an hour later, we descended by a winding path, forded the river, and proceeded up the valley
on the left-hand bank. Up to this point the country
had been fertile and well cultivated, and the fields full
of men and women gathering in the harvest ; but now
we had entered the country of the wild Beni-Hassan
tribe, and the aspect entirely changed; instead of
fields, nothing but steep mountains, covered with ar-
butus and other stunted growth, being visible, except
ahead of us, where the great bare rocky peaks of the
Sheshouan mountains stood out boldly against the
morning sky.

The next object that we passed was a ruined fondak,
or caravanserai, not unlike that which exists halfway
between Tangier and Tetuan, but entirely deserted
and out of repair. It was near this fondak that my
first adventure befell me. We had been overtaken
by two Beni-Hassan tribesmen, who, I had noticed,
had scanned me very closely—far more closely than
I appreciated ; and I was not particularly pleased to

[2] This building is used as a fondak, though really it is the
tomb of Sidi Hadj Mahommed, whose head is buried at Tangier and body here,

X

suddenly discover these two, and a third, who was holding a chesnut horse, stationary about two hundred yards in front of me, engaged in conversation, and now and again turning in my direction. There was no other course than to proceed, which I did. On nearing them, the owner of the horse placed it across the road, completely blocking my way, while his two companions took up their position on either side. On my reaching them, one, seizing my bridle, told me I must go no further, while a second pulled me from my mule by my jelaba or cloak. I knew that if I uttered a sound my chance of reaching Sheshouan was at an end, so, grasping my revolver firmly under my cloak, for the double reason of having it ready in case of necessity and keeping it from the sight of my assailants, I remained dumb. My Arab boy proved himself on this occasion—as he did on several afterwards—to be quite worthy of the confidence I had placed in him, for, lying in a calm and collected manner, he asserted that I was a Moor from Fez.

"Why does he not speak?" asked one of the men.

"Is it likely a Moorish gentleman would speak to robbers who attack him on the road, and insult him by pulling him off his mule?" responded Selim; "but he will be revenged, for when the Sultan comes" (referring to the approaching visit of the Sultan to Tetuan), "he will come here and lay your country waste."

Thereupon the men, with a still incredulous look, relinquished their hold of me, and mounting once more, I proceeded on my way. An elevation having rendered us invisible to the tribesmen, we thought it as well to place a more satisfactory distance between ourselves and them, so whipped the mules into a gallop, and were soon some way ahead.

Turning a corner, we suddenly came upon a band of some twenty or thirty Beni-Hassani working by the roadside. These we passed without any difficulty, though the minute or two that we took to pass through them was scarcely a pleasant time, as I expected every moment to hear our first assailants shouting to them to arrest my progress. Then we again proceeded at a gallop over terribly open country; I say "terribly open"—for I felt sure that before many minutes were over I should need some place of concealment. We were crossing the high table-land that exists between the Zenat and Sheshouan valleys—an elevation that is entirely ignored on most of the maps of the country—and the only spot that would offer any cover was a stream, the banks of which were overgrown with oleanders. For this we at once made, and, entering the bed of the stream, I dismounted and hid myself amongst the shrubs, while Selim led the mules to a spot some little way further up the river.

By this time the three men who had first stopped me had reached the band we had seen at work, and informed them of their belief in the presence of a Christian; and as I had expected, a few minutes later some dozen Arabs appeared in sight, running along the path we had just travelled over. In five minutes they had found our mules, and were questioning Selim as to my whereabouts. From my hiding-place I could overhear sufficient of the conversation that passed between them.

" Where is the Christian ? " they asked.

" What Christian ? " said Selim.

" The Christian who was with you."

" There was no Christian with me."

" Who was with you ? "

" A Moor ; the son of Abdul Malek from Fez, who is going to Sheshouan to see some of his mother's people."

" Bring him here."

" I don't know where he is."

Then for a minute or two the talking was carried on in whispers, and I saw my boy and an elderly mountaineer leave the group and wander off engaged in conversation. A few minutes later I was dis-covered and marched forth from the river-bed to a large tree growing near by on the plain, where I found myself alone with a dozen or so wild-looking fellows. I knew that to deny I was a Christian was useless now, so I informed them at once that I was one, and that I was on my way to Sheshouan, hand-ing them meanwhile (much to my grief) some of my cigarettes. They seemed very much surprised at the calm way in which I took matters, and not a little amused ; and five minutes later, conversation was being carried on in an animated but amicable man-ner. Suddenly my boy appeared on the scene, and never in my life have I seen a face of greater sur-prise than he wore then, on finding me seated in the group of mountaineers, who a minute or two before had been telling him to bring me out from my hiding-place, presumably to kill me—and not only seated there, but apparently on the best of terms.

On my rising a few minutes later to proceed on

my journey, they begged me to go no further, assuring
me that if I were discovered I would for certain lose
my life, and that even their own people would kill
me if they detected that I was a Christian. I told
them that I had made up my mind to reach Sheshouan at any risk, and bade them adieu, shaking
hands with all of them, but closing my ears to their
ill-omened warnings.

We had soon left the watershed, and once more
the path led us along the steep mountain-side, the
new valley running almost due south, while that we
had left ran in the opposite direction. From where
we were now we obtained a glorious view, rivalling
any scenery I have seen in Morocco, with the exception of some of the valleys of the Atlas mountains,
which it much resembled. Thousands of feet into
the now sunset sky the great mountain of Sheshouan
reared its rocky crags ; while far below, purple in
the evening shadow, lay the wooded and cultivated
valley, with its rapid river turning and twisting here,
there, and everywhere like a thread of silver.

We were now at no great distance from Sheshouan,
so, concealing ourselves in the bushes, we awaited
the setting of the sun. As soon as he was down we
resumed our journey, and an hour later, in bright
moonlight, crossing the sharp ridge of a hill, came
suddenly upon Sheshouan, and found ourselves in
the soko, or market-place, situated outside the walls
of the town. Crossing the soko at a brisk trot, we
entered the town by the Bab-el-Sok, and, proceeding
through several streets, passed under a dark archway.
Here dismounting, we knocked at a door, which,
being opened, we entered the house of my guide's

parents.   In the dark they did not recognize me as a Christian, in fact it was not till some minutes later, when we had secured the mules in the patio of the house, and ourselves in a large bare room, that my boy confided in them.   They were not at all pleased to see me, but they knew as well as I did—and therein lay my safety—that my detection meant death to their son for bringing me, as well as to myself.   Half an hour later, having partaken of some food, and rested a little, for we had been sixteen hours *en route* from Tetuan, I left the house, and with Selim's father walked through the town.

Sheshouan, which is a large town covering more acreage than Tangier, and possessing seven mosques and five gates, is magnificently situated on the slope of the mountain, which rises from the town almost perpendicularly to a great height.   The houses are different from those of any other city in the country, as they do not possess the general flat roof, but are gabled and tiled with red tiles, which gives the place more the appearance of a Spanish than a Moorish town.   But what to the natives is the great attraction of Sheshouan is the abundance of water ; for issuing from caves far above in the mountain-side are three waterfalls, whose water is so cold that the natives use the expression that " it knocks one's teeth out to drink it."   I tasted it, and found it too cold to be pleasant drinking.   From the pool at the bottom of these three falls aqueducts carry the water to the numerous mills which are clustered there, after turning the wheels of which it continues its course to the many fruit-gardens for which Sheshouan is famous. After about two hours' walk in the town, we returned

once more to the house, where I was only too glad
to roll myself in my blanket and surrender my weary
body to sleep. All next day I lay in hiding. During
the afternoon we decided that my safest means of
leaving would be after dark in the disguise of a
woman, as that would render me almost entirely
hidden from sight under the enormous haik that
completely envelops womankind in Morocco.

About sunset my boy returned from purchasing
some fowls and eggs for supper, looking very much
upset and in tears. I was sorry to see this, for up
till now he had behaved splendidly, though his
mother had been in one long fit of hysterical crying
ever since I had arrived—a circumstance which was
not warranted to improve any one's spirits. Even
when I saw Selim in this state, I never suspected
anything was wrong, except that his spirits had
given way under the strain, and it was quite casually
that I asked him what was the cause of his
trouble.

"Oh, sir," he cried, "it is all up. Those Beni-
Hassan men have told that they have seen a Christian on his way to Sheshouan, and all the town is on
the alert to catch you."

I went at once to the tiny window and looked into
the street. It was full of men hurrying to and fro.
Twice I heard the question asked, "Have you seen
the Christian?" My prospects certainly did not
look golden; but nothing could be done for an hour
or so, till it was dark; and on an empty stomach
one can do very little, so I set to work and cooked
and ate my supper. I had not much appetite, but I
made a point of eating half a roast fowl and drinking

a large jugful of milk, meanwhile carefully considering my plans in my mind. First, I determined to
abandon the woman's disguise, as being of a suspicious
nature, and instead borrowed a torn and ragged
mountaineer's brown cloak.

Supper was over, and in half an hour more it

The Author in disguise.

would be sufficiently dark for me to leave. What a
wretched half-hour that was ! Selim was in tears, his
mother in hysterics, his father sulky ; in fact, the
only persons who kept up any show of spirits were
myself—and I confess that it was nothing more than
a mere " show " of spirits—and a man whose help
had been sought, a native of a mountain village some

hours distant, and who all through never lost his cheerfulness, though the risk of losing his own life, a risk that he was voluntarily running, was very great.

At last the half-hour was over, and all our plans completed. Mahommed, my new-found friend (and verily a friend in need), was to accompany me out of the town by the principal gate, thus hoping to excite less suspicion than if we attempted to escape by one of the less important and more obscure exits, while Selim was to proceed by another way and meet us outside the soko. The mules we left for the present, arranging for Selim's father to bring them early in the morning to our next hiding-place, the cottage of Mahommed, situated in a village some four hours distant.

My disguise was light and airy, far too light and airy for such a cold night, consisting as it did merely of a brown jelaba and a pair of slippers. Creeping quietly through the door, we left the house, and walked through the now crowded streets to the gate. Every now and again I felt an uncomfortable, creepy sensation, as I heard the hurrying natives saying to one another—and saying it once or twice even to my companion and myself, " Where is the Christian ? " " Have you seen the dog of a Christian ? " At the gate was a guard placed to stop me ; but in my disguise I passed them successfully and entered the soko, where men were passing to and fro on the look-out for me. Here, to avoid suspicion, we seated ourselves cross-legged on the ground, and remained sitting for several minutes, it seemed like an hour. While in this position a native came and seated himself next to me, and carried on a short conversation with my companion. Every moment I expected detection—it seemed an impossibility that I could escape. Then we rose and were once more *en route*.

Soon we had reached the spot where Selim was to have met us, but there were no signs of him. We sat down on some rocks and waited, but he did not come. Then Mahommed left me to search for him, and I was alone, but completely hidden among the ferns and stones. While he was away, a man passed me so closely that his jelaba touched my knees ; but he went on without perceiving me. A few minutes later Mahommed and Selim appeared, the latter having mistaken the trysting-place.

We at once set off at a brisk walk across country to Mahommed's cottage. For four hours and a half we walked in the cold night, over the most terrible ground. We had not been on our way half an hour when I slipped in crossing a stream, and got my shoes soaked with water, which rendered them impossible to walk in. From that moment, till we arrived at the cottage, I walked bare-legged and bare-footed, pushing my ankles, already raw from sunburning, through the sharp thorny bushes, till the blood was trickling down over my feet. At last we reached the village, and creeping from tree to tree, Mahommed reconnoitring ahead, we entered the cottage. I was at once taken to my hiding-place, a kind of cellar, but very clean, where, half an hour later, when I had bound up my legs in some strips of sacking, we ate a supper of native bread and goat's milk, and very good it was too. My kind friends then left me, and were soon slumbering in another part of the cottage—their snore reaching me even in my cellar. I felt better; though far from safe, yet I was out of Sheshouan. I opened my red-leather bag, and drew out some cigarettes; then rolling myself in my blanket, I lay and watched the blue smoke curl up and up till it was lost in the darkness. Never did I enjoy a cigarette so much as then, and were I a poet, I would have written an ode to that benefactor of mankind, Nestor Gianaclis. It was not long, however, before I fell asleep, worn out with the excitement of the day, and the long night walk; nor did I wake till late the next morning. My breakfast—bread and eggs and milk—was brought me at once, and I received the welcome news of the arrival of my mules.

Luck, however, was against me, for one of the very Beni-Hassan men who had accosted me on the road turned up in the village by some evil chance and recognized my beasts. However, Mahommed denied that they belonged to Christians; but the suspicion of the villagers was aroused, and again I was in great danger.

It had been our intention to proceed on our way when the sun set, but towards evening we discovered that the villagers were on the look-out for me, and that it would be unsafe to leave before the moon went down, about midnight.

That day and evening seemed very long, but Mahommed never lost his cheerful mien, and kept me interested by telling me stories of himself—how he was the head of a robber-band, and only a few months before had shot two rich Moors, whom he had robbed, and whose mules he had stolen. Never for a moment did I mistrust him, as I knew that, whatever he might be, his ideas of hospitality—the greatest virtue the Arabs possess—would render impossible any treachery. The only reason I can think of why he should have rendered me such services was his love of adventure, for he positively seemed to enjoy the risk he was himself running in saving me. There was no monetary reason in his acts; for on my parting from him the next day, he absolutely refused to take what I offered him, and it was with great difficulty that I persuaded him even to accept payment for the food, &c., I had partaken of in his house.

At last the moon went down, and accompanied by Mahommed I set out, again creeping from tree to tree and hedge to hedge, once even taking refuge in an empty stable, till the village and the guard around it were safely passed. Then Mahommed hid me in a clump of trees while he returned to the village, and, with Selim, brought out my mules. The cold was intense, in spite of its being July, and I felt cramped and sore indeed as I crouched down, not daring to move a muscle. So an hour passed, then my eyes were gladdened with the welcome sight of the men and mules. Selim and I at once mounted the beasts, while Mahommed walked ahead to show us the path. When dawn appeared we were well on our way, and an hour or two after sunrise had left almost all danger behind us. At the ruined fondak, which we reached after about eight hours' ride, Mahommed left us and turned back. Never did I grasp a hand to say good-bye with more kindly feelings than I did that of this stalwart, handsome

mountaineer, who had risked his own life and had
saved mine. I tried to thank him in fitting words,
but he stopped me, and said, "It is nothing. It is
nothing." Four hours later the white walls of
Tetuan were in sight; and thirteen hours after
leaving the village, tired and hungry, with blood-
stained legs and torn clothes, I passed through the
gates with a sigh of relief such as I have seldom
sighed, and felt myself—at last!—safe from all
dangers.

The following evening I arrived at Tangier, to
receive the hearty congratulations of my friends, and
a severe blowing up for risking my life in such an
unwarrantable way.

PART IV.

ABOUT THE MOORS.

CHAPTER I.

ABOUT THE MOORS.

I CAN think of no better way of ending my book in a manner to fill up the gaps that I have left through fear of diverging too far from the path of my various travels in Morocco than by a chapter on the inhabitants of this land of an African Sultan.

Let us take the life of one individual of each sex and briefly trace its existence.

The child is born, and is more or less fondly and carefully nursed by its mother. The children are never, except in the case of the death of the mother, sent out to nurse, as any but the maternal supply of "victuals" is considered harmful. Motherless babies are, however, sometimes fed by goats and sheep.

The little boy—we will take it he is so—on reach-

A Moorish lamp.

ing his third, fourth, or fifth year, is taken to the mosque with great rejoicings, where he is circumcised by the priest.   These circumcisions are often made the objects of great fêtes, and I have seen in Fez gorgeous processions passing through the street, the hero of the hour being the small youth, seated before his father on a mule or horse.

The boy's education, such as it is, begins now, and consists in his attending a school, where a thaleb, or schoolmaster, succeeds in beating into him a certain number of the verses of the Koran ; sometimes, if he is a youth of superior degree, he is taught to read and write.

These schools are supported (?) by Government, or rather are supposed to receive some minute sum annually, but what support they really get is from small sums of money and presents in kind brought by the scholars.

The education over, the boy sets about thinking of getting married, which usually take places when he reaches an age of between twelve and sixteen. Though the bridegroom elect is not supposed to see his bride before the wedding, he generally manages to do so, usually by hiding in a room when the bride elect calls upon his mother.

The young man wishing to marry despatches a friend to the father of the girl, who announces that so-and-so wishes to marry his daughter so-and-so. The father then asks the mother, who in turn asks the girl, and she very seldom refuses, nor if she did, would it probably prove effective.

The father then asks the ambassador how much his friend will give, which depends very much upon the circumstances of the parties, some men paying a dollar or less, and some fifty or sixty pounds. This money is supposed to pay the expenses of the trousseau, and of the marriage festivities, and also to soften a little the grief of the parents at parting from their daughter.

These preliminaries arranged, a month or so elapses before the marriage takes place. Seven days before the wedding-day the two principal characters in the coming ceremony begin to entertain, the bridegroom inviting all his male friends to partake of tea and listen to music in his house, while the bride's mother entertains all the ladies of her acquaintance in her residence. Day and night tea-drinking and music are carried on, till the seventh day arrives. Then the bride, decked in fine raiment, is placed on the back of a mule or donkey, herself completely covered by a box, or frame, draped with rich silks and embroideries. In this she is conveyed with music and lanterns to the house of her husband. Here the procession breaks up, the girl entering with her women friends and relations. She then proceeds to a room where her clothes are carefully arranged for her after her tiresome ride in the box, and she is seated on a divan. Tea is then served, after which the ladies retire, leaving the wife alone. Solitary she sits for some hours till midnight, when her husband, after being escorted round the town on a horse, also with music and lanterns, arrives.

The girl is seated closely veiled, but on her husband's entering, unveils herself. It would make a fine subject for a picture, the girl throwing her veil back and exposing a beautiful face to her lover's dazzled gaze.

Each time a man marries, this ceremony is gone through, though it is usually on a much finer scale for the first marriage. A man is allowed by the Koran four wives, but the number of slaves is not stated, and some of the richer Moors keep enormous harems. The rule, however, amongst the lower and middle classes is one wife and no slaves ; in fact, except in the case of rich men, it is the exception to find more than one woman in the household.

In time the man dies ; he is wrapped in white linen and laid upon a bier and borne by his friends and paid mourners with sounds of soft music to the cemetery, where he is buried. No coffins are used, which is no doubt a healthy custom in a climate like that of Morocco. The graves are very shallow, the body being seldom more than two or three feet below the ground.

The girl's life is easily sketched. She lives with her mother in the harem till she is of an age to marry. She has no education except in embroidery and making sweetmeats, though if she be a village girl she has to work hard in drawing water from the wells or grinding corn in the handmills. It is needless to describe her part in the marriage festivities, as I have already done so in sketching the man's life. After marriage she is shut up in a harem, and if her husband be a man of means, she never stirs outside ; though if he be a villager, she has her work cut out for her.

In a house I stayed in once in Mequinez, at one end of a large high room was a balcony communicating with nowhere except the room below, whence it was reached by a ladder. The reason for this balcony was easily divined. When the owner of the house went out he bundled his women up the ladder, then, taking the steps away, left them prisoners until his return.

Much has been said about the cruelty of this confinement, but it must be remembered that their women are, thank goodness, different to ours, and literally cannot be trusted for one moment away from their husband's eyes. The wife of one of the highest native officials of Tangier not many years back used to take advantage of her husband's leniency in allowing her to visit the Hummum, or baths, every Friday, to meet her various and many lovers. At last her plot was discovered, and she was publicly disgraced and divorced. I have seen numbers of cases amongst even my own men, in which, if their women are for a moment left by their husbands, they prove unfaithful, that is to say if they get the chance.

There is one tie that holds husband and wife together, the constant dread of one administering poison to the other. This habit of poisoning is terribly rife in Morocco, in fact is a thing of everyday occurrence, and as there is no medical knowledge of any sort, and no attempt at an inquest, it is never discovered.

In this way, too, the Sultan is said to remove his enemies. He invites (commands is more expressive of his invitations) his victims to tea with him. After receiving the poor fellow with all kinds of compliments, a cup of poisoned tea is handed him, and the victim dies in a few minutes or hours, according to the dose. The man knows perfectly well that he is to be poisoned, yet so great is his superstitious veneration towards his lord and master, that he does not think of disobeying his commands for one moment.

This extraordinary superstition crops up everywhere amongst the Moors. Though democratic to a great extent, they almost worship their Shereefs and Saints. What an amount of holiness is supposed to surround the family of Wazan cannot be imagined till one has seen how great and low crawl up to kiss the clothes of the Shereefs of that ilk. How every word they utter is listened to with breathless attention, and every opinion becomes a moral law. Religion and superstition are so mixed in the country that no Moor knows which is one and which is the other, and it is only by a careful study of the Koran that one can sift them. Were the pages of the Koran strictly kept to, the power of most of these Shereefs would disappear. Superstition is most apparent in the sacrifices which are still carried out by the Moors upon occasions; and again the awful rites of the Hamdouchis and the Aissouis more resemble Fetish than Mahommedan customs.

It is this love of the supernatural that instils into the minds of the people their fear of djins and all kinds of evil spirits. Every old ruin, every river, every cave, almost every mountain is haunted by some devil, whose intentions are bad.

I once asked a small boy far away in the interior if he had ever seen a djin. He said, "Yes, but only one. He was tall, about forty feet in height, with black horns and red hair, and the tail and legs of a goat."

Nor does superstition attain only to the supernatural, but there are many strange beliefs connected with animals. I remember once passing a drove of donkeys on the road. The Arab who was driving them made no attempt to keep out of my way. The donkeys were loaded with stones in paniers, and I got my shins severely barked. Having passed the donkeys I accosted the driver.

" Why," I yelled at him, " did you not drive your donkeys aside ? "

"I tried to," he answered, " but they knew you were a Christian, so wouldn't move."

I let him know I wasn't a Mahommedan before I left him. I think he would take care that his donkeys made way for the next European they met; and I could not get my hunting-crop mended till I got back to Tangier.

The Cadis (bishops) lay down the spiritual law and arrange divorce, while all civil cases come under the Kaids and their Caliphas.

Two laws of the Cadis are worth mentioning as being superstitions for which no reason can be gathered. First, that it is haram, i.e. sinful to whistle ; and, secondly, that if one breathes on one's food to cool or blow the flies away, it is necessary to remove all the part touched by one's breath.

As I have said elsewhere, medicine is at a very low ebb. A few charms, principally papers scrawled over with meaningless characters, or bags of salt and alum, or more commonly still the distended hand, are the sole means of preventing and curing sickness. Yet it must not be for a moment supposed that when medical aid is within reach of the Moors they do not take advantage of it, though it is very seldom that it is so within reach. The English Shereefa of Wazan has vaccinated some hundreds of men, women and children ; nor did the Moors prove ignorant of the results gained thereby, as it was soon apparent what

good effect the English lady's treatment had in preserving against the terrible small-pox that sometimes
rages in the country.

All sorts of incantations are used, one, almost
obsolete now, is worth mentioning. It is a cure for
unfaithfulness on the part of a husband. The wife
prepares him a dish of kooskoosoo, which, before being
eaten by the husband, has to be stirred at night with
the hand of an exhumed corpse laid over the lady's
knee while certain words are sung. Amongst the
Jews all sorts of filthy concoctions are used as cures,
probably with exactly the opposite results to what are
intended, except that the Jews are so used to filth
externally that a dose internally is ineffective altogether.

A disease that is common in Morocco is leprosy.
This ghastly complaint is still rife in the south, where
a whole city is put aside for the lepers. No cure is
attempted, and, of course, no attempt at one would be
successful. The victims do not seem to suffer much
pain with the complaint. The leper city contains
some thousands of inhabitants who can be seen in
every stage of the disease, from its first appearance
on their hands, feet or face, to limbless lumps of de-
caying flesh, which are by day laid out in the sun by
those less afflicted, and carried in again in the evenings
to shelter. The lepers are not allowed to enter the
city of Morocco, or to hold any contact with healthy
people, except in asking alms, which they receive in
long wooden spoons. They marry, and as far as I
could discover, the children are lepers, though the
disease does not usually show itself until they reach
an age varying from twelve to sixteen, by which time

they too are married. But to return to a pleasanter side of Moorish life and change the subject from disease and foul charms to a more lively topic.

In architecture there has never been a nation to

Corner in a Moorish house.

surpass the Moors. Not that any of their buildings show great power and force of conception, except from the exterior, rather the delicate tracery and exquisite colouring is typical of effeminacy and luxuriance. Yet where in the world can be seen a more

lovely specimen of architecture than the Alhambra.
Nor is the Alhambra the sole example that remains ;
the Giralda at Seville and more so its sister tower,
the Koutubia at Morocco City, untouched by restoration, are marvellous specimens of handicraft, while
the old palace at Saffi, on the Moorish coast, is still
very beautiful, even in its ruined state.   The great
gates at Mequinez, too, are splendid specimens of the
finest style of Moorish architecture, and I doubt not
that the interiors of the palaces at Morocco, Mequinez,
and Fez are full of wonderful courts and arcades.   The
exquisite arabesque in plaister, with its delicate tracery
and interwoven geometric designs, the carved painted
and bedombed wooden ceilings, show what an eye
for beauty existed and still exists to some extent
amongst the Moors.   This love of art, however, is
fast dying away, the painting has become coarser and
less skilful in design, and crudeness is setting its
stamp on all modern Moorish work.   There is no
better example to be found than in Rabat, the carpet
manufactory of Morocco.   Formerly carpets almost
as beautiful as those of Persia and the East were
manufactured there, but to-day the Moor prefers
strips of green Brussels to the exquisite blending of
colours displayed in their own country's rugs, to the
detriment of the trade.   The carpets manufactured
now are tawdry, full of aniline dyes, amongst which
magenta predominates, and of coarse texture.   Though
the old rugs can from time to time be procured, yet
they are very scarce.

The same can be said of the embroideries, though
in Rabat, Fez and Mequinez one can to this day find
exquisite pieces, yet the modern stuff which now floods

the Tangier market is of very inferior quality, and
made simply to supply the bazaars and the oily Jews
who keep them. The old gold embroidery on velvet
is fast dying out, and it is exceedingly difficult to
procure good specimens on which the gold will never
tarnish, though on the modern imitations it will be
black in a very short time. The best specimens of
these kinds of embroidery is to be found on the
" Haities," wall coverings of panels of velvet several
feet high arranged in the form of Moorish arches and
thickly encrusted with gold. These Haities can be
but rarely picked up, and are generally very dear,
though sometimes one has the luck of getting one for
next to nothing. I brought a fine specimen away
from Fez in February this year, for which I did not
give half the value of the weight of the silver-gilt
thread with which it is thickly embroidered, while the
ground-work is the most perfect silk velvet. In all it
has nine panels of velvet and silk, the three centre
ones of which are covered in embroidery.

The old Fez brocades, long since ceased to be manufactured, are both beautiful and rare, though we procured a considerable quantity of it at reasonable prices
during the same visit to Fez. The silver work of
Morocco is not to be compared with that of the East.
It is crude and rough and the silver itself impure. The
best specimens are found on swords and daggers. A
sword which his Majesty the Sultan was gracious
enough to present to me is rich in colour and silver
work, but on close examination the embossing of the
silver is rough, as also is the damasceening of the blade.
The great silver and silk tassels that belong to the
sword-belt are perhaps the finest part, though decidedly

barbaric. In the Atlas mountains, in fact amongst all
the Kabyles of North Africa, enamel is inlaid into the
silver, though the workmanship is in this case also
very rough. Large earrings set with precious stones
or glass big enough to be used as bangles in England
are common, while anklets of massive silver can here
and there be seen. The most common articles of
jewellery noticed by the traveller are necklaces of
coral, coins, amber-coloured beads and charms, and
clasps that fasten the women's dress, one worn over
each breast, the two joined by a chain. The fasten-
ings of these brooches is with a ring and pin, and in
form exactly resembles the Celtic brooches in the
British Museum and elsewhere. The wives of some
of the richer Moors wear crowns of gold and jewels,
but these are usually manufactured in Europe. The
Sultan's wives possess magnificent jewellery, diamonds
and emeralds in profusion, much of which has come
from Paris and Bond Street. The silver daggers of
the Moors are quite one of the characteristic sights of
the country, though individually they are seldom of
great beauty. However, collectors such as Kaid
Maclean and Mr. White, our Consul at Tangier,
possess many very fine ones, collected during a long
residence in the country. The native guns can be
arranged in three classes. The Sous guns are the
most beautiful of all, with ivory stocks inlaid with
coral and silver and behung with coins and charms,
the barrels also cased in silver. The Riff guns are of
dark wood generally undecorated, though sometimes
designs in silver wire and coral are found. The butts
of these Riff weapons are unlike the first class, the
Sous, or the third, the Tetuan guns. The butt

narrows down, while a thick piece of boxwood runs at right angles to the gun, and is pressed against the shoulder, giving the whole the appearance of a hammer. The Tetuan guns are more simple, though often inlaid. Tetuan is by far the largest gun manufactory in the country. All three varieties are flint-locks. The Moors are clever at basket-work, and the size of their straw hats, worn by women in Tetuan, is unequalled ; more like they are to carriage umbrellas than hats ; so wide in fact are the brims that they have to be supported to the crown by cords of wool or silk.

The Moors possess no agricultural instruments beyond the pick, the spade and the plough. The latter is of wood, and drawn by oxen, though I have seen a plough with a woman and a donkey harnessed side by side. There is nothing prettier in all Morocco than to watch the ploughman guiding say a camel and an ox, harnessed together in the plough, over the heavy soil. Behind and around him strut the egrets, picking up the insects and worms.

Morocco, it has been said, could grow enough corn to supply their own country and half England as well. I consider this a slight exaggeration, though, doubtless, with proper care, Morocco could become, as it once was, one of the largest wheat-producing countries of the world. Grain at present is not allowed to be exported, as it is repugnant to the strict religious views of the Emperor that the corn of the righteous should be devoured by unbelievers.

In minerals Morocco must be very rich, but here, again, native stupidity is to the fore, and no mines are allowed to be worked. Gold is brought in small quantities from the Sous, where it is found in the river-beds. Copper is known to exist, as also are many other metals. Land is held on a system of military tenure, which is a source of great gain to the Government, as, on the death of the holder, ground that but a short time before was waste land, comes back into the hands of the Sultan in a state more or less fit for agriculture. Not only does the land revert to the authorities, but also any buildings the tenant may have raised, and all his personal property. There are, of course, also landholders by hereditary rights, and by purchase.

Fruit is grown in considerable quantities throughout the country, but owing to the difficulties of transport, is not utilized as an export, nor would it probably pay to do so in any case, as no competition could succeed against the large fruit-growing districts of Southern Spain.

Morocco can be scarcely spoken of as possessing any literature. Perhaps, stored away in the old libraries at Fez and Morocco, are books and manuscripts of great value, who can tell ? But the only works which can be spoken of as being in circulation are illuminated and other religious books,—for the most part commentaries on the Koran. But though written literature is almost unknown, songs and poems have been handed down from generation to generation. The earlier these poems date from, the less crude they appear to be.

It would be an interesting study to trace the origin of Moorish poetry, to follow its changes and its intricacies, to be able to put a date to the various epochs at which radical changes have been introduced,

or taken place, in its formation ; but such a study
would be the work of a lifetime,—the lifetime of one
whose knowledge of the different dialects would have
to be perfect, in whose power it must lie to travel in
out-of-the-way tribes, and there to live the lives of the
natives themselves—nor would such a sacrifice on
the part of a man ever gain repayment by the discovery and translations of the poems.

There is much poetry in Morocco, from which the
rhyme has long since disappeared, but in which the
rhythm still remains.

The subtle turning of a few words gives to some of
their poems an undercurrent of passion and love—
only half expressed but fully meant — which is
possible in no other language ; not that it must
for a moment be supposed that there ever existed
in Morocco verse of the structural purity of that of
" Saadi," known now to all men by Sir Edwin Arnold's
beautiful translations, or the " Omar Khayam," nor
can any of the Moorish work be compared to the
" Sakuntala," or other early Hindu plays and poems.

In the small space I can spare here for Moorish
literature, I can find no better way of illustrating my
purpose than by translating one short poem—if such it
can be called, for it is half in verse, and half in prose.

> " I know a garden so fair, so fair,
>   Full of oranges, red and gold,
>   And the murmuring streams that are flowing there
>   Tell of love as yet untold.

" At the gates of Tetuan sat a girl in the hot sun selling
oranges, and such were the words she sung. Presently there
passed by a youth who perceived how beautiful she was, and
oranges he bought from her, and as she counted them out, she
sung,—

" ' I know a garden so fair, so fair,' &c., &c.

" Then the youth's heart beat fast with love, and lifting her in
his arms, he cried, ' Fly with me,' and she said, ' Whither shall
we fly? ' and he sang,—

" ' To a garden I know, so fair, so fair,' &c., &c.

" So they two fled away, and for days they journeyed till they
reached a valley in the Beni M'Sara, and there they found,

" A beautiful garden so fair, so fair,
Full of oranges red and gold,
And the murmuring streams that are flowing there
Saw their love, no more untold."

One word as to climate. Morocco is not a suitable
country for invalids in the winter. Tangier is the
only town in which they can reside, and the absence
of roads, and therefore of wheeled vehicles, the heavy
rainfall and chilly winds, the bad crossing from
Gibraltar on the small steamers that ply from port to
port, render Tangier at present anything but a health-
resort to confirmed invalids. To any one, however,
whose health is sufficiently strong to allow of riding,
going out into society or sport, &c., Tangier offers a
splendid winter home. The spring is the best time
of year to travel in Morocco, and to any one intending
to make a journey through the country I should
recommend a start to be made in early March, or
even later, as the rains are generally over, or nearly
over, by that time, and the rivers passable. The
summer in Tangier is delightful, seldom is the heat
extreme, and the temperature is always several degrees
lower than that of Gibraltar, while a cool wind
prevails on most days.

There is little more for me to say on Morocco. I
have told my story—for this is not supposed to be a

book on Morocco, but an account of my travels,
extending over many happy months spent in that
country.

I have purposely left out all statistics, I have
touched but in the lightest way on the trade and
government of the country, nor have I entered into
any serious discussion of European politics in the
country.

I have striven only to give to my book as much
reality as I can; I have tried to tell to the best
of my ability what I consider most characteristic of
the country by sketching out every-day life there.
Nor does this book purpose to be a book of exploration. My travels in Morocco have always been
undertaken merely for pleasure and sport, and for
no other reason, and the pleasure I have sought I
have also found there. However, to my remark on
exploration I make one or two exceptions. My ride
to Sheshouan was considered sufficiently of an exploring trip to allow of its publication in the " Proceedings
of the Royal Geographical Society," [1] while my tour
in the hill tribes is being honoured with the same
distinction.[2]

How to conclude my book I scarcely know. All
the time I have been writing it I have been thinking
of the moment when I shall lay down my pen, more
in sorrow than relief, light a cigarette, and gaze in
pride over a pile of manuscript, and now the moment
has come. Yet, as far as peroration goes, I could
not write one to save my life. Yet there is one duty
I must perform, a pleasure rather than a duty, to

[1] January, 1889. [2] August, 1889.

Z

offer my heartiest and sincerest thanks to one to whom most of my travels in Morocco are due, to one who has on every occasion in his power helped me by his kind advice, and who put himself to great inconvenience in taking me with him on his official visit to the Sultan of Morocco. Nor is it to him alone that I owe thanks, but also to his wife, whose kindness to me has been boundless, whose home in Morocco has been like a home to me; ay, I even forgive her the day she made me wear a mustard plaster, with not a single fold of a handkerchief between it and my chest.

I cannot express in words to how great an extent I am indebted to our Minister to the Court of Morocco, Sir William Kirby-Green, and to Lady Kirby-Green.